MW00467001

THERE IT IS…
IT DON'T MEAN NOTHIN'

CHARLES P. HENSLER

Copyright © 2017 Charles P. Hensler

All rights reserved.

ISBN-13: 978-1-7239-7074-0

DEDICATION

I want to dedicate this book to my wife and kids. Specifically, my daughter Jenny for inspiring me to write it, my wife Carol for making it readable and my daughter Cathy for making it publishable.

CONTENTS

AUTHOR'S NOTE

I served with the 199th Light Infantry Brigade in Vietnam from April 1968 to April 1969. It was a year of transition for the country. America's support for the war was rapidly fading while racial strife, social upheaval, and political unrest were escalating. The Army was not immune to these changes, and the resulting ramifications rippled throughout the Army. Consequently, my story is not just about slogging through rice paddies or hacking through jungle foliage, but integrates how events and changing attitudes back home impacted our morale, discipline, and trust in what we were being asked to do. It was a crazy time in America and no less so in Vietnam.

For privacy reasons I have changed the names of my fellow soldiers and superiors.

PREFACE (AFTERWARD)

When I started this little project some time ago, I never thought I would need a preface. But along the way the reasons for writing it evolved into something more than it was first intended to be. Therefore, I'm writing the preface after it's done. It was initially going to be a letter to my daughters to fulfill a request: to write a little history of my time in the service, the way I did for my dad. What started out being for Jenny and Cathy slowly developed into something that was just as much for me as for them.

There are several reasons this came to be; first among them was a return to my youth. When I first returned from Vietnam, the war was all I could think about—morning, noon and night. This went on for quite some time. Gradually, as life went on, that part of my life eased into the background. It was always there, always a part of me but no longer front and center. There was school to attend, a career to be found, a girl to marry, and kids to raise, and all the rest that comes with it. Time has a way of slipping away from you, and before you know it you're at retirement age and wondering where it all went.

Writing about my time in the Army took me back: back to when I had a full head of hair and some muscle to spare. Consequently, in the penning of this composition, I often found myself experiencing my youth in full bloom, rekindling emotions that had been dormant for years. It was more than just recalling. It was reliving a time in my young life when everything was new and exciting, and every fresh experience left an indelible imprint— both the good and the bad. It wasn't that I'd forgotten any of it; it's just that it had been some time since I felt it. When you go to war as a teenager and experience the twin emotional roller coasters that the coming of age and combat present at the same time, it becomes difficult to think of one without the other. Being young and healthy and fit is a wonderful feeling; although, most of us don't recognize it as such at the time. As George

1

Bernard Shaw so eloquently stated: "Youth is wasted on the young." Writing about Vietnam let me recapture some of those youthful feelings. If anything, being in a war zone intensifies them beyond measure. That is one of the many dichotomies of war: the proximity of death can make one feel so much more alive.

Besides taking me back to my youth, this project gave me the opportunity to relive my experiences during the war—something I haven't done very much. Writing about it (which I've found is much easier than talking about it) served a need in me that I didn't know was there. It was kind of like a release—the putting of pen to paper. Vietnam has always felt like an open-ended story to me, one that I never finished. I had the feeling that telling my story would help me to close the book on that chapter of my life. It turned into something I hadn't planned on: a journey retaken and in some ways finally complete.

PROLOGUE

Dear Jenny and Cathy,

A few years ago, while Jen and Gaz were home for Christmas, Jen asked me if she could read the short history of my dad's service in World War II that I wrote. After reading it, she told me that it might be nice if I wrote something about my own time in the service. I thought about it a while and decided I'd make an attempt. Only thing is, I don't really know how interesting it would be to you. I'm a bit of a history buff, so doing research on my dad's unit and seeing where it fit into the narrative of World War II was really a lot of fun for me. I knew a lot about the war—times and places and people—but my father rarely spoke about it. I'm not sure exactly why. We all knew the basics but really not too much specifically. My dad was in the signal corps and his division, the 97th Infantry, was involved in the last great battle of the war in Europe, "The Battle of the Ruhr Pocket." My dad's job was to run telephone lines between the command posts of the division's various units. When I was little I remember him saying that his squad had entered a town before it was liberated from the Germans. I was probably too young to really appreciate the significance of that. I really wish I knew the whole story. My dad brought home a German bayonet from the war, but I don't know how he got it. Only a few years ago, my mother told me that my dad also brought a German pistol back and gave it to her father. She has no idea where it went after that.

Shortly before my dad passed away, I asked him about his trip across the Atlantic. I had been reading a book that described what it was like to cross over to the war in a convoy of ships. Well, I was shocked, but very pleased, to hear him describe the trip in detail. It was apparent that it was still very clear in his mind, even at 89 years old. He seemed to enjoy the telling, and I was really glad that I had asked him. My mom told me later: "You know,

I've been married to your father for 60 years and I never heard that story." Maybe my dad never brought it up much because he thought his story might be too mundane to be of any great interest. After all, he was just one of 10 million guys who served in the war. He wasn't a hero, hadn't taken part in any of the more recognizable events of the war, and his contribution to it paled in comparison to those who had lost their lives or had come home broken in body, mind, or spirit.

If that was the case, I can fully understand as I feel that way myself. I was just an average soldier in an average unit. I didn't see a great amount of action. I have nothing heroic to relate, at least not on my part. I too, played no role in any event you would ever have heard about. But when I heard my dad relate his story about crossing the ocean, it didn't matter to me that a few million other guys did the same thing. This was *my* dad's story, and it meant a lot to me to hear it. Hopefully, you will feel the same about *your* dad's story.

I'm not too sure how to go about this, so I'll just start and see where things lead. I think I should probably give a little history lesson to start just to give you a feel for the times as it plays a role in how we got ourselves into the war.

I entered the service on July 24th 1967 during what for some would be coined "The Summer of Love": named that because of the hippie movement that had started in the Haight-Ashbury district of San Francisco. The hippies were anti-war, for free love, and pro-drug—marijuana and psychedelics (LSD), to be specific. They were the beginnings of the counterculture movement that would eventually spread far beyond San Francisco. For others, it was "The Long Hot Summer." Race riots broke out in dozens of cities across the country (Detroit and Newark being the worst) with major loss of life and property damage. That summer was a harbinger of change for the nation, as the following year would prove all too well.

But before we proceed with 1967, let me jump back to 1957. That was the year I moved to a suburb of Pittsburgh from our farm near Bentleyville. It was summer, I was eight years old, and I'd be starting the fourth grade in the fall. Castle Shannon was a whole new world for me, a drastic change from rural life. Oftentimes, a big change in a person's life can cause an individual to become much more aware. I think that happened to me. I seemed more interested in everything that was going on. And there was a lot going on in 1957. Even though I was only going on nine years old, I was developing a real interest in current events. In the years to follow, I can remember being excited when each week's edition of Life magazine came in the mail. I'd lie on the living room floor and read it cover to cover. It opened up the world to me, and I soaked it up. In the late fifties, you would be hard pressed to find a news weekly that didn't have at least one article related to the Cold War. It was East versus West, the "Free World" against the communists, Good versus Evil.

The Russians brutally smashed the Hungarian Revolution in 1956; it was proof positive of their intentions to dominate the world. Our view of communism in the 50s was as a monolith, one that would, if allowed, destroy us. After World War II the Russians reneged on their promises and kept control of eastern Europe, setting up puppet states. Germany remained divided and Berlin became the epicenter of the Cold War. China fell to communist rule under Mao and came to the aid of North Korea. In 1959 Cuba, only 90 miles from Florida, fell to the communists under Castro. It felt like our very way of life was being threatened. After all, the premier of the Soviet Union, Nikita Khrushchev, promised to "Bury Us."

Even if you weren't interested in what was going on in the world, you could not escape it. I can remember seeing large public buildings, including my own grade school, with black and yellow "fallout shelter" signs posted alongside the doors. Fallout was the radioactive particles that would be present in the atmosphere long after any nuclear explosion. Common wisdom at the time held that you would need to stay in a shelter for two weeks minimum after an attack. I can remember seeing the triangular CD (civil defense) markings on boxes of rations under the stairwells at my school. Along with the rations were drums marked "potable water." I remember wondering what was the big deal was about water you could put in a pot. I don't recall ever having to duck and cover like you see in those old newsreels where the kids are hiding under their desks. But I do remember having fire drill like exercises where we left our classrooms and gathered in the gym.

If you happened to be at home during an attack, you would go to the basement and, if you *really* planned ahead, into your own fall-out shelter. I remember a place along Rt. 19 south (toward Canonsburg) that sold prefab fall-out shelters that you could bury in your backyard. Every now and then they would have a newscast telling people how to stock them with provisions. In truth, I never knew anybody or even heard of anybody that ever had one. If you did have one there was a system in place to let you know when to leave your home and how long you had to get to the shelter. It was called the "Emergency Alert System," and it was a set of three different sounding sirens. I think one was a warbling sound, one a series of blasts, and one a steady note. Each had a meaning and a warning of how long you had before an expected attack. I don't remember them all, but the one I do was "Attack Imminent—Take Cover." The Castle Shannon Fire Hall tested their siren every Monday at 11:00 AM. The local TV stations broadcasted this information as public service announcements.

Then if you were lucky enough to make it to your shelter and you wanted to find out what was going on, you tuned in to the "Emergency Broadcast System." In the event of an attack, all regular TV and radio stations would leave the air. The reason for this was to prevent Russian bombers from using radio direction finders to home in on—let's say— 50,000 watt KDKA radio 1020, and lead them directly to Pittsburgh. The government had a name for this program; it was called CONELRAD. The anagram meant "control of electromagnetic radiation." You turned your AM radio dial to either 640KHZ or 1240KHZ. These were low wattage stations that could not be used as homing signals by distant enemy bombers. Not to worry if you forgot the numbers. The government mandated that all radios manufactured in that era have two white triangles marked on the dial at the proper locations to easily find the emergency broadcast system. If Uncle Steve happens to have his old Pontiac out at the house some time you could ask him to take a look. The radio stations were mandated to test the system on a regular basis, so they would usually do this in the middle of a song you really liked.

Worst case scenario: the bombers are closing in on Pittsburgh. Back in the day, Pittsburgh was the main steel producer in the nation and a prime target for any Russian nuclear attack. Because of this the Army had 12 Nike missile sites ringing Pittsburgh. Their mission was to shoot down Russian bombers. Some of the locations will be familiar to you: Elizabeth, Finleyville, West View, and North Park. The North Park location is now home to the Allegheny County Fire and Police Academy. Every Veterans Day or Memorial Day would generate at least one newspaper article about the Nike sites.

As you can see, the Cold War was part of the background of everyday life; even Santa Claus couldn't escape it. The US had built a line of radar sites across Alaska, Canada and Greenland near the Arctic Circle to spot Russian bombers headed toward America. It was called the "DEW LINE," for distant early warning. Well, every year on Christmas Eve (and this was usually the job of the local TV weatherman) a report was issued when Santa and his reindeer were picked up by the DEW line. Then they would show a little blip on a radar screen, and that would be Santa headed toward your house. Most folks got used to hearing about the Cold War and didn't worry night and day about nuclear annihilation. However, there was enough happening in the world on a regular basis to bring it all back into focus.

In 1957 Russia was the first nation to launch a satellite into earth orbit. What a fuss that started! The idea that the commies had a satellite flying over America, and we could do nothing about it, drove people nuts. The launching of Sputnik proved that the Soviets had a missile capable of sending a nuclear weapon over the pole and hitting American cities. This shifted the balance of power and initiated the space race to close the "Missile Gap."

The Strategic Air Command started continuous airborne alert. We had B-52 bombers in the air prepared to counterstrike in case of a surprise attack—24 hours a day, 7 days a week.

A communist insurgency began in South Vietnam, sponsored by North Vietnam.

In 1958 the communist Chinese attacked the Taiwanese Islands of Matsu and Quemoy with artillery, prompting the US to send carriers into the Straits of Taiwan.

The Berlin crisis began when Russian Premier Nikita Khrushchev demanded the West leave Berlin.

In 1959 Cuba fell to a communist revolution led by Fidel Castro. This inspired other insurgencies throughout Latin America.

In 1960 the US deployed nuclear missiles to England and Italy, putting the Soviet Union in range.

A US spy plane was shot down over the Soviet Union. Communist insurgents in Malaya were defeated.

A Communist revolt in Laos began.

In 1961 the US deployed nuclear missiles to Turkey. Moscow was in range.

The Berlin wall was constructed, tensions mounted.

In 1962 the Cuban Missile Crisis occurred. The Soviets were trying to introduce nuclear missiles to Cuba. The US initiated a naval blockade around Cuba. The crisis lasted 13 days, and most Cold War scholars believe we came as close as we ever have to nuclear war.

Well, you get the idea by now; stuff was happening all the time. Plus, we had a member of the family on the front lines (so to speak) of the Cold War. My older (by 6 years) brother Mike joined the Air Force not long out of High School. The Air Force sent him to Syracuse University to study the Russian language. I should add here, he was really intelligent. After training he was sent to Berlin where the tensions between the East and the West were at their highest. My brother's job was to listen in on Russian military communications in order to gain intelligence on the enemy. Mike had a

Top- Secret clearance and was not allowed to reveal anything he intercepted over the airwaves. Berlin was constantly in the news at that time, and I would never let an opportunity go by to remind my friends that he was there AND that he had a TOP SECRET clearance. I was really proud to be his little brother!

As I mentioned before, the West at that time looked at communism as a monolith (an evil bent on world domination). In the early sixties it looked to us like South Vietnam was its next target. A prevailing opinion at that time was the "Domino Theory." It concluded that Vietnam was the first domino in Southeast Asia: if we let them fall to the communists, the other dominos (Laos, Cambodia, Thailand, etc., etc.) would soon fall in turn.

As you can see, the groundwork was in place for us to get involved in Vietnam. As always, politics play a role in foreign affairs whether or not we go to war. John F. Kennedy was elected in 1960. He was a Democrat and one who made sure that the Republican mantra of Democrats being "soft on communism" was not going to stick on him. Truman, a Democrat, was accused by the Republicans of having "lost China": a reference to the Mao-led communist revolution in China. Kennedy was having none of that; he became a true cold war warrior.

Khrushchev had stated publicly that the Soviet Union would support wars of "national liberation" (like Vietnam) wherever in the world they were taking place. JFK was a believer in the domino theory and felt he had no choice but to try to contain these communist advances. By 1963 there were 16,000 advisors in Vietnam, sent there by Kennedy.

In the beginning, the effort was fairly well received by the public, and the media was supportive. Kennedy was a charismatic politician, and he made the mission in Vietnam seem like an obligation that we as Americans had no choice but to follow. His most famous quote from his inaugural address was: "Ask not what your country can do for you, but what you can do for your country." He also said: "Let every nation know, whether it wishes us well or ill, that we shall pay any price, bear any burden, meet any hardship, support any friend, oppose any foe, in order to assure the survival and the success of liberty." Vietnam would be a test for this doctrine.

Some of the people who were asked to implement this doctrine were the Special Forces. Who better? Their motto was "De Oppresso Liber"—free the oppressed. Kennedy was responsible for rebuilding the Special Forces, and he authorized them to wear the Green Beret. He visited their base at Fort Bragg; his tour there generated a lot of publicity for them. This carried over to their mission in Vietnam and produced some good media for the war effort. The good feeling was perpetuated by a book by Robin Moore called the "Green Berets," which chronicled their adventures in the early days of the war. It came out in 1964 and spent months on the New York Times Bestseller list; it peaked at number 2. In 1966 Sgt. Barry Sadler released a record called the "Ballad of the Green Beret," which rose to number one on the Billboard chart and stayed there for weeks in 1966.

President Johnson took over the presidency after JFK was assassinated in 1963. He went on to win the election in 1964. He promised to keep in effect those policies that JFK had initiated. He soon found himself with a major decision to make. At JFK's death there were 16,000 American troops in Vietnam, mostly advisors and support troops. North Vietnam had started to escalate their involvement in the south, and there were fears that the South Vietnamese Army was not up to the task of defending the country. At this point we probably could have withdrawn without losing too much face; we were only in the country in an advisory capacity. Johnson's primary focus in politics had been domestic issues, but he also believed in the domino theory. In 1965 he made the choice to escalate and send American ground forces in large numbers into the country. By 1967—the summer of love and race riots—the levels had grown to over 400,000. Kennedy may have initiated our involvement, but LBJ had now taken over full ownership; it was Johnson's War.

I was 18 years old that summer of 1967, a year out of high school, with no particular prospects. (I attended the community college in the fall of 66 and the spring of 67.) I was always a pretty indifferent student: doing enough to get by, taking the easiest classes I could find. By the end of the spring term, I knew I was not going back. With no particular aim in mind, I found it difficult to apply myself and study for studies' sake. I was working as a groundskeeper: cutting grass, trimming hedges, etc., etc. That job would end on Labor Day and I had no idea what would come next. I started thinking about going into the service.

To be sure, the first rumblings of protest against the war had begun in earnest that spring, but they seemed far away from Pittsburgh and did not involve too many people. Pittsburgh is a conservative town when it comes to national defense. Allegheny County has one of the highest proportions of veterans in the country. So, in general, those early protesters were not looked upon with too much favor in these parts. No doubt the bloom was off the rose, but the majority of the people still felt the war was necessary when looked at in the light of cold war containment policy.

That was the situation when I decided to join the Army that spring. While I was a pathetic student in most subjects, an exception to that was current events and history. I was fully aware what was going on in Vietnam while a lot of guys my age couldn't find it on the map. I signed up in July. I can't honestly say my reasons were patriotic. I wasn't thinking I would go in and help save the world from communism. No, I was 18 with no plans. Maybe I was thinking I'd "learn something," or maybe I was looking for some adventure. At any rate, I lost my student deferment when I left school so it was a sure bet I was going to get drafted. So why wait around? I figured I'd go ahead and get my two years over with instead of wasting time waiting to be drafted. However, with the history of the time it never occurred to me that I was doing something that down the road quite a few people would consider a total waste. From the time I went in until the time I got out spanned only 20 months. Yet the whole perception of the war changed during that time. The public soured on the war and to a certain extent on those whom the country asked to serve in it.

Dad dropped me off on his way to work. I got out at the intersection of Grant and Liberty and walked into the Federal Building. It was Monday morning, July 24, 1967, and my world was about to change. I spent practically the whole day there. I wasn't alone, of course; I had plenty of company. We took our physicals, did tons of paperwork, and were sworn in. Mostly, we learned that the military way of "hurry up and wait" was no myth.

I got my orders to report to Fort Polk, Louisiana. I arrived at the base mid-morning the next day and it was already blazing hot. We got off the bus and were greeted by a drill sergeant who immediately started yelling at us. I had seen enough war movies and heard enough stories to know this was par for the course.

The first week of Basic doesn't really count toward your 8-week course, hence the name "zero week." This week is spent taking tests, doing paperwork, getting shots and hurrying up and waiting. They take your civilian clothes away from you, and you won't see them again till graduation day. You get your army fatigues and your buzz cut. Then they allow you a visit to the PX to pick up some items you need to maintain a certain look they deem necessary: namely, shoe polish and Brasso. While there, I saw my first newspaper since I left home. I remember distinctly the headline and picture on the front page: "Detroit Ablaze." This was above a picture of a National Guard jeep patrolling a Detroit street. Yet another city was hit by riots that summer, and the effects of the riots would spill over into the military. This racial tension would manifest itself in Vietnam, particularly on the main bases.

We were confined to the company area the weekend before week one. The only exception was Sunday worship; you could go to church if you wanted to. Just about everybody went, mostly to get out of the barracks. Attendance the following weeks would never come remotely close to the first one.

Week one started pretty early, somewhere between 5 and 6 Monday morning. We were roused by the drill sergeant, dressed quickly and formed up in the company area. Of course, forming up in those early days was actually pretty comical. You didn't dare laugh or you would find a drill sergeant. breathing down your throat, asking you: "What's so fucking funny?" Then you would find yourself doing all kinds of push-ups. Or worse yet, he'd make the whole platoon do push-ups while the offender stood and watched. But sometimes you couldn't help yourself, you had to laugh. Some guys just didn't pick up on the moves and would turn the wrong way and run into another guy, then that guy would trip—well you get the idea. We did a lot of extra push-ups.

We spent a lot of time drilling and learning the commands: left face, right face, about face, marching in cadence. We learned how to keep our foot lockers looking militarily correct (all the socks rolled just so, lined up in rows), how to make our bed, and how to hang our clothes. And most importantly, how to wear your clothes. Don't show up in morning formation with a button unbuttoned or your hat too far back on your head. The point of all this was to make everybody the same. Individuality is not an asset in basic training. This was harder for some guys to learn than others, and they always paid a price for it—or I should say, we all did. The whole idea of this was for everyone to think of themselves as part of a unit, and to think of the unit first and foremost. The other reason was to learn to follow orders immediately and without question.

Our lead drill sergeant, Jason Stalls, was great at berating you. He was African-American, short, and stocky. His complexion was kind of rough and he had a gold tooth which was quite evident when he smiled, which he often did with a sense of bemusement as he belittled you. I can hear him now, "You fucking dud! Charlie's gonna git ya. Heh, Heh, Heh!" Charlie was the nickname of the Viet Cong (Vietnamese communists) who we were fighting in Vietnam. Sgt. Stalls seemed to take delight in pointing out how our stupidity was going to get ourselves killed. Over and over we would hear it, "Charlie's gonna git ya, Charlie's gonna git ya, Heh, Heh, Heh!!!"

The group dynamics of the platoon were interesting. We had whites, blacks, Hispanics, and even a couple of Cajuns who, if you didn't know any better, seemed to speak a foreign language. We had northerners and southerners, big city boys, and down-home types. It's a bit of a test for the Army to bring these guys together. They did this by providing a common enemy: the drill sergeant. It was the one thing that got everybody on the same page. It's all part of the plan.

Drill Sergeant Snead was our other instructor. One weekend, while he was off duty, Sgt. Snead showed up to get something from his office and we saw him crossing the company grounds. He was wearing shorts and you could see ugly purple scars up and down both legs. I think he knew what he was doing and was sending us all a none-too-subtle message: this war is serious business, and it's all too easy to get hurt or killed if you don't know what you're doing.

Most of the drill sergeants and course instructors we came into contact with were Vietnam combat veterans. Curiously, I never heard a one of them mention the Army mission in Vietnam as being of vital importance to the country. There was never any talk of patriotism or why we were there. Basically, I think they felt they were going to do the best they could to prepare us for a bad situation.

We had to take a lot of different classes. The least exciting included: first aid, military courtesy, army general orders, and chain of command. I liked weapons training the best. Bayonet training was on the agenda. Just the thought of needing to use it left a queasy feeling in my stomach. The instructors did their best to get you into the swing of things. First, they inspired you to learn the techniques of bayonet fighting by constantly yelling out the question, "What are the two kinds of bayonet fighters?" To which we would all scream out in unison, "THE QUICK AND THE DEAD." All this training was meant to instill the "spirit of the bayonet" in all of us. The instructors had a course laid out with life-size figures stuffed with straw which the trainee would traverse, practicing his bayonet thrusts. Before each run through the course, the instructor would yell out to the trainee: "What is the spirit of the bayonet?" To which the trainee would scream in return "To Kill…To Kill!!!" I'm not sure about the other guys, but even though I would respond correctly to the question, I don't think I ever really captured the "spirit of the bayonet."

Considering the diverse backgrounds of everybody in the platoon, I think most folks got on pretty well. It was really interesting to get to know people from different places and backgrounds. A lot of the guys were draftees who, for the most part, took their involuntary conscription with equanimity. Some didn't, like my bunkmate Juan who had a perpetual scowl and seemed to warm up to no one during all of Basic. One guy had a hell of a time adapting and he seemed quite troubled. One day he went for sick call. When the rest of us got back from our day of training, his bunk was stripped of bedding, his foot locker empty, and we never saw him again. Some guys were homesick, though few would admit it. I was never really bothered by that. However, I did experience a curious reaction regarding what was going on at home. I called Mom & Dad every weekend, but one week I called and no one was home. I called the next weekend and found out they had gone on vacation with my sisters. My first thought was: "Hey, you can't go on vacation without me." For some silly reason I was shocked to realize that life at home went on without me.

All through Basic rumors ran rampant among the recruits. You are pretty isolated as new inductees and, being new to the service, kind of vulnerable to any wild story that floats around. I'm sure they were pretty standard fare for every class. Of course, they always happened at some other company down the road. One of the first ones we heard was about the recruit that couldn't hack it and committed suicide. Another was the recruit that panicked on the live fire infiltration course and stood up into the stream of bullets that flew a few feet overhead. The grenade throw range served up one about the trainee who froze after pulling the pin on his grenade.

As the weeks went by we learned more and were harassed slightly less. We had courses in first-aid, land navigation, camouflage, field sanitation, and hand-to-hand combat, as well as field exercises in cover fire, infiltration, and close combat maneuvers. The scariest exercise in Basic was a cover fire course. It wasn't really physically demanding, but it was very disconcerting: knowing that the man behind you firing live ammo, in many cases, had never fired a weapon before Basic Training.

Another memorable, if ineffective, part of the course was the section on STDs. Always a problem for an army at war in a foreign land, it was incumbent on the Army to reduce the number of cases it had to deal with. It felt the best way to do this was to scare the hell out of you with graphic pictures of private parts belonging to some unfortunate souls who had contracted particularly virulent strains of these communicable diseases. The visual impact had the desired effect: it produced audible groans in our group along with some nervous laughter. It was a good try on the Army's part, but I would say the effect of the pictures probably weren't long-lasting. The traditional teenage view that "it can't happen to me," along with the peak hormonal levels of a fit 18-year-old male, guaranteed that if you had a mind to, those pictures weren't going to hold you back. Besides, for most guys, once you were in Vietnam STD's were the least of your worries.

Looking back on the experience 50 years later, it's surprising how much you do remember considering the length of time that has gone by. Again, I guess it's that first time, "something new" syndrome. Basic was something completely foreign, a different world than anything I had ever experienced. You meet all kinds of different people from all kinds of different backgrounds. You are exposed to people more worldly than yourself (not too hard to do in my case) and puts the whole growing-up process into fast forward.

While I was in Basic…

A group called "Vietnam Veterans against the War" began to protest US involvement in the war.

Troop levels in Vietnam reach 464,000.

Gallup poll results shows 42% of Americans believe sending troops to Vietnam was a mistake.

Muhammad Ali is convicted of refusing induction into the US Army after being drafted. Ali: "I ain't got nothing against them Viet Cong."

US Supreme Court strikes down state laws prohibiting inter-racial marriage.

Race riots take place in Detroit, Newark, Buffalo, Memphis, Boston and others.

The Beatles release "Sgt. Pepper's Lonely Hearts Club Band."

Rowan & Martin's "Laugh-In" debuts.

During my 8 weeks of Basic, the US suffers 1,066 deaths, bringing the total for the war to 9,453.

I got orders to report to Fort Lewis in Washington state to begin infantry training. My orders stated that my MOS (Military Occupational Specialty) would be Infantry, designation 11C. The C meant that I would receive mortar training for two weeks during the 8 week course. I was assigned to C-2-3: Charlie Company, 2nd Battalion, 3rd Training Brigade. I was assigned to the second platoon.

My memory of Infantry Training isn't nearly as clear as Basic is to me. I guess because it wasn't all new like Basic. It was training but without near as much harassment. As we were learning new weapons and tactics, we were getting used to a new group of people. One thing we all had in common in this group: we were all training for the infantry. As usual with the Army there were people from all over. I started to pal around with a guy named Dan Morris. He was from Montana and had lived on a ranch there with his folks. He was a draftee and was really missing life back on the ranch. Having lived on a farm, I felt a bit of a connection with him. I really didn't have much to talk about since I was only 8 when I left the farm. Yet all it took was that slight connection and we became fast friends.

Training continued on with communications, land navigation, more first- aid, mines and booby-traps, and patrolling. Our weeks soon came to a close. There was no graduation ceremony. At least none memorable enough for me to remember it. Everybody's focus was what our new orders would say. Dan and I talked about it every night, weighing all the possibilities and debating on the veracity of all the rumors we heard.

Finally, the word came down: we would hear where we were going on Sat. afternoon. We all gathered in our company area, each platoon in formation. The company commander announced that he would be reading aloud each person's name followed by his assignment; they went in alphabetical order. The first few went to the 6th Battalion 31st Infantry, one of the two new battalions being formed on the post to be sent to Vietnam as a unit. Then some were called for the 5th Battalion 12th Infantry. That was the other unit being formed. They finally got to my buddy Dan. "5th & 12th" was hollered out. The way things were going it didn't look like they were going to call out my name and say Hawaii—or anything like that. So, I was hoping that at least I would get assigned to the same unit as Dan. A minute or two later my name was called, followed by "5th & 12th". Well, no more suspense; at least I was going to be with Dan. Monday morning we would be bussed to the other side of the base to our new digs and find out what was next in store for us.

While I was in Infantry Training....

The US matches the enemy escalation; nearly 500,000 troops by years end will be deployed to South Vietnam.

US Navy pilot John McCain is shot down over North Vietnam. He would eventually spend 5 ½ years in a POW camp. He was the Republican presidential candidate in 2008.

At the University of Wisconsin, protests against Dow Chemical, manufacturer of "Agent Orange" (controversial defoliant used in Vietnam), turn violent.

150,000 demonstrators congregate on the Washington Mall by the Lincoln Memorial to protest the war. Later, 50,000 protestors "March on the Pentagon."

The musical "Hair" debuts off Broadway.

Premier edition of "Rolling Stone" is published.

The Beatles release "Magical Mystery Tour."

1,416 troops are killed in action, bringing the total for the war to 12,338.

I was assigned to Company B of the 5th Battalion 12th Infantry. My buddy, Dan Morris, was going to be in Company C. I would be in the fourth platoon, or weapons platoon, most often referred to as the mortar platoon. There were 27 men in the platoon, the average age was 21. Lt. Stockman at 25 and Sgt. Browning at 30 were the oldest. The most common age was 20. Myself and one other guy at 19 were the youngest. Ten men were married.

Since July when I was inducted the winds had shifted on how the country was looking at the war, and we were not immune from this gravitation. Again, just like Basic and AIT, there were no Rah, Rah speeches as to how important our mission was. No call to fulfill your patriotic duty. Just, this is your job and this is the best way to do it.

The first few weeks were spent reviewing things we learned in Infantry Training and getting to know each other. It always takes a little while to gel with a new group and get a "feel" for things. Almost all of us were two-year people, the vast majority drafted.

Unit training was much more relaxed than what I was previously used to and it was different in that I knew I'd be going to Vietnam with these guys. Now knowing that we were actually going to Vietnam, everyone took the training more seriously. However, that being said, there was also a certain attitude among the troops that was pervasive. The sentiment was: yes, I'm in the army; I'll do what I have to do, but I don't have to like it. And if I don't like it what are you going to do about it? Put me in the Infantry? I'm already there. Send me to Vietnam? I've already got my ticket. It can't get any worse. So what can you do to me?

This was pretty much the mindset in regards to all things military except for what might help you survive the coming year. I think the lieutenant was wise in recognizing this and did not push the issue. Nobody was harassed for haircuts or boots not polished enough. We didn't have inspections of our personal stuff but did have to keep our mortars in tip-top shape. No one was threatened with having leave revoked. The weekends were pretty much ours to do with as we pleased. If we trained well they left us alone. I remember the early morning police calls (police, as in cleaning up the area). We would all get in a line and walk around the company area looking for trash or cigarette butts to pick up. We did the walking but nobody ever picked up anything. Hey, whatta ya gonna do to me?

With what was going on in the country at that time, it could hardly be any other way. We watched TV every night and could see that sentiment for the war was evaporating. On the battlefield itself things were not going well. The marines were surrounded at Khe Sanh and everyone was worried about another Dien Bien Phu (Site of French defeat in the first Indochina war). The Tet offensive began at the end of January. It was a countrywide offensive by the North Vietnamese Army and Viet Cong against nearly every provincial capital and every major city and military installation in the country. The Viet Cong even breached the gates to the US Embassy in downtown Saigon. How could this possibly be; didn't General Westmoreland (Commander of all US troops in Vietnam) say we were winning? But then again, he had asked President Johnson for over 200,000 more troops. It was the beginning of the end for the US involvement. Those troops would never be sent.

In February the anti-war presidential candidate, Eugene McCarthy, got way more votes than expected in the New Hampshire primary, reflecting the growing unrest with the war. A Gallup poll for the first time showed that 50% of Americans thought the war was a mistake. Protests against the draft increased. Demonstrations against the war occurred not only in the states but in places like London, Paris and Berlin.

Walter Cronkite, the CBS evening news anchor, visited South Vietnam after the Tet offensive. Cronkite was once rated in a poll as the "most trusted man in America." So when he returned from Vietnam and announced that the war was not winnable it sent shock waves through the Johnson administration. A few weeks after the Cronkite editorial, President Johnson announced he would not run for re-election. LBJ became a casualty of his own war. All of this could not help but have a deleterious effect on the troops' mental attitude.

Nonetheless, training went on. We went to the range often to practice with our mortars and fired many live rounds. We were all issued M-16's, our personal weapons that we would take to Vietnam.

I remember one cold, full moon night when we set up an assault exercise on a defended position. The objective was across an open field, maybe 200 yards from the treeline where we would begin our assault. The air was clear and the moon super bright. There was no way we were sneaking up on anybody that night. It was to be a company assault over all that open ground.

The theory of a ground assault on a fortified position calls for a minimum of a 3 to 1 ratio of attackers to defenders because the opposition has the advantage of cover and protection. The reality of this situation is that we would lose a lot of people. The actuality of that hit me hard as I moved across that wide expanse. It wouldn't matter what you knew, how skillful you were, or even how brave. If you were in the open and the enemy had clear fields of fire, the only thing that would see you to the other side of that field would be luck or good fortune. It would be out of my hands, and I didn't like that feeling. It was the first time I really felt my destiny was only a matter of odds or chance. I was troubled by this long after the exercise, even though it should have been obvious to me. I could never quite quash the heebie-jeebies I'd get every time I'd think of actually being in a position of having to do something like that. I would carry those jitters to Vietnam and tote them in my pack as long as I was there.

Training began to wind down about halfway through March of '68. We started cleaning and packing all our weapons and gear that would be shipped over ahead of us. We were issued our jungle fatigues and boots. They were lighter than the standard uniform and looked better too. The shirt was worn like a light-weight coat; it was long and not tucked in. The pants had extra pockets and ties at the bottom of the legs. The boots were made of nylon and leather and came with eyelets in the insteps for drainage. These features were used to help cope with the high temps and wet conditions we would encounter in-country. The boots also had spike protection built into the soles to protect against punji sticks penetrating into your foot, if you were unlucky enough to step into a punji pit (an extremely nasty booby trap).

A one week leave was granted to everyone before our departure date. I flew home to Pittsburgh toward the end of March. I don't remember much about the leave except for the airport on the way back. Mom and Dad took me out in the morning to catch a flight to LA. I was going to visit my brother Mike before going back to Fort Lewis. I don't think any of us knew quite what to say at the gate before boarding. You would think that the occasion of going off to war would demand something to be said of a memorable nature, but all three of us were at a loss for what that might be. In the end, it was hugs and kisses, a "be careful," and off I went.

Mike met me at the airport and we spent the day together. He took me to Venice Beach, known more for what went on ashore than on the beach itself. It was a bit of a counterculture refuge and there were a lot of quirky people who were entertaining to watch. You guys never really knew my brother Mike, but if you did, you wouldn't be surprised that he more than made up for the paucity of words at my goodbye in Pittsburgh. Not only were there many, but they were heavy and deep. He meant well, but I just wanted to have a good time and not dwell on what was coming up. He was really worried about me, and while I appreciated that, it kind of put a pall on the day.

Got back to base and found out our departure date would be April 1st. We also learned that the whole battalion was going to meet at one of the base movie theaters for a talk by our battalion commander. All enlisted personnel would attend as well as the officers and their wives. Nobody seemed to know what the meeting was going to be about. One thing for sure, no one was interested in a "pep" talk. What was happening to the country could not help but be reflected in the troops' attitudes. For many of the guys, any convictions about our mission in Vietnam had crumbled.

The meeting started off with each of the 5 company commanders saying a few words. Mostly, they told us how they were proud of us, how we were well-trained, and that we were prepared for the challenges ahead. Then Colonel Behm spoke, reiterating what was said before and adding a few thoughts of his own. I guess he felt obligated to be inspiring and motivating. He was trying to get us "fired up" with his pep talk style speech. On the whole, I'd say it was received rather tepidly. Personally, I was a bit offended by parts of it. One thing in particular was troubling. He wanted to create a pool of money that would be given to the first person who brought him the ears of a NVA (North Vietnamese Army) or VC (Viet Cong) colonel or above rank. Now, admittedly, this practice had occurred during the war to varying degrees, but to hear it condoned by a lieutenant colonel in the US Army was a bit shocking to me. I'll concede my naivety at the time, but I was thinking: "Aren't we supposed to be the good guys in the white hats?"

On March 31st President Johnson made a speech to the nation about Vietnam. Most of us in the barracks that evening went into the day room to watch it on television. He began by telling the nation that the recent Tet offensive by the NVA and VC did not achieve any of their goals and that the US was committed to "stay the course." He acknowledged that there was division in the country over the war and alluded to the "house divided" speech by Abraham Lincoln before the Civil War. He announced his willingness to talk with the enemy, to negotiate with them, and to unilaterally commence a bombing halt over North Vietnam. Lastly, in order to spend all his energy in the pursuit of peace, he would not accept his party's nomination to run for re-election as President. It was a shock to everyone, but I immediately began to wonder if the speech would have any consequences for us. Would the NVA respond with a peace proposal? Could there be a cease fire? Would there be any lessening of hostilities? I was doing a lot of wondering on the eve of our departure.

The following day, we boarded buses after evening chow and drove the short distance to McChord Air Force Base. The buses drove right out next to the plane. We would be flying on a Continental Airways Boeing 707 320-B. It looked new, gleaming-white with an orange, maroon, and gold accent stripe running the length of the fuselage. The vertical stabilizer was all gold. In fact, Continental's advertising slogan was "The Bird with the Golden Tail." I hadn't anticipated going off to war on a commercial jet.

Our company got off the buses and got into a formation. Much to our surprise, the post army band was on hand to play some "see you off" tunes. I thought it was a little late in the game as far as this war was concerned for an "Over There, Over There, The Yanks are Coming" kind of music. Thankfully, nothing like that was played. It definitely would have been inappropriate for the mood of the audience. I can't remember what was played, but I do remember how: perfunctory and muted. I don't think the band could get up for a "send you off" to Vietnam performance. They probably just wanted to get it over with, put the brass away, and head to the base club. After the performance we boarded the plane: all 189 of us in our brand new olive drab jungle fatigues and boots. We were welcomed aboard by pretty stewardesses outfitted in cute, brightly colored, little uniforms. The juxtaposition of their attire and ours made the whole scene somewhat surreal.

We took off about an hour before dusk and chased the sun across the Pacific. It seemed odd to see that red disc hanging in the air so long.

Because the plane was traveling west at over 500 miles an hour, it took twice as long for the light to dip below the horizon. Our first stop was Hawaii. While we were refueling, I got off the plane and had my picture taken under a palm tree. It was 10 and a half hours to Manila. We landed there mid-morning. Then it was off to Bien Hoa, Vietnam.

While I was in unit training…

Marine base at Khe Sanh is surrounded by North Vietnamese Troops. The siege lasted 77 days.

TET offensive begins; over 100 cities and towns attacked across the country. US Embassy grounds breached by Viet Cong.

Hue City Massacre takes place in Vietnam's Imperial City during the TET offensive. The one-time capital of the country is held by North Vietnamese and Viet Cong troops for 28 days. During that time, citizens who work for the South Vietnamese government, public servants, elected officials, and members of the armed forces are given trials. These trials ended in executions, if you were lucky. If not, many victims were bound, tortured and buried alive. Reports vary, but somewhere between 3 thousand and 5 thousand civilians were killed or went missing.

My Lai Massacre takes place in a small village in Quang Ngai Province in northern South Vietnam. Elements of the US Army's 11th Brigade, under the command of Lt. William Calley, take out their frustrations on villagers, old men, women, and children. The soldiers of C company were told the hamlets of My Lai were suspected of harboring enemy troops of the 48th Viet Cong Regiment. The American troops had many casualties from mines and booby-traps in the preceding months. Resentment of the local population was building because oftentimes villagers would know where the mines were placed but would never inform the GI's. The morning the troops entered the village, they were given ambiguous orders by the officers in command. An incident occurred with a civilian that should not have; a GI stabbed a man and threw him down a well. This act of brutality spread like a contagion to other troops and didn't end until no less than 347 civilians were killed.

Martin Luther King Jr. calls for a massive march on Washington D. C. to protest the war in Vietnam.

Robert F. Kennedy announces he is going to run for the Democratic nomination for the presidential election.

Richard M. Nixon announces he is going to run for the Republican nomination for the presidential election.

Protests of the war in Vietnam occured in London and West Berlin, tens of thousands involved.

President Johnson announces a bombing halt over North Vietnam, calls for peace talks, and declares he will not seek his party's nomination for re- election to the presidency.

First 911 emergency telephone system is inaugurated in Haleyville, Alabama.

Mr. Rogers Neighborhood premieres on public television.

Planet of the Apes" hits movie theaters.

"(Sittin on) the Dock of the Bay" is released by Otis Redding.

The first three months of 1968 produced 1,519 Americans killed in action. This brings the total KIA count to 13,857.

CHAPTER ONE
IN-COUNTRY

We were about two hours out from Manila when we first spotted the coast of Vietnam. The plane was rather quiet, or maybe I was so deep in my own thoughts that I didn't notice anyone else. I think I was in a *Wow! This is really happening* place. I was nervous, of course, but also anxious to get there to see what this was all about.

As we cleared the coast the plane was still at high altitude. Out of my window I spotted an air strike occurring in what looked like dense jungle. The fighter jets just looked like specks, but the smoke that billowed up after a bomb strike was clearly visible. I was trying to imagine what was going on down there on the ground. It seemed strange to see a possible life or death situation going on out the window of a commercial jet as the stewardess is telling you to fold up your tray, straighten your seat back, and tighten your seatbelt; and the pilot is announcing that the local time is 12:30 PM and the weather at Bien Hoa is 96 degrees and sunny.

Our approach to the airport was a lot steeper than normal as a precaution against any enemy ground fire. Our wheels hit the concrete runway about the time the pilot said we would, and after the run out we turned onto a taxiway that took us to the terminal. Along the way we passed aircraft revetments with warplanes parked inside those protective walls. There were sleek F-100 Super Sabres, low slung A-37 Dragonflies, and old prop-driven A1-E Skyraiders laden with bombs and rockets—all at the ready. They were in their wartime livery of matte brown and green and olive drab camouflage and exuded an intimidating menace.

Finally parked, the stewardesses opened the doors and let a bit of Vietnam inside. Our first hint of the heat to come wafted down the aisle carrying with it unfamiliar odors. Everyone was on their feet shuffling toward the bright outside. I think everybody on that plane remembers their first step out of the aircraft into a whole new world. We all left a cool, damp, 45 degree Washington state less than 24 hours ago. Now we were entering what felt like a blast furnace. The heat seemed to envelop you; the air felt heavy, thick, and hard to breathe. Sweat began to pour off me before I reached the tarmac at the bottom of the steps. Along with the heat was a smell that was just as engulfing. It wasn't coming from somewhere; it was everywhere. Depending on who you talk to, it was a combination of any of the following sources: rotting vegetation, garbage, diesel fumes, outdoor plumbing, rice paddies, and stagnant water. It was a shock to your system, mentally and physically.

I now had completed my "FTA" flight, which meant "FREE TRIP TO ASIA." Our plane would be refueled and readied for a return flight to the states. One hundred and eighty-nine troops who had just completed 365 days were anxiously waiting to board. For them, the day had finally come; they were getting on the "FREEDOM BIRD" for a return to "THE WORLD."

We assembled in an open area to wait for transportation to our base. The sun was high overhead, a lot higher than at home thanks to being at 10 degrees of latitude. April is the hottest month of the year in Vietnam, averaging 94 degree highs. It was April 2, 1968, and we were above average. Dark green buses arrived to pick us up and take us to Long Binh, our unit's main base. We boarded and sat down, happy to be out of the sun. I was thinking, "I'll never make it here." I felt sapped already, not yet an hour in-country.

The drivers drove off the airfield and into the city of Bien Hoa. All of us were wide-eyed, of course, taking everything in. The road was paved but only about a lane and a half wide. The thoroughfare was crowded with motor bikes, bicycles, Lambrettas (3-wheeled vehicles), cars, and military vehicles. Businesses and residences hugged the street: they were one and two-story buildings that had stucco exteriors, mostly white, beige, or dull yellow in color. Many had windows with shutters. What little space was left between structures and road was taken up with pedestrians wearing loose fitting clothes (sometimes referred to as P J's) and straw-like conical hats.

It was soon apparent that if the country had any rules of the road they were taken as only suggestions. I didn't envy our bus driver as he navigated his way through the free-for-all that was our route. We came to a stop when traffic jammed up in front of us. I was staring out the window watching all the people pass by when I noticed an older lady squat down by the side of the road, pull one leg of her very baggy pants off to the side, and begin to urinate on the street. "Toto, we're not in Kansas anymore." One of the guys asked the driver why there was a wire mesh screen over the bus windows. He replied, "To keep people from throwing a grenade in."

Along one section of road, evidence of fighting was apparent; the exterior walls of many homes were stitched with pockmarks from bullet strikes. Some houses had large holes in them or partial roofs from rocket-propelled grenades and mortar round hits. The Bien Hoa /Long Binh area had been hit hard just two months previously during the Tet offensive. Now I was looking at places I saw on TV just a short while ago.

Long Binh was about 3 miles from the air base at Bien Hoa so it didn't take long to get to our destination. At its peak 50 to 60 thousand troops worked on the base, making it the largest army base in Vietnam. Long Binh was the main logistical center for the southern part of the country: it held the command center for all of Vietnam and furnished two evacuation hospitals for troops in the field. Our unit, the 199th Light Infantry Brigade (LIB), was located on the northern fringe of the base.

As our little convoy pulled off the road and up to the main gate of our portion of the base, I noticed a large sign next to the gate. It read: "Camp Frenzell-Jones." I was to learn later its name came from the first two casualties the unit suffered in Vietnam. The buses traveled up what looked like the main street of the base. There were 2-story wooden barracks on either side of the street. We passed a mess hall, a Post Exchange, and various other buildings before arriving at our area. We were the fourth and last battalion to join the brigade. No buildings were ready for us; tents would be our home.

Our company area was located on a dusty plot about 50 yards from the perimeter fence. The fence was made up of barbed wire and concertina wire. Bunkers made of sandbags and PSP (perforated steel planking) were standing every 25 yards or so just to the rear of the fence. Every 50 yards were observation towers, maybe 25 feet high, sandbagged and manned by machine gunners at night. April is the tail end of the dry season in Vietnam, and the dirt our camp was sited on was bone dry. The soil was powdery and you kicked up puffs of the fine grained earth as you walked.

Our tents were set up on wooden platforms that served as a floor for the tent. The tents held maybe 20 troops each. The tent sides were rolled up for ventilation, so basically you had a floor and a roof. This was fine since it would have been absolutely unbearable to be in a tent with the sides down in that heat.

We all picked a cot out and put our personal stuff underneath it. Then we just hung out until a scheduled 4:00 PM formation with Captain Conner. He gave us the lay of the land: where the mess hall was, the showers, the PX, the Enlisted Men club, etc., etc. Then he told us that we would start building bunkers the next day since we had none in our area. He also told us that we would attend the Redcatcher Combat Training Center before we went on our first mission. Redcatcher, by the way, was the nickname of the 199th LIB.

After the meeting Jerry Fuller and I walked over to the mess hall for dinner. We had to cross an open area to get there, and we noticed some holes in the ground that looked like small craters. We had a hunch what they were. We asked someone at the mess hall to confirm our suspicions and he did. He told us the area was hit by rockets last week. I decided I wasn't going to mind filling sandbags the following day. I don't think Jerry was going to mind either. Jerry and I were practically neighbors, he being from West Virginia. I think from up in some hollow. He fit the stereotype with the way he talked and his chewing tobacco habit. I was a smoker at that time so no stranger to nicotine. Jerry would bug me about trying a "chaw." When the unit was in the field, the Army supplied us with SP packs, the "S" meaning sundry. They included: candy, hygiene items, cigarettes, and even chewing tobacco. Jerry picked out a plug of tobacco. A plug is chewing tobacco compressed to a solid chunk. Usually a sweet syrup is added to keep the plug together and to give it flavor. It sounded a little better than the loose-leaf tobacco, so I let Jerry talk me into trying it. It didn't go well. I bit off a nice chunk, chewed a little too enthusiastically, turned green, and barely suppressed barfing. I was happy for Jerry, though, as it really made his day.

I was a bit nervous that first night; sleep didn't come easy. There were new sights and sounds to take in. We could see out in the distance helicopter gunships raking over a ridge line with their mini guns, and outgoing artillery pounded the hills all through the night. Flares punctured the darkness with their unnatural amber glow and star clusters of red and green arched upwards from units already out in the field, signaling I knew not what. A lot had changed in a day. I was 10,000 miles and 12 time zones away from home.

The low temp that night was 30 degrees above the high for the day where I left. It was a big first day: nineteen hours on the plane, new country, new culture, a war zone, and the possibility of rockets or mortars falling out of the air. Only 364 more to go.

The sun rose around 5:30 AM. Since the tents had no sides, it had no problem making its presence known. There was no relief from the heat overnight. We woke to a 75 or 80 degree morning, had a nice breakfast, and then formed up to see what the new day would bring. Captain Conner informed us that Bien Hoa Air Base where we had landed just yesterday was hit last night by mortars.

I soon learned that my second day in-country would be spent constructing bunkers for the company area. Roy Farley and I were assigned to begin filling sandbags. Roy was a class clown, always goofing around during infantry training back in the States, and he liked to have a good time. He spent a lot of his free time at the club back at Ft. Lewis along with the other drinkers in the platoon. I wasn't one of them, but we got along just fine. I don't think we were shoveling dirt for more than 10 minutes before we were both dripping wet. I kept worrying that I wasn't going to be able to hack the heat; my only consolation was that most of the other guys weren't faring too well either.

We had help filling the sandbags from local Vietnamese laborers. That was a big shock to me: seeing all these Vietnamese on our base when we first rolled in on the buses a couple of days ago. It seemed that the lure of cheap labor outweighed any security concerns. The mess halls were manned by Vietnamese to do the work that nobody likes to do and to perform a lot of the general labor around the base. We learned that all the troops permanently stationed on the base had "hooch maids." They entered the base every morning, came to the barracks, make their beds, cleaned their areas, polished their shoes, and did their laundry. All this for literally pennies a day.

The base troops had permanent barracks with their own living space assigned to them. They had electricity so they could have fans, mini refrigerators, and stereos. There was also an enlisted men's club they could go to every night. The field troops only had tents and no space that they could call their own. Not that it mattered since we would hardly ever be there. Over time, this disparity of living conditions between the guys in the field and those in the rear led to some hard feelings. The guys on the base liked being "in the rear with the beer." The troops in the field had their own name for them: "REMFs," as in rear echelon mother fuckers. The REMF's far outnumbered the field troops at the height of the war. When the US had 540,000 soldiers in Vietnam less than 80,000 were in the field.

Our bunkers were built between our tents. In the event of a rocket or mortar attack it would only take a few seconds to get to it. They were built with a wood frame and half pipes of corrugated metal for roofs. Then the entire structure was enclosed with sandbags. I was pretty much ruined by the end of the first day working on them. I was hot, sweaty, and filthy dirty. I headed for the showers that were just cold water, gravity fed from overhead tanks. But it felt great to get clean. Had supper at the mess hall afterwards and was feeling pretty good. We all sat around on our cots BSing about our day until 9 PM or so.

About 1:00 AM sirens start going off, scaring the hell out of me. For one thing, I didn't know what they meant. Lieutenant Stockman showed up and told us it was a general alert and to prepare for a ground attack. Holy Hell!!! We all ran down to the armory to get our weapons. After that, we were deployed along the bunker line on the perimeter to wait—for nothing. This turned out to be the first of many false alarms and bogus intelligence reports that would lead us to a healthy skepticism of just about everything they told us. Not that we didn't think trouble was around; that was more than evident. We just didn't think they had any clue as to when or where it would happen.

We had another day or two of bunker building before we started

Redcatcher Combat School. We were told where to report and when. The night before school started we got the word that Martin Luther King Jr. was assassinated in Memphis, Tennessee. We didn't know much more than that for a while, but you didn't have to be in the Army long to know this was going to have an effect. The Army may have been in the forefront of civil rights, but it was made up of folks from civilian life who brought their prejudices along with them when they entered the military. There were lots of blacks who were having a hard time reconciling being drafted to fight for their country while discrimination was still an issue at home. The Civil Rights Act was only passed in 1964, and it was resisted in many parts of the country. Laws can't change attitudes overnight.

The mortar platoon was underrepresented racially. We had only one black guy; his name was Greg Jackson and he was from South Philadelphia. Greg was a leader for the second squad, an E-5 buck sergeant. While there was never any overt racism in the platoon, there was an undercurrent (among a few) of less than harmonious feelings toward blacks.

I guess when you think about it this tension shouldn't have been too surprising. The majority of the platoon was probably like me; they had likely gone to schools that were homogenous. In my high school there were exactly zero people of color. I had no interaction whatsoever with diverse cultures; therefore, when I did meet people of different ethnic backgrounds, there was a good chance we'd have little in common. And the fact is, commonality is the foundation of many friendships. So, when a white suburban kid like me meets a black inner city guy like Greg, odds are long that we are going to be great pals. Greg might as well have been from a foreign country for all we had in common.

I never heard my parents utter a racial slur or demean or disparage anyone of another color. Not everyone in the platoon had the benefit of such an equitable example. So it should be no surprise that people coming from racially insensitive backgrounds carried that baggage along with them into the service. My fellow squad member and class clown, Roy, was rather like that. Not a bad guy at all and a lot of fun, but somewhat insensitive to cultural differences.

The next day school started. I walked down with my best buddies in the platoon, Jim Wallace and Mark Byrd. Jim, who I called JP, was the third squad gunner and Mark was an ammo bearer like me. It wasn't too far a walk to the school, but JP and Mark were sweating up a storm in no time. They both were a little stockier than I was and weren't acclimating quite as fast. It was probably our fourth day in-country and I could tell I was already starting to adapt.

The school started out with most of the battalion assembled around an outdoor stage, probably around 400 people. An officer introduced himself and after a few preliminaries he asked for a show of hands of how many thought the United States should be involved in Vietnam. A handful of troops raised their hands. He made no comment on the result and started into his spiel. It was the first and last time I heard anybody from the Army try to give a good reason why we were there. I don't think he made many converts. He didn't ask for another show of hands when he was done.

After that, various instructors got up and explained what we would be doing the coming week. One of the first things was going to the rifle range so everyone could make sure their personal weapon was zeroed in and in fine working order. Of particular emphasis were mines and booby-traps; these were second only to small arms fire as a cause of death in Vietnam. Our brigade, in particular, worked in an area that was notorious for them. The school also had a typical Vietnamese village set up to teach you how to cordon (enclose and guard an area) and search a hamlet.

They showed examples of what might be found when we got out in the boonies: everything from punji pits to 155 mm artillery rounds rigged with tripwire igniters. It wasn't just what they looked like but how they could set up an enticement to draw a troop to it.

We reviewed claymore mines (A lens-shaped, ground-emplaced anti-personnel mine whose blast is focused in the direction of the oncoming enemy), M-72 LAWs (light anti- tank weapons) and grenades. We all threw live grenades at the range. The instructor told us the school had two accidents at the grenade range since it opened, killing a total of 8 troops. Vietnam was a dangerous place, even outside of combat; it wasn't too hard to accidentally kill yourself or your buddy. The Army had various names for this: misadventure, accidental self- destruction, accidental homicide, or just plain accident. I have no idea what the criteria was for each category. The death toll from them was in the thousands.

I'm not sure how long the school was, maybe five days or so. We spent those days getting our equipment ready to go and hump the boonies. At any rate, we were "off to the field" in a couple of days. Leaving the base usually was referred to as going to the field. In Vietnam the field was usually referred to as the boonies or the bush. For some units it was "Indian Country." The phrase "humping the boonies" usually meant days or weeks out in the field carrying heavy packs. The dictionary defines boonies as rural country or jungle and humping as a slang term for carry, especially on the back. In case you were wondering, there it is.

Typical for units in Vietnam, a few people in the company stayed at the main base while the rest went to the field. These included: the first sergeant (the top NCO in the company), the executive officer (second in command), the company clerk, and the supply clerk. I didn't remember any of their names, but I was searching websites some years ago when I ran across some pictures that one of the members of the company had posted online. There he was, "Supply Sergeant RAMBO." How could I forget!! Of course, it would have meant nothing at that time.

Nobody was going to feel sad that the first sergeant wasn't coming along with us; he was universally disliked. He epitomized the gulf between the enlisted men and the NCO's (non-commissioned officers). These were the career sergeants: usually platoon, first, and master sergeants. They were derogatorily called "lifers" by the enlisted personnel.

I arrived in Vietnam shortly after the Tet Offensive. It was the watershed event of the war. The aftermath of which split America in a way not seen since the Civil War. The sight of holes blown through the yard walls of the US Embassy and dead Viet Cong soldiers lying on the ground made an indelible impression on the American public. The idea that the American embassy could be attacked within the capital city of Vietnam flew in the face of years of upbeat reports by politicians and generals on the progress of the war.

In November of 1967, President Johnson summoned General Westmoreland to return to Washington and engage in a public relations campaign to shore up support in Congress, curry favorable press, and assure the American public that we were winning the war. The president wanted Westmoreland to point out in regards to the war, "that we could see the light at the end of the tunnel." That phrase would become infamous in the wake of the Tet Offensive and General Westmoreland's post-Tet request for 200,000 more troops to augment the half-million he already had. The TV images of the offensive and the Army's insatiable desire for more troops for a war we were "winning" caused a large portion of the American public to lose heart. A corner had been turned.

Ironically, TV pictures nowithstanding, the Tet Offensive proved to be devastating to the Viet Cong. They took horrendous casualties, their ranks were decimated, and the "General Uprising" did not materialize. The communists were counting on the general public to rally to their side once the offensive started, but the support was not there. In truth, they suffered a massive tactical defeat. Irony didn't stop there though. The tactical defeat the communists suffered during Tet was not recognized by the American public. The credibility of the president and the generals was now in question. The reports on the nightly news of the cities of Saigon, Danang, Hue, My Tho (and many others) being attacked, as well as large US bases like Long Binh and Cam Ron Bay, did not look like the results of a winning effort. In addition, the saga of the embattled and encircled marines at Khe Sanh played itself out for 77 days every night on the networks. When the siege ended, the Marines had lost 274 men. The fact that the North Vietnamese lost many thousands to the B-52 bombings that pummeled the encircling enemy troops was lost on the folks back home. The tide of public opinion had shifted. At the end of the day, the communists scored a strategic victory. What they couldn't win on the battlefield, they won in America's living rooms. You can't successfully wage war without the support of the citizenry.

We were in the post-Tet offensive era of the war. The US had turned the corner on the war, and the troops were generally ahead of those at home. 1968 was the transition year for the Army. The troops were still doing what they had to do but weren't happy about it. They weren't much interested in hearing any crap about how long their hair was or their lack of military bearing. The career sergeants were not adapting well to this new reality, and it caused a lot of grief for everybody involved. I might add that our platoon sergeant, Sgt. Browning, was also in this category. But to be fair, there were some good ones. The young officers, 2nd and 1st lieutenants, were actually much more in tune and, in general, coped with the situation a lot better.

Lt. Stockman had a platoon meeting and informed us of the date we would go to the field. He also told us we would be taking our mortars with us. This meant each man in the weapons platoon would be burdened with about 25 pounds more gear than the 3-line platoon members. We were given a list of what we would take to the field and began to put everything together; it was a daunting load. I'll start with the lightest: I threaded my dog tag chain through my P-38 can opener. It was all downhill after that. I had my M-16 along with 21 magazines containing 18 rounds of 5.56 mm ammo for a basic load of 378 bullets. The rifle weighs 8.8 pounds loaded, the magazines at least 15. My personal protective gear included a helmet, 2.8 lbs., flak jacket, 9 lbs., and four fragmentation grenades, 1 lb. each. We had a rucksack (knapsack) where we kept our personal stuff: toothbrush, shaving gear, writing pad, mosquito repellant, and cigarettes. Also our poncho, poncho liner and air mattress, four canteens of water (8 lbs.), individual compress bandage, and C-rations for three days. If we weren't carrying the mortars, we carried an assortment of other gear like the line platoons: claymore mines, M-72 LAWs, machetes, C-4 explosive, extra machine gun ammo, smoke grenades, trip flares, entrenching tools, etc., etc. But since we were carrying ammo—and I was an ammo bearer—I would be carrying three 81mm mortar rounds, weighing in at 7 lbs. each. Others would be carrying the tube, baseplate, and bi-pod. You could safely say that I carried at least 70 lbs. on my back!

If I had to guess, I'd say maybe we left for the field around the 10th of April, give or take a day. We were assigned a medic from the 93rd evacuation hospital. His name was Mike and once you heard him talk there was no need to be told he hailed from Boston. He seemed very enthusiastic; I had no doubt that he would see to it that everyone took their anti-malarial pills. The SOP (standard operating procedure) for the pills was that the medic had to watch you take the medicine. There were two reasons for this. One was that the once-a-week pill (a large orange one) came with some unpleasant side effects, mostly dealing with how fast you could get to a bathroom. The other reason was that troops who were seeing a lot of action might prefer getting malaria to staying in the bush.

On the eve of our departure for the field I'm sure all the guys were wondering what was to come. There obviously was a war going on, you could see it out in the distance. Every night you could see the gunships' tracers ripping into the hills only a few miles away. You could hear the roar of the F-100's climbing out of Bien Hoa air base on bombing missions. So, it was hard to pretend otherwise. There were a few guys who seemed gung ho about it, but I think they were a distinct minority. I think most of the guys were in a "well if this is what I have to do, I guess I'll do it," mode.

With all that was going on back in the states regarding the sentiments of the war and the decided lack of enthusiasm in Nam, I struggled to make sense of it all. It sure would make things easier if you believed in what you were doing. Still, there was a little part of me that wanted to see what it was like, a curiosity that was set apart from the politics. Maybe I thought of it as a test and wanted to see how well I would do.

Morning came after a fitful sleep. Then it was off to the mess hall for the last real breakfast I'd have for a while. We were going to be airlifted to our area of operations a little later in the morning. We were assigned different helicopter lifts. I had all my stuff ready to go when called. It seemed like more than enough to me, but some guys went over and above what was called for, figuring more is better. Lt. Stockman told us to saddle up and move out. The lift pad was a few hundred yards from our tents. Byrdy and I put on our rucks, strapped on or slung the rest of our equipment, grabbed our M-16's, and headed down the road to the helipad.

As on every other day we had been in-country, the wilting weather was an ugly mix of heat and humidity. It was only midmorning, but the rising heat was already spawning dust devils. As I mentioned before, Mark Byrd had a husky build. His weight plus all we were carrying was killing him already. Just our basic load was bad enough, but those 3 mortar rounds (21 lbs.) were just too much. We were about halfway to the pad when I looked over at Byrdy. He was bent over at the waist with sweat pouring off of him. I wasn't feeling so well myself. All of a sudden, I just burst out laughing at the absurdity of it all. Mark looked over at me asked: "What the fuck is wrong with you?" I was thinking about how we were supposed to jump off the chopper, run out away from it, and form a perimeter. I'm thinking: "Damn, with all this equipment, I'll be lucky if I can even crawl into it, let alone jump out of it and run. This is never going to work."

We formed up on the helipad in groups of 5 or 6 to board the choppers.

The choppers were running, and the downwash from the rotors was kicking up all kinds of dust and dirt and grit; some of it even stung a little. I squinted to lessen the chance of getting something in my eyes. I was not surprised when it became apparent that boarding and situating yourself on the floor of the chopper did not go as smoothly as everyone would have liked. We were just carrying too much—plain and simple.

Nonetheless, it was exciting! This was the first helicopter flight for just about all of us. Everyone sat on the floor; there were no seats other than those for the crew. There was quite a bit of vibration as the pilot spooled the engine up to speed, pulled pitch, and let the rotors dig into the air. You could feel the chopper get light on the skids and then gradually lift into the air. After rising 2 or 3 feet, the nose dipped down and we started to climb. The doors of the choppers in Vietnam were always left open so we had a great view as we banked over our tent city below. We topped out at about 1500 feet for our cruising altitude. This third flight of 6 choppers was headed northeast from Long Binh. My first helicopter ride didn't last very long; we were on the ground again in no time.

CHAPTER TWO
THE ROCKET BELT

Our LZ (landing zone) was only a few miles northeast of the Long Bien/Bien Hoa military complex. Our mission was to patrol an area out to about 6 miles or so beyond the bases to try to stop the Viet Cong from rocketing the airfield at Bien Hoa and the supply depots and ammo dumps at Long Bien, not to mention the 50,000 troops stationed there. The air force base was hit not 12 hours after we arrived 10 days ago, and several spots on the sprawling Long Binh base were hit since then. Just as I suspected, our "combat assault" looked pitiful as we dragged our heavily laden bodies out of the choppers and attempted to run out and form a perimeter. I wasn't concerned, I didn't think they would throw us into the lion's den the first time out.

After all the lifts were completed, we headed out toward our first NDP (night defensive position). It was already mid-day and I knew we would probably stop around 4:30 PM to dig in for the night. Sunset was a little after 6:00 PM. The company was spread out in a long single file line, walking through fields left fallow since the war started. The vegetation was mostly light green and brownish grass with clumps of brush scattered over a mostly flat landscape bordered by dense jungle. We walked about 3 or 4 hours that first day before reaching our overnight position. Those overweight packs just killed us, and everyone in the mortar platoon was dragging by the time we reached our destination.

Our first night was a template for many to come: arrange a perimeter, dig foxholes, prepare your C-rations for dinner, and get ready to go out on ambush duty, if your squad was selected for such, or maybe LP (listening post). Lt. Stockman called out the ambush squads that evening. For most of us, just being out in the field was adventure enough for the first night, and I was hoping not to be selected. I wasn't, but there were others who were.

One of the guys who was picked was none too happy about it. I heard him say to no one in particular: "Hey! I'm married." I had to laugh to myself, no way that was going to get anybody out of going out on ambush if their name was picked.

It was dusk when we heard an unwelcoming call emanating from the bush, "Fuck Yo-o-o-o-u, Fuck Yo-o-o-o-u." Damn, what the hell is that! It didn't sound quite human; yet, those were the words, no doubt about it! It was definitely unsettling. After hearing it a few more times, I thought it might be a bird. It was not. We were to learn later that it was actually a nocturnal lizard, some kind of Gecko apparently. At any rate, it was a crazy initiation into the Vietnam night.

I recently Googled "fuck you lizard" just for fun. Sure enough, I got a hit. So I'll give you the Etymology of the term—It was named "fuck you lizard" during the Vietnam war, as the lizard's cry sounds like "fuck you." The "fuck" sound is quite clear and short in duration, followed by about a one-half second pause, and then the "you"—elongated as yooooou. I always thought the elongated, yo-o-o-o-u made it sound much more personal.

The ambush squads headed out right before sunset as did the LP's. The listening posts were usually 2 or 3 men set out about 50 yards in front the NDP. Their job was to act as an early warning system to detect anyone attempting to get close to the perimeter. Several posts were set up every night. The ambush squads were made up of 6 to 8 men and several of those were sent out every night, typically one from each platoon. All of us, those in the NDP, the ambushers, and the LP's would be pulling guard duty throughout the night. I think we did an hour or two at a time several times a night depending on how many men shared your position.

Our first night was uneventful in reality, if not perception. I don't know about the other guys, but my first night's guard hours were filled with things I thought I saw and things I thought I heard. The eyes play tricks on you in the night, and if you stare at an object directly in the darkness it sometimes appears to move. We were taught to look slightly away from the point of interest to alleviate that problem. I was all eyes and ears those early days.

One of the first things we heard from troops who were there a while was: "We owned the day and Charlie owned the night."

The LP's and ambush squads returned to the NDP shortly after sunrise. We ate our C rations and prepared for our first full day in the bush. We were going to hump the boonies. We had a certain amount of territory to cover during any given day. We marched as a company to a point on the map and then broke up into platoons. The search method was called a cloverleaf. Each platoon would head out on a different compass heading, about 90 degrees apart—let's just say north, south, east and west. The object was to go out and backtrack a line that looked like a leaf. All four platoons doing the same thing described a four- leaf clover if drawn out on a map. We might do this several times a day. We were looking for bunkers, arms caches, food supplies, or anything else of value to the enemy. Also, our presence would hopefully disrupt enemy movement and deprive the Viet Cong the opportunity to set up rocket launches at night.

Our initial foray into the Vietnamese countryside produced little more than a few heat exhaustion casualties and one serious laceration from an errant whack of a machete. One good thing came of the heat casualties: they decided to send the mortars back to the BMB (brigade main base) at Long Binh. From now on they flew them out at night on the resupply chopper. That was great news for me; I suddenly had 21 pounds less to carry. It was still hard going, especially between the hours of 10 AM and 3 PM when the sun was high overhead, the temp bordering on 100 degrees, and the humidity nearing the century mark.

Guys like JP and Byrdy suffered: they still hadn't adjusted to the climate, and they couldn't get enough water. We were carrying 4 canteens (a gallon of water), and it was never enough for them. One day JP was tapped out of water early in the afternoon and was really hurting. I gave him a canteen; you would have thought I'd given him a quart of gold, he was so happy to get it.

April 18th was another long, hot walk in the sun. We had just finished setting up our NDP when the call came in on the radio that Charlie Company was in contact with the enemy, and the battalion commander wanted us to go to their aid. We were to take a direct route which meant going through heavy jungle.

By the time we were ready to move out, it was dusk. We entered the jungle already tired from a long day in the heat. Now we had to hack our way through heavy vegetation in the darkness of a jungle night. We made pitiful progress. For one thing, it wasn't just dark; it was like inside a cave dark. You literally had to keep a hand out to touch the guy in front of you to keep track of him. The footing was terrible; you couldn't see roots or fallen branches. The poor guys in front had a terrible time trying to hack away at the tangled undergrowth. After a few hours, it was obvious that whatever Charlie Company had gotten themselves into we were not going to play a role in it. The trek turned into an all-night affair. The distance might have been only an inch on the map (to whomever ordered this march), but a mile in that night jungle was like 10 out in the open. Everybody was super ticked-off by now at whose idea this was to tromp through this impenetrable growth in the dark. Cussing and grumbling were heard all night long as guys lost their balance after tripping or slipping on unseen tree roots and crashed to the jungle floor. Once you got a bit off-kilter, it was hard to stay upright with all that weight on your back. I was getting scratched up from the unseen rough edges of branches and tree limbs that snapped back into you after the guy in front of you pushed them aside as he walked through. The fact that a lot of guys were out of water didn't help. Exhaustion was beginning to set in, and guys who had stocked up on extras of everything back at Long Binh were beginning to "lose" stuff. With all the tripping and falling during the night, they figured they had a legitimate excuse if ever questioned.

We finally arrived at Charlie Company's location around 11 AM, long after we might have done them any service. We dragged ourselves into their perimeter, fairly well wasted. Considering that most of us had 4 or 5 hours sleep the night before, it was no wonder. We had been up for about 30 hours straight, most of those on the move. I soon noticed that the troops of Charlie Company looked worse than we did. Yeah, we had a rough time of it, but nobody was shooting at us.

My buddy Dan from Advanced Individual Training was in Charlie Company. I didn't see him around anywhere but didn't think too much of that as it wasn't unusual to have the company split up in different locations. We started to hear what had transpired during the night. The company had suffered two KIA's (killed in action) and a number of WIA's (wounded in action), including the company commander who lost his leg below the knee.

It was April 18th; we had been in-country 2 weeks. To the best of my knowledge, these were the first deaths in the battalion. Lt. Stockman gathered us around and told us that the battalion commander, Colonel Behm, was flying out to the site and would say a few words. A short time later we heard the low pitched, whup, whup, whup sound of the Huey's rotors as the colonel's chopper approached our position. The pilot flared the craft a few feet off the surface and touched down in a cloud of churned-up dust. When the dust settled, Colonel Behm got out and was met by one of the lieutenants. After a few words, they announced that we would be having a service for the deceased in about an hour.

I watched as a couple guys from Company C made up two field crosses side by side in a grassy clearing. The soldier's M-16 had its bayonet attached, then the rifle was stood stock end up, and the bayonet was stuck in the earth to hold the rifle upright. A pair of boots was placed in front of the bayonet and a helmet placed on the butt end of the stock. Several men formed an honor guard, rifles in hand to give a gun salute after the service.

Colonel Behm began to speak, saying something about how these men had not died in vain. He then called the lieutenant over to read the names. The platoon leader hesitated for a few moments, as if gathering fortitude. He then called out: "Specialist 4th class, Robert C. Klein" then, after a respectful pause, "Private First Class, Dan W. Morris." Hearing my buddy's name sucked the air right out of me. I felt a little light-headed and I wanted to sit down. God Damn It! I started feeling a little numb. The service continued with the rifle salute, ready—aim—fire. Then, again, ready—

aim—fire. Then a third volley to complete the tribute. I felt kind of hollow afterward, out of sorts I guess. Trying to get a grip. This rifle salute was a far cry from the first one I had ever witnessed. Up until now, the salute was always associated with good feelings, remembering back to my childhood days in Castle Shannon.

It was 1958, my first year in Little League baseball, and I was going to march in the Castle Shannon Memorial Day Parade with my teammates, wearing our Cardinals' uniforms. It being only 13 years after the end of World War II, there were plenty of veterans to take part in the community event. And kids too, even if they weren't in the parade. Back in the day, youngsters used to decorate their bikes with red, white, and blue crepe paper threaded through the spokes and attach colored streamers to the hand grips and little flag holders on the handlebars. Traditions going back to when Memorial Day used to be called Decoration Day. In fact, my Grandmother, who lived with us back then, still called it Decoration Day.

We used to form up at the school on Myrtle Ave, march down to Willow through "downtown" Castle Shannon, then up to Baldwin Street where we hung a right and climbed up to St. Anne's cemetery at the top of the hill. There used to be a tall cross at the very top of the hill and some open grassy area around it. The dignitaries gathered on that lawn and gave a speech or two. A priest or a reverend said a prayer. A military guy would say a few words, usually followed by a 21-gun salute by the VFW honor guard and then the playing of Taps.

As soon as the salute was over and the guard dismissed, we would run over to the grass and try to find a brass shell casing that was ejected from the rifles during the salute, a cool souvenir to have on Memorial Day. Next on the agenda was a walk down to the VFW where you got a free hot dog and a bottle of Regent pop. All in all, a very Norman Rockwell kind of day.

I was just ten years old back then and didn't really appreciate what the day was all about. But now, nearly a decade later, I understood all too well. My main problem (as with most of my compatriots) was this: did Dan and Robert really die for something? Colonel Behm's words not-withstanding, I would struggle with this issue my whole tour.

I didn't know Dan all that long, a little over two months actually. But sometimes when you make a connection with someone and you are with them 24/7, you can know them better than someone you may have known for years. Dan loved the ranch he lived on in Montana, and he let me know that he was terribly homesick for it. He liked to talk about it a lot and the plans he had for it when he got back home.

It's hard for me to say exactly how Dan's death affected me after the initial shock wore off. I just know that I didn't dwell on it. The world didn't stop because of it. We got up the next morning, saddled up, and headed out like any other day. I'm sure there was some psychology at play. As if by not thinking about it, I wouldn't have to acknowledge how easy it could happen to me. It was the beginning of a pattern.

Captain Conner said we were going to fly a few klicks (kilometers) northeast from our present location, and some of us would be guarding the communications relay station on Signal Mountain. Choppers picked us up in the morning for the short flight to our new area. Off to our left we could see Nui Ba Den, a singular mountain that seemed to rise up out of the flat plain around it, almost like a gumdrop in the middle of a cookie sheet. It was very distinctive as it was the only hill for as far as the eye could see. At 3200 feet high, you could see it from many miles around; therefore, it was a landmark for the troops and was used as a navigational aid by pilots. The mountain had many legends attached to it. The most prominent was the story of Ba Den, the namesake of the mountain. Ba Den was a young girl whose betrothed went off to war and was subsequently killed in battle. Ba Den was so distraught that she climbed the mountain and committed suicide so she could be with him. The English translation is "Black Virgin Mountain." We banked right and headed east toward Signal Mountain, much less impressive—it's not near as tall—but similarly distinctive as it rises up out of the fields.

The landing was uneventful and we headed out on patrol a few klicks away from the mountain. About 5:00 PM we stopped and set up our NDP. A couple of ambushes were sent out and some LP's, and the rest of us settled in for the night. We would climb the mountain tomorrow. Actually, even though it's called Signal Mountain, it's more like a hill.

The night was quiet, and after some breakfast we headed out on patrol. About mid-day we started climbing. The top of the hill was small and crowded with communication gear, so there was only room for one chopper to land. That's why we were climbing up. It wasn't too steep at the bottom, but soon the angle sharpened and we slowed considerably. With the weight of our rucksacks trying to pull us over backwards, we had to lean into the slope to avoid losing our balance. Toward the top we had to hold on to the trees to help pull ourselves up, and our footing was becoming less and less sure as the troops in front tore up the ground scratching their way to the top. We reached the apex about 90 minutes before nightfall. It was a tough climb and I was pretty well beat.

A resupply chopper landed shortly after we arrived, and we got some fresh water, C- rations, and our mail. I hadn't received any mail for a couple of weeks and was anxious to hear my name called. Happily, I got a handful. As would happen on several occasions during my tour, mail would get delayed for some reason, then you got a pile all at once. I decided to wait until I was done with everything else before I read the letters.

I completed my foxhole and heated up my rations for supper. Afterwards, I sorted my mail by postmark date to read them in order. Mom had been writing to me religiously every day since I left for Vietnam. It's not easy to come up with something new to say every day, so it was a bit of a struggle for Mom to do so. Consequently, I read things like, "Mary Kay wouldn't drink her orange juice today." But you know what? That was all right, because hearing something familiar in my all too unfamiliar world was just what I needed. It was a connection that helped me "keep it together," especially the first two, two and a half months. Those early months were the hardest for me. For days on end we patrolled all day, went out on ambushes at night, got little sleep, and repeated the process over and over. Nothing happened to our company, but you never knew when it might. It was stressful and tiring and scary. Those letters from my mom were a high point, sometimes the only one, in my day. I could put aside, if only for a moment, my cares and woes and return to a safer, more secure world.

Some Stars and Stripes newspapers were handed out. The paper had articles about the aftermath of the Martin Luther King assassination and some talk about the potential for peace talks in Paris. I turned to the sports pages and was saddened to see that one of my favorite race car drivers, Jim Clark, was killed on a race track in Germany. Clark had won the Indianapolis 500 in 1965.

I was bummed about Jim Clark, and while there was nothing wrong in that, it does reveal a dichotomy in my feelings. Only a few days ago, the brigade lost 9 men (one who I knew and considered a friend). After the initial shock, I somehow was able to block out any feelings regarding those losses. How was it I could mourn a race car driver I didn't really know, at a time I should have been grieving a lost friend. It certainly wasn't a conscious decision, and I don't think I was aware, at the time, of how I was dealing with the situation.

I finished the letters while sitting on a ledge overlooking the flat fields down below. I was looking west and the sun was setting. The azure sky transitioned into a horizon burnished in red, gold, and orange. It was a stunningly beautiful evening. It was a tad cooler at that elevation, and a slight wind was caressing the top of the hill. I was enjoying the view and appreciating my mom and the warmth that comes with knowing that someone loves you and is thinking of you always. It was a sweetly comforting moment.

After leaving the hill, we resumed patrolling the fields around its base. One night I was picked for an ambush, and we moved out into position shortly before dark. There were probably 8 of us at that location. Paul Randle and I were rear security. That was unfortunate for me because Randle, for some unknown reason, liked to give me a hard time. I'm a naturally passive person, so I always pretended what he said didn't bother me. But in truth he was getting under my skin. I figured I could live with it since I got along fine with everyone else.

Frank Jordon was along with us that night as well. Frank could have been a poster child for ADD, had that label existed back then. Frank was hyperkinetic and showed way more enthusiasm than most of us. Captain Conner appreciated his interest and took him under his wing. The captain taught him about explosives and how to set booby-traps. Frank was really getting into the spirit of things. I was sleeping when the explosion awoke me. I grabbed my rifle and scanned in front but was unable to see anything. Apparently, no one else did either because there was no firing. Frank swore he saw movement in front of his position and threw a hand grenade. I don't know if there was or not, but we checked out front at first light and found no evidence that anyone had been there.

We headed back to join up with the rest of the company, had some breakfast, and started our patrolling for the day. Like many other days, it was just a long hot walk in the sun. We were setting up our NDP and digging foxholes when someone spotted a lizard running into a hole in the ground. One idea led to another and a plan was hatched to catch the lizard. I'm not sure if it was the same hole the lizard went down or another close by, but a green smoke grenade was tossed down a hole. The details escape me now; at any rate, a newly dyed, bright green reptile was captured. It didn't swear at us like our first lizard encounter, which was surprising as he wasn't too happy with the situation. Then came the best idea: we'll send it back to our beloved first sergeant. When the supply chopper left that evening it had a passenger onboard. Our little (12 to 18 inches long) green monster was packed away in an ammo box with the first sergeant's name on it. We really, really would have loved to be there when he opened it!

The next day we continued our patrolling of the Rocket Belt. The routine would be the same for the next couple of weeks: up at daybreak, a bite to eat, saddle up, and move out for a long hump in the boonies. I don't think we accomplished much in those days in regards to the war effort, but we did learn how to deal with our new environment. The heat and humidity were oppressive but became more tolerable as time went by. I can't say the backpacks ever began to feel lighter, but I think we started walking a little less hunched over. After a long day beating the bush I wasn't totally spent. I'd still have some water left and enough energy to dig my foxhole in a reasonable amount of time.

The fear factor had waned some, too. A distant gunshot no longer produced a knot in my stomach or a strangely metallic taste in my mouth. Not only had I put Dan's death into a deep recess of my mind, but I soon realized that fear drains you just as much or even more than the physical demands of the day. You would never make it if you dwelled too much on the danger. I put myself into a state of mind where I wasn't going to worry about things that might happen. Not to say I didn't have anxiety; I just suppressed it until there was a palpable reason to have it. I'm not saying this was a conscious choice on my part; it was more of a subconscious decision to stay sane. This coping mechanism, turning a blind eye to things that happened or maybe could happen, served me well—for the most part. Especially while I was in-country. In the end, it would cause me to doubt my humanity.

Bien Hoa and Long Binh were still being rocketed despite the presence of our battalion in the area. Trouble was, the Rocket Belt covered a wide area and since we were in their backyard, so to speak, I'm pretty sure they had a good idea where we were most of the time. Besides that, it took very little time to set up and fire a rocket. A lot of times the Viet Cong would forgo the use of a proper launcher and merely prop up a rocket on a pair of crossed bamboo poles. They looked like a big letter X. We ran across a number of these while patrolling. The VC laid the rocket in the notch of the X, aimed it in the direction of the airbase or maybe the ammo dump, and let it fly. Launched this way it wasn't very accurate, but the airfield and supply base were huge, so it was likely to hit something. It was unnerving for the troops stationed there because the rockets hit so randomly. Not being close to a prime target gave no assurance that a rocket wouldn't fall on your head in the middle of the night. By using the bamboo instead of a launcher, the VC could high- tail it as soon as the rocket was launched. This was important because camp and base radar could triangulate the launch position and send artillery counter-fire within minutes.

We covered a lot of ground every day, sometimes fallow farmland, sometimes thick jungle. We encountered no enemy soldiers but found evidence of their presence besides just the bamboo poles. We found enemy bunkers stocked with food and armaments. The Army called these "caches." The word comes from old French and means to hide or conceal. It was disheartening to find bags of rice in enemy bunkers labeled with US markings and the phrase "a gift from the people of the United States" stenciled on the bags. We were all new but learning fast that things were a lot different than what we were led to believe.

We also found small pieces of paper scattered all over the landscape. They were leaflets usually dropped from helicopters over enemy territory. The leaflets carried a message encouraging the VC to defect to the government side. In theory, an enemy soldier could use the leaflet as a safe conduct pass. The program was called Cheiu Hoi. Loosely translated, it meant "open arms." The general consensus among the troops was that the Cheiu Hoi program's main accomplishment was supplying the enemy with toilet paper.

The Army runs on rumors. A persistent one was a coming offensive by the North Vietnamese Army and Viet Cong. Word was that a high-ranking VC officer was captured and told his interrogators that a major push would occur toward the end of April or the beginning of May. With this in mind, we were dug in one night in defensive positions about 6 miles north of Long Binh. We got word that a recon unit spotted about 100 VC headed toward our position. Upon hearing this, I dug my foxhole a little deeper. Shortly thereafter, the brigade's artillery battery started pounding the area to our north for pretty much the rest of the night. It was a restless night and I didn't sleep well, even when it wasn't my turn to pull guard duty. Morning dawned without us taking any fire through the night. Patrols were sent to check out the area that was hit by the barrage. Nothing was found that indicated the enemy was hit. Either they headed off in a different direction after being spotted, or they were the result of an overactive imagination on someone's part.

Guys were edgy as it was, being new and all. Plus, all the rumors didn't help ease the tension. A couple of days after the night of the artillery barrage we got word again that a lot of VC were in our area. Our position that night was in an open area covered in waist-high grass. We were in fairly close proximity to other units in our battalion, and one of those units spotted some enemy troops and engaged them.

Captain Conner decided to call for a flare ship. Flare ships were old C-47 aircraft from WW II, equipped with guns. Bien Hoa Air Force Base was close by, so it didn't take long for one to arrive. High overhead, we could hear the drone of the old radial engines as it passed over our position. Soon we heard a pop as a flare ignited above us. The flares came in metal tubes about 3 feet long and 5 inches in diameter, weighing about 30 pounds. They drifted down on parachutes, staying lit for over 3 minutes. Several were dropped in a delayed sequence on each pass of the aircraft, so the ground below was continuously illuminated. The flares were incredibly bright (2 million candlepower) and lit up a large area.

The night was eerie. There was a fair breeze, and the tall grass was swaying in the wind. The flares burned with an amber color, bathing the landscape in an unnatural glow. The flares, floating down under their parachutes, were oscillating with the currents of air causing the sea of grass to cast multiple moving shadows from different directions. It was almost disorienting and definitely spooky.

The plane stuck around for about an hour. The last flare in the sky was burning out when I heard the plane passing overhead. Then I heard a whistling sound. The sky was pitch-black and I couldn't see anything, but the sound was intensifying. A couple of seconds later I heard a thud out in front of my position. When morning came I searched out in front of my foxhole and found a flare tube imbedded a foot into the ground.

Apparently, it was a dud of sorts as it did not ignite and the parachute did not deploy. This flare didn't put out any light, but it came within a few feet of putting out my lights. Lucky!

The next night one of the guys flipped out in the early morning hours. It may have been 3 or 4 AM. I don't remember the guy's name, but I recall that he was a big, husky black guy who usually had a placid demeanor. I don't know if it started with a bad dream or what, but he started screaming and yelling, most of it was unintelligible. A couple guys tried to calm him without success. He became belligerent and started getting physical. In the end it took about 6 troops to subdue him. He was sent back to the brigade main base on the next supply chopper. He didn't come back.

Captain Conner told us that we would be staying at our next NDP for several days in order to search the area more thoroughly for arms caches. Our new position was in a small clearing abutting some thick jungle. We began setting up as usual, clearing some lines of fire and setting up claymore mines and trip flares, when a couple of guys spotted a bamboo viper in the undergrowth. They are relatively small and light green in color which makes them hard to spot. They are just one of the twenty or more poisonous snakes that call Vietnam home. The bamboo viper seemed to be the one you most often heard about. It had the nickname "Two Stepper." Supposedly, that's how far you got before dropping over dead. I'm sure that was just one more legend of the boonies, but I certainly didn't want to find out. The fact that I basically slept on the ground every night made me feel vulnerable. Once the snake was spotted, our new NDP was immediately named the "snake pit."

The snake pit offered up a couple of more surprises that evening while we were digging our foxholes. Seems we opened up some shallow graves. The spot was probably the scene of some fighting, maybe years ago since the bodies were completely decomposed except for the bones. The VC always tried to bury their dead quickly before leaving the site of a battle so our army wouldn't know how many of them were killed. Young males, being in general an irreverent bunch, saw nothing wrong in utilizing some of the remains for an impromptu game of skull soccer. I know it should have bothered me to see someone's cranium used as a soccer ball, but it didn't. Time and place having something to do with that, I suppose.

The monsoon season in southern Vietnam is officially from May to October. It was the end of April and we had already seen a few showers, so we started making little lean-tos, since while on guard duty you were exposed to the rain. We cut off branches from trees for tent posts and tied our ponchos to them with nylon rope.

One night we had a big storm: thunder and lightning, and a torrential downpour. The rain fell from thousands of feet high, meaning those drops were cold. I sat there shivering and soaked to the bone. I couldn't see or hear anything other than the storm. Someone could have driven a tank up in front of me and I wouldn't have known it. Luckily, I had a poncho liner to wrap around myself; however, it wasn't waterproof like my poncho. I couldn't use it anyway since it was set up as my shelter. The liner did afford some warmth: it was like a small blanket made with polyester batting and a nylon rip-stop covering. It was a valued possession out in the field and sometimes hard to come by. For some reason, they were in short supply. Yes, no one thinks of Vietnam as being cold. In general, that's true. But, I've had more than one night sitting on the ground in a cold hard rain and got to the point where my teeth were actually chattering.

We began patrolling deeper into the jungle. Sometimes the heavy undergrowth made travel very difficult with "wait-a-minute" vines snagging you or your equipment. Occasionally, there was no other way but to hack through with machetes which we all carried. Other times the jungle floor was somewhat clear due to a couple of layers of higher growth that blocked out the sun to the point that not much grew on the jungle floor. These jungles were called double or triple canopy, as in three layers of growth at different heights. They were dark and sometimes smelled of rotting vegetation.

There were bugs aplenty, insects of all sorts: spiders, scorpions, red ants, black ants, and no end of mosquitoes. One of the mysteries of the jungle were the red ants. They were small but had a bite that hurt like hell. You never got bit by just one—and there the mystery lies. They lived in trees and bushes of the tropical forests. It was impossible to walk through the jungle without brushing into the undergrowth. We usually traveled in single file, one man following in the footsteps of the man in front. So, the ants either dropped on you or were knocked onto each troop as they passed by the colony. The ants then made their way under your fatigues without you knowing.

Then, as if on command by some Head Honcho ant with a silent whistle, the attack began. Suddenly you were being bit on your back, your neck, your legs, and places where you least wanted them. Besides yourself, there might be four or five other guys simultaneously starting the fire ant dance. First you swear, then you start throwing down your gear and ripping off your backpack while pounding the life out of the little creeps through your fatigues. This entailed bending, twisting, and turning to get a good shot at whacking the little guys wherever they might be on your body. Lastly, you take your clothes off to search for any that might be hiding out for a later attack. It could have been a funny sight if they didn't hurt so badly.

Another denizen of the jungle was the leech. And while they didn't hurt like the ant bites or itch like the mosquito bites they carried a level of revulsion unmatched by the other irritants. Basically, they suck the blood out of you. I know they are just another one of God's creatures and all, but they are ugly as sin and very easy to hate. They range from an inch or two in length, colored black or reddish-black, and are slimy as snot.

Most often you get them from wading through standing water; however, sometimes they get on you when you're not even near the water. Naturally, we took precautions. I tucked my pant legs into the top of my boots and tied the laces tight. The leeches still found their way in. They were prevalent enough that we regularly stopped for leech checks. So, there we were, in the middle of the jungle with our pants down, checking for leeches. Strange sight, no doubt. It wasn't unusual to find one of the little suckers blown up as big as your pinky finger, engorged with your blood, latched onto your calf.

There were two standard methods for removing the leeches. You didn't want to just grab them and pull them off: their little teeth might stay embedded in your skin and get infected. So, we used insect repellent or a lit cigarette to cause them to release and fall off.

I guess you have to give the little slimes credit for the ingenious way they have of latching on without you knowing it. First, they secrete an anesthetic onto your skin so you won't feel it when they sink their little teeth into your flesh. Then they inject an anticoagulant into the wound to keep the blood flowing freely. Once you give it a "bug juice shower" (the repellant) or touch the hot end of a smoke to the leech, it falls off. You keep bleeding for some time until the anticoagulant is flushed out. It wasn't unusual to see several guys with little rivulets of blood flowing down their legs after a leech check.

One time when we were up in War Zone D and had a leech check after wading through some waist-high water. We were proceeding with the check when I heard Sgt. Trout yell, "God Damn It!" Ordinarily, finding a leech was so common that it didn't invite swearing with such emotion, so I knew something else was wrong. Well, it was a leech, but poor John had found it on one of his testicles. Clearly, the removal process would be of a more delicate nature than usual. The bug juice works fine, but it is slightly irritating to the skin and actually burns if applied to more sensitive areas. Bug juice ruled out, it was time for Fred to light up a cigarette.

I think the platoon collectively felt John's anguish. Still, there was a certain element that could not help but perceive a level of amusement value watching John—ever so delicately—dispatching the disgusting creature. In our defense, comic relief was in short supply out in the boonies, so you had to grab a laugh anytime the opportunity presented itself. Unfortunately, Sgt. Trout's encounter with the leech in such a sensitive area reinforced fears that a certain rumor about the disgusting creatures just might be true. Word was that a particular species of tiny leeches had the ability to worm its way up into a certain organ unique to men. While the rumor was probably apocryphal, once an idea like that gets embedded in your head it's hard to dislodge.

The days were starting to blend together. There were no weekends, no days off, no kicking back with a beer in the evening, no TV, no radio. It rained more days than it didn't. We stayed up on guard duty or ambush for hours every night. I usually woke up wet and went to bed wet, wore the same clothes for weeks, didn't have a shower for ages, and stunk like hell but was oblivious to it. I'm so thankful for the letters I got from home, sometimes, they were the only bright spot in the day.

The days were just so full that I had no time for anything. Just trying to write a letter home was a chore: my paper got soaked by the rain or by the sweat pouring off my face when it wasn't raining, ballpoint pens quit working, or my envelopes refused to seal. One nice thing, we didn't have to pay for postage. We just wrote the word "Free" in the upper right hand corner, put it on the next resupply chopper, and off it went back to the "world."

Everybody had their own little rituals when it came to eating: what they ate and how they prepared it. It was one of the few things we had any control over, so it took on more importance than was justified. Sometimes we carried two or three days of C- rations with us. They came in cans, and I used to carry them in a sock. You could stack quite a few cans in a sock. Then I tied it onto my rucksack. The C-rations or "C-rats," as they were sometimes called, came in cases that were dropped off by the supply chopper. There were 12 meals to a case, and they came labeled as B-1 units, B-2 units, and B-3 units. I always tried to get at least one B-1 unit and one B-3 unit for every day. I liked the B-1 unit because it had fruit and the B-3 because it had cookies and cocoa. I started every morning with cookies and cocoa; that was my ritual and I was bummed if I didn't have it. Of course, they had a lot of other stuff in them, but I never ate much of it.

Everyone made themselves a little C-ration stove. You took a short can, removed the top with your "P-38" can opener, then used a beer can opener to put little triangular openings all around the bottom to let plenty of air in. We were supposed to have heat tabs which were small blue tabs made of a substance like Sterno that you could light and heat your C-rats with, but we never had them. Instead we used C-4, which was an explosive. All of us carried sticks of C-4 to blow up bunkers with; however, it was safe to light and burn. So, you pried off a chunk of C-4, rolled it in a ball, placed it in your stove, and you were ready to cook. One thing about C-4: once it's lit you can't put it out, and it burns crazy hot. Anyway, I opened up the cookie can, emptied it and filled it with water, poured in the cocoa mix, added the cream and sugar packets from the accessory pack, and heated. I'd dip my cookies in the cocoa and eat them one by one. After that I had my morning smoke.

My lunch was usually a can of fruit. We didn't have much time to sit around and cook anything, so the fruit was quick and easy. Now, you could eat the meat that came in the cans cold, since all the food was pre-cooked. But just looking at cold pork slices in congealed fat (let alone the sucking sound it made when I tried to pull one out of the can) was enough to destroy my appetite. So, fruit it was. My favorites in order of preference: pears because the syrup wasn't thick, and if you were around a stream, you could put the can in and drop it a few degrees before eating, making it a bit more refreshing; peaches because if I was lucky enough to have a can at night with a can of pound cake, I could put the peaches on the pound cake and that was absolutely as good as it got; fruit cocktail—and last and most definitely least, apricots.

We usually had a little more time for the evening meal, so cooking was in order again. You could trade around for something that was to your liking as everyone had different tastes. I liked the Turkey Loaf, Beans and Wieners, Spaghetti and Meatballs, Boned Chicken and Meat Loaf. Ham and Eggs was ok if you didn't look at it. That covers about half of the canned meats. The worst of the rest was Ham and Lima Beans. It had such a bad reputation that I never tried it.

Cooking with C-4 explosive took some getting used to because it burned so hot. You definitely missed your stove after making a few attempts to save time by cooking without it. I can remember just tearing off a chunk, laying it on the ground and lighting it, then holding my can of cocoa water over it. If you cut the top lid off a certain way, you could make a handle to hold the can with. Anyway, if you did this and a wind shift caught you off-guard, you usually ended up burning all the hair off the back of your hand. My first attempt at spaghetti and meatballs ended in disaster. The C-4 burned so hot and so fast that the contents of the can rose up out of it a third of the way. The top third was cold, the bottom third burnt, and I ate the middle.

Other items of interest were the aforementioned Pound Cake, not bad at all. Pecan Roll was also pretty good. Then there was the Fruit Cake; let's just say you had to be starving. Then there was White Dread—whoops, Freudian slip there. I meant White Bread. It was pretty much inedible. It came with jam which you could use on the crackers that came with processed cheese (which was also inedible). Then there was peanut butter which more often than not had the oil separate in the can, leaving a dry hunk of I don't know what. It took a full quart of water to get it down.

When we were down south in the more populated areas, the kids were always begging us for food. One day we were riding through Saigon in stop-and-go traffic, slow enough that we attracted a bunch of kids. They ran alongside, yelling for us to throw them C- rations. So, we all started tossing them some cans. I saw one kid make a fine catch of a can, look down at it, and then throw it back in the truck—White Bread! You couldn't give it away! The accessory pack that came with each meal contained a plastic spoon, coffee, salt and pepper, sugar and cream, chewing gum, toilet paper, and 4 cigarettes and matches. There were 9 different brands of smokes; Marlboro, by far, was the most popular with the troops. Salem were another one, easily the most popular brand with the Vietnamese. Smoking was something that I'll bet 80% of the guys in the Army did. I don't think I gave it much concern as a health issue. My Dad smoked; Tareyton was his brand. Those were the days when you could send your kid down to the corner store to buy them for you. But back to the point, I enjoyed a smoke: like that one after my cocoa and cookies in the morning or that last one at dusk after a hard day humping the boonies.

CHAPTER THREE
FIRE SUPPORT BASE PARIS

Rumors continued to fly about an offensive by the VC and NVA (North Vietnamese Army). Two NVA regiments were supposedly in the area. The powers that be apparently took them seriously enough to move us closer to the Long Binh/Bien Hoa complex. We set up a base along Highway 1 a few miles east of the big base. Our company was going to provide security. Base might be too strong a word for what it was: there were no amenities there, just some fortified bunkers and a communications station. Some of us got to stay there on a revolving basis while others went out on patrol. We didn't need to dig foxholes every night. Compared to the previous three weeks, it was a little bit of luxury.

I was on bunker guard one night when I spotted tracers. Tracers are bullets that have some phosphorus or other ignitable material in the tail. After the bullet is fired, the phosphorous ignites and burns a bright red, enabling the shooter to follow the path of the bullet. In the distance, maybe a mile from our position, the tracers were flying both ways; somebody was in a firefight. We hurried up and grabbed a radio and started checking the frequencies of our sister companies. When we got to D company we found out who we were looking at across that mile of jungle.

One of D company's platoons was engaging the enemy in a fierce firefight. We tuned into the involved platoon's frequency and heard the platoon leader describing what was happening to his company commander. You could hear the intensity, anxiety, and fear in the lieutenant's tone. He had troops wounded, and he had to get them medical attention soon or some of them might not make it. He wanted a medevac helicopter in the worst way, but the gunfire was too heavy to risk a dust-off attempt. His despair about not being able to get his men to safety resounded in his voice. His emotions were so raw, his feelings so personal that I was stressing out just listening to him. The VC disengaged shortly thereafter, and the firing came to an end. Medevac choppers were able to land and evacuate the wounded. The next morning, we learned that D company suffered 6 wounded but that all of them would make it.

We headed out that morning to patrol the area around FSB Paris. We didn't get very far when we spotted the wreckage of a plane about twenty-five feet up in some trees. It was a small plane, piper cub size, used for recon or artillery spotting. It was olive green in color and possessed the markings of the US Army. The wings were sheared off and the fuselage was inverted. One couldn't help but wonder: "What was the story here? Did the pilot live or die? Was he shot down or did he have a mechanical failure?"

We occasionally encountered these markers (ersatz memorials to what had gone on in the years before us) while out on patrol or when traveling down the dirt roads of the provinces. The carcass of a burnt-out truck or Armored Personnel Carrier was left to rust where it lay, testimony to some long-forgotten ambush or firefight that snuffed out somebody's father, son, or brother. When we passed those steel skeletons, there were no shared memories of what happened in that place and time. No one could have known who died there or how. Somehow the thought of that anonymity always made me sad.

FSB Paris, built alongside Highway 1, enabled us to come into contact with the locals for the first time, although, the manner in which it occurred was a little disconcerting. Many times after sweeping certain areas we ended our patrols at some point along Highway 1. We left the jungle to intersect the road only to find a group of Vietnamese within a few hundred yards— waiting for us. How did they know where we would be coming out? But our concerns about security breaches didn't keep us from enjoying what these traveling road shows had to offer.

The Vietnamese showed up on their little motorcycles or Lambretta utility vehicles (their version of a pick-up truck but smaller and with 3 wheels) with cold cokes that were packed in ice within Styrofoam containers. After beating the bush all day, a cold coke can taste really good. There was a rumor going around that the locally bottled Coca Cola had formaldehyde in it, but that didn't stop too many people from partaking in the refreshment. They also brought souvenirs for GI's to buy. They did a pretty good business. We had all been in the boonies with absolutely no place to spend any money.

I got to talking with this one fellow who was selling watches. He had this wooden case that he strapped to the back of his little Honda 50 motorcycle. It held his stock of wristwatches. He spoke English fairly well so we had a nice conversation. I wasn't in the market just then for a watch, but I let him give me his sales spiel anyway. It wasn't hard to tell that the watches were all cheap knock-offs of well-known brand names. Even though I think he would have been happy to rip me off, he was still fun to talk to, and he seemed to know a lot about real quality watches. After he gave up trying to sell me something, he started telling me about the best watches to have. His first choice was Longines, followed by Rolex, Omega, and Bulova. This was back in the day when watches still had mechanical movements and employed jewels to reduce friction and improve accuracy. The advertisements for watches boasted of 17, 21 or even 25-jewel movements. He told me he could tell the quality of the watch just by listening to it.

The Vietnamese, we were learning, had a standard rating system for everything. It was an easy 1 through 10 rating system. Number 1 was the best and number 10 the worst. What seemed funny about it was that every Vietnamese, whether they knew one word of English or not, always knew number 1 or number 10. Of course, everything they were selling was always number 1. Anyway, after my watch education I asked my new friend what he thought of my Timex. He said Number 14!

We also talked about motorcycles. I told him about my Yamaha 250 and what bikes were popular in America. He introduced me to some of his fellow hucksters, and I chatted with them for some time as well. I was enjoying myself; it was great to be out of the jungle and having some interactions with the local population. He also offered me a Pall Mall cigarette, a generous gesture I felt was impolite to turn down. Of course, he assured me they were number 1. Well, with apologies to my brother Fran who smoked Pall Malls, it tasted terrible. But I didn't want to seem ungrateful, so I smoked the whole thing.

Along with the hucksters came the girls: females who showed up wherever the army had a base or on a road in the middle of nowhere, where we happened to be that day. Like the hucksters, they were selling their "wares." I never felt like participating in those festivities. I can't say it was a moral issue as I never felt that those who did were committing horrible sins. Maybe I was one of the two guys in the unit who remembered those graphic pictures from Basic or saw the rolling pin size hypodermic on the wall back at the medic's shack in Long Binh used as a scare tactic against contracting the clap. Heck, I didn't daydream about girls any less than any other guy, but none of my musings ever involved pulling out my wallet. I guess I'm just a romantic that way. I felt sorry for the girls; I could never imagine anyone doing that kind of work unless they were so desperate that they had no other choice. For me, it just didn't feel right.

We continued our sweeps of the areas around FSB Paris, and I was continuously amazed at being met by the road show that appeared at every road crossing. Nevertheless, it was always fun to see them—security issues aside.

We all started to learn the lexicon of the Vietnam War from the

Vietnamese road show and from troops from other units at FSB Paris who had been in-country longer than us. Communicating with the locals who followed the troops around was accomplished by using pidgin language: simple words and phrases combining two or more languages. They made their living off the troops, so they had a good incentive to learn English. We learned some Vietnamese from them: some things useful like lai dei and dung lai (which means come here and stop, respectively) or boo koo (from the French beaucoup), meaning a lot, and ti ti, meaning a little.

The "working girls," also known as "boom-boom" girls or "short time" girls, solicited the troops with come-ons like: "Hey G I, you want short time love, boo koo boom-boom, ti ti money?" And it really wasn't very much money. If a troop had some cigarettes, he could use those to barter. If a guy wasn't too particular what the girl looked like, a few packs of Salems did the trick (pun intended).

We learned that xin loi (pronounced sin loy) means I'm sorry. However, most Vietnamese use it more like "sorry bout that" in a tone lacking any sincerity at all. Consequently, most GI's used it disingenuously as well. Like in faux sympathy for the VC after an air strike—as in, "Xin loi, Motherfuckers."

Di di mau was another useful phrase; it meant, "Get out of here, quick!" My favorite pidgin phrase combined French, English, and Vietnamese. Beaucoup Dinky Dau—It was the phrase for crazy in the head. Choi-oi! Was an exclamation of surprise often heard when you offered too little to buy something they were selling.

As mentioned previously, the rating system of #1 and #10 was used for just about anything. Curiously, with the exception of my watch salesman buddy, I never heard any Vietnamese use any of the numbers in-between. While number 1 was just number 1 (with no superlatives added to make something special), number 10 did have some extras to get the point across to show just how bad any particular item, idea, person, or place could be. More often than not, these extras were directed at people. The first of these was "Number 10 thou" (thousand). Granted, a big leap from 10. The worst of these was "Number fuckin 10 thou." The latter almost always directed at a person, and never uttered without true vehemence in their voice.

Some guys learned some Vietnamese phrases they thought might do them some good but, without fail, proved utterly useless when dealing with pretty girls in the local populace. You might be able to say chou co (hello miss) or chou ong (hi honey) or add a beaucoup ban dep (you are beautiful) or at a stretch amh yeu em (I love you), but you were getting nowhere. If she wasn't a "working girl" or trying to sell you something, you were studiously ignored. If a response was forthcoming, you might get a "never happen G I," or "No biet" (I don't understand).

We were also learning the GI lingo of the war. I have to address the word fuck, first. Granted, the word wasn't invented in Vietnam; but it was used in every conceivable fashion there—Noun, Verb, Adverb, and Adjective. Likely used more often than any other words in the dictionary with the possible exception of "a" or "the." Swearing was as prosaic as "pass the fucking salt." Not that I never swore, but I refrained from over-indulging, preferring to save my swearing for maximum stress relief for when I really needed it. Anytime you overuse something, it loses its potency.

Most GI's in Vietnam felt they were getting screwed over by being there, at least in the post-Tet Offensive years when the country turned the corner on the war. First, they were drafted, put in the infantry, then sent to Vietnam. It became apparent, even to the lowest private, that with the way things were run we were never going to win. Caught between poor strategy and increasing tensions between the career soldiers and themselves, it was no wonder that they started looking at their situation unfavorably.

Consequently, they felt the need to give affirmations to every crummy thing that happened. "Fuckin A, man" was one, or "Damn straight." "There it is" was usually used when there was no need to comment any further on an absurd situation. "Don't mean nothin" was a phrase that was used to hide feelings that were the exact opposite. Maybe you lost some guys in a firefight, maybe someone was killed in a "friendly fire" accident or guys were being maimed regularly by booby-traps. And for all of that, you had nothing to show for it: no territory won, no ground gained, no local citizenry thanking you for your efforts, and the folks back home skeptical of the whole venture. If it all got to be too much to take, you could get numb to the point that: "It don't mean nothin." A coping mechanism, to be sure; you do what you have to do to get by. A verbal shorthand developed to cover practically any situation. "There it is" covered the insanity; "It don't mean nothin" covered the result.

One of the major problems contributing to the GI's consternation over war policy was the ARVN (Army of the Republic of Viet Nam). It was apparent that the US troops were getting assigned to the harder missions. So, it was like—Hey! Aren't we supposed to be HELPING them? It seemed like the other way around. Whereas the US Army went on "search and destroy" missions, the ARVN's went on "search and avoid" missions. This stuck in the craw of the troops. Also, particularly in Saigon, you saw a lot of young guys who were obviously not in the service. Here we were drafted, coming 10,000 miles to fight, while they're zipping around Saigon on their motor scooters. There were rumors that if you had money and connections you could get out of serving (Not unlike our own country).

As in most wars, the enemy is easier to kill (in a psychological sense) if he can be de-humanized. In Vietnam one way to do this was to refer to them by disparaging names. So, the Viet Cong or NVA were referred to as

Dinks, Slopes, Slants, Zipper Heads (don't ask), or Gooks. Gooks was probably the most popular. Problem was: Everybody was Vietnamese— friend and foe alike. Considering the not so sterling reputation of "our" Vietnamese, it was easy to see how some GI's came to the point that a Gook is a Gook is a Gook, no matter what. I should add here, most of that animosity was directed at the Vietnamese as a whole and not on an individual level. On personal levels, there were a lot of friendly relationships.

Continuing with some of the slang of the Vietnam war:

"Charlie"... The enemy, officially the Viet Cong (Vietnamese Communist) or more often the VC. The military uses the word Charlie for the letter C in the phonetic alphabet. Hence, the VC, becomes Victor Charlie, which 99% of the time is shortened to just Charlie. Occasionally, he would be referred to as Chuck, Charles, or even Sir Charles, usually by the black guys.

"Rock and Roll"... Firing your weapon on full automatic.

"Dust-Off"... A medevac helicopter, probably so named for all the dust it kicks up when picking up a casualty.

"Shake N' Bake"... Name given to "quickly made" sergeants who attended a 3 month class back in the states.

"Wasted" or "To Waste"... Killed or to kill, respectively.

"Puff the Magic Dragon"... Name given to old WW II, C-47 transport plane turned into a gun platform. It had 3 guns capable of spitting out 6000 rounds a minute. When doing so, especially at night, the tracers formed a continuous red line from plane to ground just like a laser beam. In addition, so many rounds were fired so fast that no individual round could be heard going off, just an unearthly roar. Very scary!!

"Crispy Critters"... Name given to enemy burn victims of napalm. Derived from a popular breakfast cereal of the time.

"The World"... Back in the USA

"Freedom Bird"... Usually the commercial jet that would fly you back to "The World."

"Mad Minute"... At night at a fire base a time would be picked arbitrarily to begin firing from every position out into the bush in front of the bunkers. Supposedly this was done to dissuade the enemy from trying to sneak up on positions in the dead of night.

"Stoners"… Those who preferred Marijuana. "Juicers"… Those who preferred Alcohol

"Chop Chop"… Food

We were still patrolling out of FSB Paris when the long-rumored offensive began. Paris was a little elevated and we could see for many miles. Artillery shells were exploding in the distance, helicopter gunships were raking over the hillsides, and flare ships were illuminating the sky with their eerie orange/white light. It was quite a pyrotechnic show, but for us at Paris all was quiet.

However, tensions were high. The not knowing if or when we might be caught up in the hostilities was causing a lot of anxiety among the troops. For one guy in the third platoon, it got to be a little too much. His lieutenant ordered him to do something, and the guy refused the order, flipped out, and threatened the officer with his M-16. The confrontation was resolved without incident when the troop realized he had screwed up bad and dropped his weapon. Nevertheless, pointing a weapon at your platoon leader was not something that would be let go without consequence. The soldier was sent back to Long Binh the next morning and was incarcerated in the stockade to await judicial proceedings.

What we had witnessed in those early morning hours was the opening shots of what would be called "Mini-Tet." Its duration was shorter than the more famous Tet Offensive, but it was much bloodier in its initial phases. The Viet Cong/NVA attacked 119 targets that night, including Saigon. Bien Hoa, some 5 or 6 miles down the road from us, was hit by over 60 rockets.

The brigade sent a couple of companies from our battalion south to protect Saigon. Our company B was left at Paris in support of Bien Hoa/Long Binh. We lucked out as the fighting was much more intense around Saigon. Alpha company was one of those sent who suffered an ambush during the offensive one night. It was a fierce, close in fight. Alpha killed 13 enemy troops but lost 4 of their own; one of them was named Kenneth Lee Olson. Olson was throwing a grenade at an enemy position and was struck by a VC bullet in mid-throw. Upon being hit, he dropped the grenade. Seeing that this put his fellow troops in mortal danger, he threw himself on top of the grenade, absorbing the blow and saving his buddies. He was killed instantly. (He was awarded the Medal of Honor for this act of self-sacrifice.)

Meanwhile, back at Paris things were still calm. A bunch of mail came in at once; it had been delayed somewhat due to the offensive. I got my usual bunch from Mom who was still writing every day. I also got a "care" package from home with some items I had requested: pens, paper, envelopes, and film for my Kodak Instamatic camera. I also got peanut butter cookies— a couple still in one piece! I got letters from Mary Ellen which included Kool-Aid packets.

I can't actually recall asking anybody for the Kool-Aid. I think word got out back home that some troops were asking for the packets to cover up the bad taste that water took on after purification tablets were added to their canteens. At any rate I started getting the flavored powdered drink mix from my family. I believe the Army used either Iodine or Halazone tablets to purify the water that troops might have to find from local sources out in the field. I was lucky in that regard as we were regularly re-supplied with clean water. Even so the water rarely tasted refreshing. By mid-afternoon the water in your canteen was as warm as the hundred degree air and seemed to take on the flavor of the polyethylene plastic that the canteen was made from. Not even the Kool Aid could mask that.

I also got letters from Big Posey, Little Posey and Fran. Little Posey sent me candy and Kool Aid, and I got a prayer card to St Joseph from Fran. The prayer supposedly would spare you from any number of nasty things that can happen to you in war. I didn't really believe in that kind of stuff, but carried it with me, more out of respect and affection for my brother than any faith in its protective powers. In fact, I've kept it all these years since, a bit worse for wear now, but for pretty much the same reasons.

CHAPTER FOUR
A O LOS BANYOS

We were told that we would soon be leaving Paris for A O (area of operations) Los Banyos. Paris was pretty sweet duty compared to where we were before and where we were headed. Once again, we would be living out of our backpacks for days on end, and the rains (which were getting heavier and more frequent) only added to the misery index. So it was goodbye to the traveling road show, the swimming hole we found close to the base, and the occasional hot meal trucked in from Long Binh. No more easy patrols through brush land and fallow fields that didn't require a machete to traverse. No more light loads; we wouldn't be returning to the same place every night. No more bunkers; we'd be digging in at the end of every day. I wasn't looking forward to the move.

But move we did. The long predicted offensive had begun while we were still at Paris. It would become known as the "May Offensive" or "Mini-Tet". It would prove to be the bloodiest month of the war and was still in high gear. You wouldn't have known that at FSB Paris, though, another reason I didn't want to leave that sanctuary. Our first night back in the jungle reminded me of the original first night but minus the lizard. And this time we had rain. The jungle made me feel uneasy; it was Charlie's backyard, and I always felt like we were being watched.

Nighttime in the jungle, particularly if you are out on an LP (listening post) far from the company NDP, can make you feel so alone. Especially on rainy nights when the darkness feels absolute, no moon or starlight can break through the overcast, and the blackness envelopes and isolates. Yeah, there would be another guy with you, maybe two, but they were sleeping while you pulled your shift. The time drags, and your two-hour shift feels like four. If you happened to have the last guard shift of the night, you couldn't wait to see that first hint of light on the horizon. Those first rays not only brightened the day but invariably your spirits as well.

Conversely, on clear moonless nights when the sky was studded with uncountable stars, you could lose yourself in the grandeur of it. Particularly in the wee early morning hours when the nighttime creatures had finally called it a day and a quiet stillness prevailed. I'd sometimes lay back after my guard shift was over and just watch the heavens. There was no ambient light out in the jungle to diminish the stars' brightness, and it seemed like I could see a million more stars than I ever saw from my backyard in Castle Shannon.

On some occasions, depending on your state of mind, the isolation felt more like solitude when you were under that star-lit canopy. The grandness of those wee small hours often created an atmosphere conducive to philosophical pondering. If nothing else, peering millions of light years out into space made you feel small and insignificant. I wondered, with all of that area to look after, "Does God really know I'm down here, lying on a jungle floor of a small planet in an average size galaxy somewhere in the far reaches of the universe?" War inevitably focuses the mind on mortality so it's not surprising that lying under a still, star-lit night, feeling alone and vulnerable, you sought comfort by funneling these queries toward the heavens, hoping for some solace. Unanswered as they were, I was left with my solitude.

I well remember some of those nights when the moon was full. It seemed bigger and brighter than at home, maybe because there was no pollution to fuzz up the picture. At any rate, it could easily cast shadows, and my young eyes could even read a book under it. Many a night was spent keeping track of it as it traversed the heavens. I tried to guess how much time had passed by while on guard duty by the moon's position in the sky. However, it didn't matter how beautiful the Vietnam night sky was, it was still Vietnam and the night still belonged to "Charlie," so I was always happy to see another sunrise.

After weeks in the field we finally got clean clothes to wear. A chopper dropped off a few large bags containing fatigues. You had to root through them to find your sizes. They had come from different units and had names and patches on them that had no relation to our unit, but they were clean!!! It felt really good to get out of my filthy fatigues. It would have been even better if we were clean, but that was down the road a way. No clean underwear came in the bags, but it didn't mean no never-mind to me, as I (like most guys there) never wore any. Especially during the rainy season when you got soaked twice a day; your underwear never dried out, and it bunched up and caused all kind of chafing. It just wasn't worth the trouble.

We didn't get any clean towels either. Towels became an unofficial part of our uniform. They were green, of course, and we wore them looped over our neck. They had multiple uses, one was to cushion the straps of an overweight backpack from digging into your shoulders. Another was to use it as a pillowcase for the flak jacket that was your pillow. A third use was as a filter: we wrapped it around our mouth, nose, and ears when we were in swampy areas where the mosquitos were especially thick. The mosquitos could drive you crazy, buzzing around your eyes, ears, nose, and mouth. On moonlit nights, you could see so many you were afraid that you would inhale them. The towel could also be used as a towel. So commonly used by so many troops in uncommon ways that the sculptor of the "Three Fighting Men" statue at the Vietnam Veterans Memorial in Washington D.C. saw fit to include the towel. You can see it draped around the neck of the troop on the right.

It wasn't too many days until we were back in the rhythm of humping the boonies or beating the bush or whatever else you wanted to call it. We had no real time to ourselves; the day was full from sun up to sun down. We accumulated little annoyances along the way: ant bites, sucker marks from leeches, itchy mosquito bites, and cuts and scratches that wouldn't scab over because they were always wet. I was fortunate up to this point. I didn't have any real health issues yet. Some guys had real problems with blisters. Your feet being wet all the time didn't help that any. One guy came down with (lacking a more accurate description) jungle fever. Another guy contracted malaria. It was funny what we got used to doing without a second thought: walking along in torrential downpours, slogging through mud, or crossing streams that came up to the neck with no more concern than crossing the street back home.

Drowning was a real concern in Vietnam, especially for troops who served in the delta. My unit, the 199th Light Infantry Brigade, served part of its time in Vietnam in the delta, and it suffered 30 deaths from drowning.

You didn't have to be in the delta: one of the guys in the second platoon almost drowned while we were up in the Rocket Belt. It was a night patrol and James Vanderwall was crossing a swift moving stream when he lost his footing and was swept downstream. Luckily, someone was able to quickly throw him a rope and he was pulled to safety.

Occasionally you got a break in the all-day drudgery and had some time to write a letter, clean your gear, or just relax. Sometimes you hoped for some rain during a break so you could get a little clean. If it was raining hard enough you could strip down and soap up in the downpour. The rains over there could start and stop on a dime so you had to be careful and not get caught all lathered up and then have the rain end abruptly. You did your best to keep from getting too scruffy with a shave every now and then. My almost next-door neighbor buddy, Jerry Fuller from West Virginia, gave me a haircut while I was sitting on a log out in the middle of a jungle clearing.

That same clearing held host to our first visit from a chaplain who happened to be a Roman Catholic priest. He choppered in with some supplies and spent a few hours with us. He offered confessions to anyone interested and then held Mass. He used the C-ration cartons he flew in with as a makeshift altar. I did attend the Mass, but it made me think of Sundays, and that made me think of bacon and eggs, and then that made me think of sausage and baked beans on Saturday nights, and it just got worse from there. In a way, church wasn't that much different in that jungle cathedral than it was at home; I did a lot of daydreaming there as well. I don't know if the whole Mass thing did anything for my soul or not, but it sure didn't do anything for my psyche. I had been doing really well at not thinking about home too much, but church triggered a lot of thoughts—which wasn't too healthy since there was nothing to be done about them anyway.

In some ways, I still feel a little guilty about how my focus was so myopic in Vietnam. It was a while before I realized just how hard this was on my family. One of the things that brought that home for me was a card I got from my grandma, your great-grandmother. I don't have a memory of a time when my grandma didn't live with us. She was part of the family. Grandma was probably 90 years old when I left for Vietnam. At first, my mom and dad kept that information from her. Later, not sure of that decision, they decided to tell her. Shortly thereafter, I received a card from my Grandma, a bit of an unusual card considering the circumstances. It was a card for someone who had taken a trip. On the front, it had images of a globe and various forms of transportation: planes, trains, and ships. It read: This is a travel card...it traveled all the way from me to you, to say good-bye...have fun!! Then at the bottom, in unsteady script:

Bye bye honey boy God bless you
and bring you back safe home

Love Grandma

I still have that card. I took pains to keep it safe and dry until I could get it back to the main base and put it with my stuff until I came home. That card from Grandma kind of represented the fact that I wasn't really doing this alone. That others were with me every step of the way and that their lives were deeply affected as well.

I also got letters from a few friends: Rich and Bob and Dave. Dave, in fact, had bought me that Timex watch as a going-away present before I left for Vietnam. It was gold in color with a black leather band. It was a really nice gesture and one that I appreciate now even more than I did then. I've lost track of him over the years—kind of wish I could thank him again. Back in the day, they used to advertise Timex as the brand that could "take a licking and keep on ticking." They had commercials that showed the watch taking all kinds of manufactured abuse. Then their spokesman, John

Cameron Swayze (as the camera zoomed in on the sweep hand), announced that the water- resistant, dust-resistant, and shock-resistant Timex was still ticking. Apparently, they forgot to test them in a southeast Asian rain forest. It didn't take long before the leather band began falling apart, so from then on, I carried it in my pocket. In short order, the heat and humidity breached the watch case's integrity and formed its own little atmosphere under the crystal to the point that I could no longer see the hands. In the end, I somehow lost it—sad to say. I felt like I let Dave down by not taking better care of his present.

Too bad the watch salesman from out in the Rocket Belt wasn't around, I could have used him then. Now I had to add another item to my nightly rituals. After digging in, rigging up a shelter, heating up some C-rations, dousing myself in bug juice, rolling down my sleeves and buttoning up my collar to defend against the nightly onslaught of mosquitos, I'd have to bum a watch off someone for guard duty. With towel in hand, I was ready for the night.

CHAPTER FIVE
THE RAILROAD TRACKS

I think we were beating the bush for about 10 days when we got the word that we were moving again. We came across some VC supply caches on our patrols: 200 pounds of salt, some sleeping mats, bags of rice, and some aiming equipment for mortars. We also found 30 shipping containers for the 122-millimeter rockets that the Viet Cong had been firing into Bien Hoa and Long Binh, but the cat was out of the bag on those. At any rate, word was that they expected another assault on Long Binh, so they were going to move us into a defensive position closer to the base. We marched out of the jungle until we intersected a dirt road where trucks were waiting to transport us to our new location. We climbed aboard the 2½ ton trucks, glad to be getting a ride for a change. While not walking was nice, the trucks had no seats so you had to sit on the steel bed of the cargo area. Being 2½ ton trucks, they were very stiffly sprung and the weight of a few troops in the back wasn't enough to make the springs flex, so every bump in the road was transmitted full force through your tail bone and up your spine. The road wasn't very good, and the anticipatory joy of riding instead of walking was soon gone.

Our new position was located along some abandoned railroad tracks not far from the Long Binh army base. We immediately began building bunkers for our defensive positions. We dug down about three feet, making a hole approximately six- foot square, then used the dirt to fill sand bags which we used to make a two foot high wall around the hole's perimeter. Then we placed PSP (perforated steel planking) across the sandbags to form a roof and added a couple layers of sandbags on the roof for protection against mortars. With a few sandbags left out of the wall for firing ports it made a nice little fort.

It took a couple days to complete several of these bunkers, so there was no patrolling. In addition to the bunkers, we cut some fields of fire so that the brush could not conceal any approach by the enemy. Frank Jordon, under the tutelage of Captain Conner, was keen on placing booby-traps outside our perimeter at night. He placed claymore mines out to the front of our bunker positions and alongside the trail that led to a nearby village.

The claymore mine was standard issue, and each squad carried at least a couple of them. They were directional: placed to fire in the direction the enemy was expected to come from. They were usually command detonated, meaning that the soldier set the mine off himself. He did this electrically by squeezing a triggering device called a clacker. The clacker generated an electrical charge which traveled through a wire and set off a blasting cap that had been inserted into the mine. Upon detonation, the mine sent out 700 steel balls—4000 feet per second—at the enemy. There was a back-blast, so you wanted the mine a safe distance from your own position. Since the mine could send those steel balls out over 250 yards, you wanted to make sure it was pointed in the right direction. To facilitate this, the Army considerately had the words "FRONT TOWARD ENEMY" embossed onto the mine's plastic case. You could also set the mines off by using tripwires.

In that case, the mine was actually triggered when someone hit the tripwire with his foot. Frank was setting up double claymore mines this way along the trail. He did this come evening when a curfew was in effect and no one should be on the trail. Then at first light he went out and disabled them.

With the bunkers built, we started to do some patrolling again. One day we entered an area that had been sprayed with defoliant. Agent Orange, so named because it came in 55-gallon drums that had an orange band painted around the middle of them. It was sprayed on jungle areas to deprive the enemy of cover. The trees in the area we entered were totally bare of leaves. They looked like a Pennsylvania woods in January. It looks very strange to the eye, and your mind doesn't want to accept the picture you are seeing when it is 95 degrees out. Added to that was the fact the area had been hit by an artillery barrage, and many of the trees had branches ripped off. Some trees were split down the trunk, many just splintered into many jagged pieces. It reminded me of those pictures of the "no-mans land" that lay between the opposing army's trenches during WWI.

We passed through the area without any thought of the potential danger that exposure to the herbicide could cause. It wouldn't be until after the war that the dangers were revealed. Dioxin, an extremely toxic compound, was found to be present in Agent Orange. During the war, fully 12% of the country was sprayed with over 20 million gallons of the herbicide. By the end of my tour I had spent quite a few of my days patrolling in areas sprayed by Agent Orange.

A couple of days later I had my first experience of "walking point." As the name suggests, you lead the way. Being in the 4th platoon usually meant not getting that assignment because when the company moved as one unit, the weapons (4th) platoon usually accompanied the command group. More often than not, the command group stayed back from the front when patrolling. The command group usually consisted of the company commander (Captain Conner), the forward observer (the officer who called in artillery support), and several RTOs (radio operators). Since moving to the railroad tracks we had been patrolling separately at the platoon level, thus increasing my chances for drawing that assignment.

I was a little nervous my first time out on the point, but luckily, we were not in an area that had many booby-traps—not that you ignored the possibility of them. In fact, in a lot of areas we patrolled that was job one. So much so that the man right behind you, called the slack man, had as his responsibility looking out after the point man. As the point man is concentrating on the ground looking for tripwires and such, the slack man is looking out ahead and up into the trees for anything suspicious. This was particularly important when using trails. In addition, you may have men guarding the flanks. Typically, the flank men travelled parallel to the direction of travel, maybe up to 50 yards out from the unit depending on terrain and cover. (Dan Morris, my buddy from training, was on flank security for his unit when he was shot and killed by a sniper.) There also was a man at the back responsible for rear security; he was constantly checking behind the unit. My first day on the point went without incident, other than being a little more fatigued than usual. Being on a higher state of alert for several hours takes something out of you, mostly because you realize how totally vulnerable you are, no matter how good you may be.

When you are moving through areas of dense undergrowth, it's very unlikely you would detect the enemy before it's too late. If he wants to lie in wait for you, you are toast; it's so easy to stay concealed in thick vegetation.

The fact is, an American rifle company on the move through the jungle is anything but stealthy. They know you're coming from a long way off. I felt like walking point was a game of chance; the more you played it, the worse your odds. I was very fortunate in not having to roll the dice very often. We seemed to be riding a real lucky streak. The railroad track location was just as quiet as FSB Paris had been. Again, things were happening all over the brigade's areas of operations but not where we were.

We settled into a routine of daylight patrols which usually had us back at the railroad tracks around 4:00 PM or so. Since our bunkers were already built, we usually had some time to relax before sundown. Sunset came earlier in the tropics than it did back home for that time of year. Back in Pittsburgh, in the middle of May, the sun was still shining at 8:30 in the evening. In Vietnam, we had two hours of darkness already. The area of Vietnam I was in is only about 10 degrees above the equator; consequently, the hours of light and darkness don't vary as much. No long summer days or long winter nights. Another thing that seemed different to me was the transition between night and day. In the summer at home twilight lingers far longer than it does in the lower latitudes. In the tropics, you don't ease into the night.

We often had the kids from the village come up to see us and try to sell us stuff. One little guy sold me a bottle of coke. I took the coke and asked him if he had a bottle cap opener. He took the bottle back and proceeded to hook the cap on one of his lower teeth. Realizing what he was going to do, I yelled: "No, No! I'll get an opener." He looked at me and said, "no sweat G I" and popped the cap off with his tooth. Damn!

We had bunkers but no one wanted to sleep in them at night. They were dark, dank, and musty inside and a habitat for creepy crawlers and sometimes rats when we were close to populated areas. Mostly we slept on the ground beside the bunkers and pulled our guard duty sitting on top of them. Sometimes, if it was really pouring, you might go in. Other than that, we pretty much avoided them.

One night, while Jerry Fuller was sitting on top of one of the bunkers, he got bit by one of those creepy crawlers. A giant centipede to be specific. Their bite is toxic, and while not fatal, it makes you very sick. He was bitten on his arm and was soon in a great deal of pain. His arm began to swell and after a couple hours looked twice its normal size. He had a very long night and was miserably sick by morning when he was medevacked.

Jerry would miss the barbecue. The following night a small deer tripped one of Frank's claymore mines. We found it in the morning—legless. Someone suggested that we shouldn't let it go to waste. We had a few hunters in the platoon who could gut it and butcher the meat. Deer steaks sounded like a great idea. We dug a shallow pit, collected firewood and strung a grill together from the wires that bound our C-ration cartons. The fire was started and we had a good blaze going. We waited till the flames died down and we had red hot embers glowing in the pit. The deer meat was placed on the makeshift grill and soon was sizzling. Anticipation was high! Unfortunately, expectations fell far short of reality. The venison just wasn't all that good. It was tough and stringy and got caught in your teeth. Some of the guys said they liked it, but I saw an awful lot of hot sauce being applied. Nonetheless, it was great fun to try and a nice distraction for an afternoon.

Later on, that evening, I was lying down on my poncho liner a couple of yards away from the entrance to our bunker when the air above me was suddenly crackling with the sound of bullets zipping by overhead. Things started happening in my mind pretty fast at that point, and not all of it on a conscious level. I instinctively grabbed my M-16 which was always within arm's reach and dived headlong down into the bunker, heedless of the possibility of breaking my neck in the process. Apparently, there is some section of your brain that calculates and weighs the options available to you in the face of danger and sets you on your way long before your conscious mind can decide on a course of action. In this case, that collection of cerebral cells tasked with saving my butt decided that going headfirst might spare me a half second of exposure to automatic weapon fire. Using the calculus of life and death, my brain chose the appropriate action. Once safely inside, I crawled to a firing port, aimed my rifle out the opening, and waited for what came next.

Some part of me actually wanted something to happen. I guess I just wanted the experience. It didn't have anything to do with how I felt about the war. Besides, I thought we were being attacked; therefore, there is no moral ambiguity. You have every right to defend yourself. So, it was like a free pass to "rock and roll." I had to laugh at myself a little later for my "bring it on" attitude. It's a lot easier to have a little bravado when you are tucked away in a fortified bunker.

I think Phillip Caputo, author of the Vietnam War novel "A Rumor of War," said that "war will always be a lure to young men who know nothing about it." There is probably a lot of truth to that. I don't know how much growing up in the fifties might have influenced kids in my generation to be susceptible to that lure, but I'm thinking it definitely played a role.

Many kids my age had a Dad, an uncle or two, or at a minimum some neighbors who served in World War II. It was called the "good war," and we felt America saved the world. It doesn't get much better than that. The war was heroic in the grand scheme of things, and those who served could bask in that glow. That good feeling was reflected in the TV shows of the post-war 50's and early 60's: shows like Hogan's Heroes or McHale's Navy which, admittedly, were unrealistic comedies but still added to the allure. Even the more realistic shows of that era like "12 O'Clock High" and "Combat" didn't really touch on just how ugly war can be. Sure, there were casualties, mostly to minor characters so it would not be too traumatizing to the viewer—and nothing graphic.

Every day at 5:00 they played the "Big Movie" on Channel 2. They played plenty of war movies, a lot of them from the forties; many were made while the war was still on. They were very heroic, as you can imagine, but not very true to life. In those movies, a guy got wounded in the shoulder and you saw a spot of blood on his fatigue jacket. In real life war, his arm might be gone. In the movies, a guy might die in his buddy's arms saying a few last words before closing his eyes and letting his head slip off to the side. In real life, he might be horribly wounded, alone, screaming in pain, and calling out for his mother.

I was steadily getting closer to the real deal. My buddy Dan was killed by a sniper, but I wasn't there when it happened. I had seen firefights going on in the distance and listened in on them on the radio; yet again, I was not there. Other units in the brigade were in heavy contact but not ours. How long could all this stuff keep going on around me before I ran into it? That was the question.

The tracers over the bunker ended as quickly as they began, and once again we were spared any contact. The only casualty was the watch I borrowed from Byrdy for guard duty that night. I caught the crystal on the PSP roof while diving in the bunker and destroyed it. Now I had to buy two watches when I got the chance.

The following morning dawned calmly after the harmless scare we experienced overnight. We easily fell into our daily routine: a patrol in the bush, back at the bunker by 4:00PM, fix something to eat and hang out with the kids from the village for a bit.

As dusk approached the kids headed back down the trail toward the village. It was time for Frank to set up his booby-traps for the night. He usually set up a double claymore (two mines daisy-chained together so they would both go off at once) on the trail, 1400 steel balls blasting out at nearly a mile per second.

The supply chopper was late that evening, arriving just before dark. We quickly unloaded cases of C-rations, a number of five-gallon water jugs, and spare batteries for the radios. After the Huey flew out we started to divide up the rations and fill our canteens with fresh water. We were heading back to our respective bunkers when the blast took place. My first thought was another deer had tripped a claymore. It didn't seem likely to be the Viet Cong and I fleetingly shuttered at thought of it being one of the kids from the village, when I heard several voices call out, "Medic, medic!" I had no idea what had just happened.

Somehow, two members of another company in our battalion, that was located not far from us, had lost their way while heading out to an ambush position. Apparently, confused about their position, they turned down the trail that led to our base camp. One of them had tripped the wire that crossed the trail, setting off the blast. They were close to the mines when they discharged a metal wall of ball bearings. Their legs took the brunt of the blast. Flesh was ripped and shredded. Two guys and one traumatically amputated leg lay in the middle of the trail.

I don't think the medic could have done much good. A medevac was immediately called and arrived in mere minutes since we were so close to Long Binh. The dust-off landed, and as they were getting ready to load the casualties on the chopper, Sgt. Trout yelled out for a poncho liner to wrap the dismembered appendage in. I heard the call but ignored it, as did most of the other guys. I didn't think my poncho liner was going to do that guy's leg any good. Poncho liners were hard to come by, and if it rained that night I'd be wet and cold without it. I felt guilty about it then—still do in a way. I think it would have been different if I had known them. I wouldn't know their names until I started doing research for this memoir.

I was right about it not doing the guy any good, although I didn't know that for sure when they put them on the chopper. I assumed they had to be dead: I didn't see how anybody could survive a close up, double claymore detonation. I talked to Frank many, many years later. I didn't bring the subject up but he did. He had found out that neither troop had survived the booby-trap that he had set up. He told me he felt very guilty about the whole episode. He didn't go into detail why, only that it has always troubled him and haunts him to this day.

As for myself, unconsciously, I quickly tucked the incident away, along with others that might be unhealthy for me to dwell on. I guess I was trying to keep my sanity. I wasn't entirely successful though, I kept hearing over and over in my mind, Sgt. Trout saying how he couldn't get over how heavy that soldier's leg was that he carried to the chopper.

CHAPTER SIX
CLAK-CLAK

As usual, life went on after the incident: back on patrol, looking for arms caches, and hoping to disrupt rocket attacks and enemy infiltration. After a few days word came down that we were moving back to the jungle. Damn, I hated the jungle!! Back to the ants and leeches, the cuts and scratches, the digging in every night, C-rats 3 times a day, and always, always feeling tired and fatigued, with absolutely no time to yourself. It was hard to even get a letter written.

We were going to be airlifted by Chinook this time. The Chinook was a large tandem rotor helicopter that could hold about 35 troops, basically a bus with a rotor at each end. The word Chinook is the name of an Indian tribe in the Pacific Northwest. The Army names all its aircraft after Indian tribes. Sometimes the names stick, such as the Chinook, sometimes they don't. Well, mostly it stuck. A lot of guys called them "shit hooks." The most common helicopter of the Vietnam War and practically a symbol for it was the Iroquois. Its other name, the Huey, is very well-known by anyone who has ever seen a movie about Vietnam. It comes from the Army's official designation: helicopter, utility, model A1. Put together, HUAI morphs into Huey.

I'd had a few rides in Hueys by this point. They were fun to ride in: the doors were always slid back and you had a great view out the wide- open side, and if you were just plucked out of a rice paddy on a 95 degree day, the rushing air felt fantastic. I liked the open doors for another reason as well. Choppers got shot at a lot and I always liked the idea of having a better chance of getting out of one in a hurry if it were shot down or crashed. That might have been more wishful thinking than reality—but hey, what's the harm if it makes you feel a little better? I had good reason to be concerned. The Army lost 5,000 helicopters during the war: half to enemy fire, the rest to operational accidents. There were many more that went down and were salvaged to fly again.

The Chinook, however, was closed in. There was a ramp in the back that you entered and exited. It felt claustrophobic and I always had an uneasy feeling while in one. Also, it was louder inside than anything you could ever imagine. You literally had to scream to be heard by the guy sitting next to you.

We loaded up the next morning and boarded a Chinook for our new AO. After a noisy flight, the big chopper settled into our landing zone. The ramp dropped, and we started filing out. As I was about to step off the ramp into the tall grass that covered the area, I heard a machine gun open up. I had no idea what was going on. I just knew I wanted away from the Chinook as fast as possible. It was a big target and if something was going down it would draw a lot of fire. I started hightailing it through the waist-high grass as fast as my loaded down body allowed. In my haste, I didn't notice the old bomb crater hidden in the high green cover. The bottom dropped out before I knew what was happening, and I tumbled down the slope of the bowl-shaped depression, landing no worse for wear at the bottom. 500- pound bombs can leave a hole in the ground as large as 30 feet across and 15 feet deep.

It turns out someone had thought they saw movement in the tree line and opened fire. I crawled up out of the hollow. The machine gun was quiet and the Chinook had just taken off. We formed a perimeter around the landing zone and waited for the other lifts to land with the rest of our company. Once we were all on the ground we headed out in single file toward our nighttime destination. The terrain was rolling hills covered in dense vegetation at ground level, a little less so under the tall trees. It was double canopy, at least. Some trees at mid-level were maybe 25 feet high, then another layer that was 50 feet or more. The area felt primordial: fit for the time of the dinosaurs. You almost felt as if you were the first humans to see it. It was the perfect place for the Viet Cong, a remote sanctuary usually safe from intrusions such as ours.

The rain came down hard along the way to our night position. It was strange at first. In a double or triple canopy jungle, you heard the rain long before you felt it. The cover was so thick that the trees acted as umbrellas: the drops collecting on the leaves then dripping down to leaves underneath. If it was just a passing shower you hardly got wet at all. But when the rains hit hard the torrents of water could not be held back for long. The leaves bent under the weight of the drops and poured down on others in a cascade effect that produced sheets of water which soaked us through and through. With the water running off the lip of my helmet in a steady stream I couldn't keep a cigarette lit. I couldn't believe how loud it was either: the pounding on the foliage by the big drops was incredible. If it was a thunderstorm the deluge from on high could chill you in no time. It was weird how you could go from a sweltering, muggy, 95-degree day to having your teeth chatter in a few minutes—and then back again before you knew what happened.

Downpours or not, there was no doubt in my mind that the Viet Cong knew we were there. Either from their intelligence network or from the fact that it's hard not to notice several big Chinooks landing in your backyard. I was sure our movements were being tracked.

A position was chosen on top of a hill for our NDP. The ground cover was thick and there were some very tall trees around us. We probably stopped around 4:00 PM to start getting ready for the night. The digging went easy in the dark, wet, pungent soil. I didn't need any encouragement to dig deep, the place exuded a palpable dread. Uneasiness was the watchword for the night. The tension was infectious, and everybody was going about their business with deadly seriousness. After my position was dug, I heated up some C's for supper. I was running late and decided to forgo rigging up a shelter. The sky had cleared following the afternoon rain, and it looked like the night should pass without any more precipitation. I'd just roll up in my poncho liner while not on guard.

I placed my claymore mine out in front of my position, inserted the blasting cap, then strung the electrical cord back to my foxhole. Nobody hooked up their firing devices until everyone was done out in front of the positions. We set up trip flares out in the brush. If tripped, they set off a bright light, hopefully illuminating whoever may have triggered it. There was a lot more activity out in front of the perimeter that night. Guys were adding extra Claymores and flares than was usual due to everyone's edginess. I was not immune. I used the dirt from my foxhole to form a berm in front of my position and positioned my hand grenades and my ammo magazines on top for easy access.

I settled in and waited for the rest of the guys to clear before hooking up my firing device. Suddenly, a loud pop. Out of the corner of my eye I saw a bright light then streaks of white smoke arcing outwards from the flash point. Somebody had rigged a line to a trip flare and accidentally snagged it, pulling the pin and igniting the flare. The flares contain phosphorous that burns crazy hot. Some of the phosphorous splattered on the guy's face; he was right next to the flare when it ignited. You can't put the stuff out; it just burns until it's gone. You don't get minor burns from it. He was in a lot of pain but deemed ok enough to wait for a morning medevac.

After the sun went down, it seemed to cool off a little more than usual. The air above us was crystal clear, but the ravine in front of our position that separated us from the next hill over was getting misty and added to the eeriness we already felt. Visibility was not too bad since we were under starlight and a crescent moon. As time went by, the mist thickened into a fog that filled the little valley between the mounds. The opposing hill looked almost ethereal, floating on a white cloud.

We had a forward observer with us from the 2nd Battalion 40th Artillery. Captain Conner decided it would be prudent to set up some DEFCONS around our perimeter. DEFCONS are defensive concentrations of artillery fire. The FO (forward observer) started by calling in a marker round. He then made adjustments off that to plot the DEFCONS. The FO was as new as the rest of us—learning on the go— and he mistakenly called his first round in a little too close to our position. I don't think they called for a delay fuse, either; it went off in the tree tops. There was a bright orange flash, a huge kaaruuumph sound, and a compression wave from the concussion that seemed to travel right through you. Simultaneously, sounds of the twisted, torn metal of the artillery round whipping through the trees, shredding foliage, and lopping limbs from their trunks added greatly to our unease. Thankfully, adjustments were made and soon our perimeter was pre-plotted. Now if we were to be attacked we could have artillery on the way a lot quicker.

That done, I settled in for the night. A couple hours later I was on my first guard shift when I heard the noise for the first time. It was an unnatural clacking sound and I soon heard it again. Then, seemingly in answer to it, a clack-clack sound came from a different direction. Then again from different locations on the hill opposed to us. The Viet Cong were known to use bamboo sticks to signal with. It was obvious that that was what was going on. Point was, what did the signals mean?

Captain Conner called for 100% alert, so everyone was up. The clack sounds were relatively close: near enough for our own artillery to be a hazard to ourselves if used at that range. It wouldn't be called in unless we were actually attacked. We didn't want to fire our own weapons at the sounds since that would give away our positions. So, we waited. It was up to Charlie to make the next move. The clacking stopped sometime in the early morning hours, and we went back to 50% alert. It was an odd feeling knowing that they were out there, and it was hard to relax enough to get any meaningful rest that night. I don't think there were many days when I was happier to see the sun come up.

In retrospect, it was unlikely that any sort of attack would have taken place. We had the high ground, we were well dug in, and we had artillery support if needed. There would have been no element of surprise and they would have taken a lot of casualties. Having said that, I don't imagine I was thinking coolly or rationally that night. Those clacks really gave me the heebie-jeebies.

The experience just reinforced my gut feeling that we were never going to get the drop on these guys. They knew we were there, and they would be the ones to decide where and when anything happened. For that reason and others, you felt like you had no control over your own destiny and that it was all a game of chance, and Charlie was the one throwing your dice. We were just your average infantry unit; we weren't Seals, Special Forces, Rangers, or Recon. No attempt was ever made to enter an area unnoticed. The American strategy was to go into an area, hope the VC took a stand and fought, then we would bring our overwhelming firepower into play. Once contact was made, we had gunships, artillery, and fighter bombers. Basically, we were a tripwire, and you know what happens to those closest to the tripwire.

Speaking of chance, that reminds me of a fellow in the company named Logan. A day or two after "clack clack" night, while we were still in the same general area, we found a trail. Now, this trail out in the middle of nowhere was clearly only used by the enemy. Captain Conner told Logan to take the point and lead us down the trail. Logan did so and proceeded to ditty bop down the path without a care in the world. Any sane person would be moving with the utmost caution, checking for booby-traps and for signs of the enemy. The captain called the company to a halt and asked Logan what the hell he thought he was doing. Logan professed to believe in predetermination: basically, what is going to happen is going to happen, no matter what you do. Nonplussed, the captain pulled him from the lead. I thought to myself: that was either the stupidest move or the ballsiest move I ever saw to get yourself off the point. As time went on, I got to know Logan a little better and I think he may have actually believed in that predestination thing. He certainly never bragged about getting himself off the undesired duty.

We spent a few more days in the area patrolling, occasionally finding some VC bunkers with supplies in them. Usually we just blew the bunkers and supplies. If there were weapons involved we sent them back to base on the supply chopper.

The supply chopper brought some new toys for us. We got "starlight scopes", one for each platoon. The starlight scopes came in aluminum briefcases. When you opened the case, the scope lay in some shock-proof protective foam of some sort. The instrument weighed about 6 pounds. It was relatively new technology at the time, at least for ground troops to have them. The scope was able to take the ambient light from the stars and moon and amplify it to the point that your night vision was improved many, many times over. New technology is always expensive, and the scopes supposedly cost $6,000. That would probably be 40 thousand dollars in today's money. Of course, nowadays you can buy one for as cheap as a couple hundred bucks from a sportsmen's store. Back then it was so new that we had orders to destroy it if there was any chance of it falling into enemy hands. I've never looked through a new one, but in Vietnam the picture you saw through the lens was kind of grainy, and very tiny flickers of white light jumped all over your field of vision. The whole picture was green in color, but you really could see at night—far, far better than with the naked eye.

Got word that we were moving again, this time to a Fire Support Base named Choctow. FSB Choctow was in the Rocket Belt area just north of the Dong Nai River. Our company was used for base security. Sounded good to me. I never felt bad about leaving the jungle. We arrived the next day and relieved the company that had been securing the base. Even better, the base was already built and the bunkers in place—no filling sandbags for days!!

The base was the forward command post for our battalion. It had a TOC (pronounced talk) that meant "Tactical Operation Center" for the battalion. It was the communication's center for the battalion and coordinated the various companies with each other and all the support units available such as transportation, supply, etc. It also had a battalion aid station for minor medical issues. It was located in a sparsely overgrown area that might have been farmland before the war, it was flat and could be crossed by vehicles. The TOC and medical aid station were in the center of the perimeter of bunkers that our company was manning. In addition to the bunkers for defense, we also had a couple of Quad 50s mounted on the back of deuce and a half trucks. Quad 50s were four 50-caliber, heavy machine guns that were ganged together on a rotatable platform. It was originally designed for anti- aircraft use but in Vietnam was used for base defense and convoy escort duty. All four going at once could throw out 4,000 rounds a minute. We also had the battalion's 4.2-inch heavy mortar platoon on hand as well as our own 81 mm mortars.

The base (well, that's too generous a term) was a muddy mess for the most part. Trucks and APC's (armored personnel carriers) had torn up all the land. It was a combination of large dirt clumps and puddles of water everywhere. It was nothing to write home about, but for the first time in a while I was able to do just that. Another nice thing about it was getting some hot chow on occasion. The evening supply chopper flew in and dropped off mermite cans. The cans were insulated containers used for transporting hot food. It wasn't great, but after eating C-rats it was gourmet dining. We usually had one hot meal a day while we were at the base.

I also enjoyed being able to take my boots off for more than a couple of minutes at a time. When you are out humping the boonies, you keep your boots on 24/7. You might take them off to change into some dry socks if you were lucky enough to have any, but that was about it. It sounds like a small thing, but you have to take your pleasures where you find them. On my first full day at the base after too many in the jungle I was lying on top of a bunker and basking in the sun. I had taken my boots and socks off, removed my shirt, and rolled up my pants. Just the feeling of being dried out was wondrous: the warm air circulating between my toes, the sun baking out the soggy white wrinkles in my skin. And I could just lie there soaking it all in. I didn't have to go on patrol. I didn't have to dig in. I would have some real food for dinner. The bunkers were large and could accommodate a lot of guys which meant fewer guard shifts. If you had the first or last shift you could actually sleep through the night undisturbed. Wow, could it get any better than this? Everything is relative, isn't it!?

Even had some time to visit with other people at the base. Byrdy and I went over to the four deuce mortar pits and chatted with some of those guys. One of them had a pet monkey. The four deuce guys could do something like that because they always stayed at battalion base camp; they didn't have to walk anywhere. It just felt great to relax and let the tensions of the jungle ease away.

All good things come to an end, so the saying goes. It was true for us. Every evening the officers went to the command post for a meeting with the command staff. They reviewed operational plans, intelligence briefings, etc, etc. I think it was the evening of May 30th, the traditional Memorial Day, when Lt. Stockman came back from the meeting and called us all together to tell us the news that we were moving north in a couple of days. There was something about his demeanor that was unsettling. He informed us that they had very reliable evidence of a base camp location for the 7th division of the North Vietnamese Army. The base camp was up in War Zone D, a name location left over from the Vietnam war with the French. We were going in to find it. The brigade commander promised contact. War Zone D was a very sparsely populated area north of Saigon. It was a heavily forested, double and triple canopy jungle. The contour was rolling hills: hard to travel in and affording limited visibility. It had long been a safe sanctuary for the Viet Cong. They used it as a training and rest area as well as a staging area for attacks against Saigon, Bien Hoa and Long Binh.

Lt. Stockman wanted us to get all our gear in order and clean our weapons. He said we were getting all new ammo, and we would be having a "mad minute" tonight to get rid of the old stuff. Well, so much for the good life. They called for a mad minute around 11:00 PM. The execution of the mad minute was for every weapon on the perimeter to be fired at maximum rate for a minute or so at a predetermined time. The theory was that this kept the enemy off-guard. If they knew that at any time thousands of rounds could be coming their way, they might be more hesitant in trying to set up an attack on a base camp. The mad minute was pretty impressive; the Quad 50s definitely made their presence felt. Tracers always put on a good show at night, and we gave anybody out there something to look at.

The next morning, we prepared in earnest for our move to War Zone D. We would leave the following day by Chinook again, so we'd been told. We had been promised contact before without it coming true, but this time it had an entirely different feel to it. Captain Conner and Lt. Stockman both seemed a little more tense than usual. I had a real sense of foreboding, the signs were ominous. I just knew we were headed for some type of engagement. We had been running through the raindrops for too long; we were bound to get wet sometime.

We did get wet that afternoon, but that kind of wet was the norm. The skies cleared toward evening, and we had a most peculiar sunset. There were very dark black clouds on the horizon, backlit by a very orange sky. The orange sky was reflected off all the puddles in the camp, and the clumps of dirt looked like the clouds—all black. The picture was almost the same above and below the horizon line. My mood was gloomy as my thoughts turned dark. I wondered if I'd ever see anything like this again. That knot had returned to my stomach and that metallic taste was once again present in my mouth. We got a late start the next day and didn't get to our LZ (Landing Zone) till mid-afternoon. It was a large open area covered with grass, on a bit of a slope, and surrounded by trees. It started raining shortly after we arrived and stayed raining till 4 or 5 in the morning.

CHAPTER SEVEN
A O TULSA WAR ZONE D

Woke up about 5:30 AM, cool and wet from the all-night rain. The first glimmer of light was on the horizon and the clouds were clearing out. It felt like a high- pressure front was sweeping the dampness from the air, giving us the promise of a dry day. Most mornings out in the bush start fairly quiet, but that morning was almost somber. Almost everybody had picked up on the officers' deadly serious attitude and felt that something was in the air. Everyone seemed to be moving slowly; no one was in a rush to start this day. I had my usual cookies and cocoa, a morning Marlboro, then packed my gear. We were living out of our rucksacks again so I had at least 50 pounds of personal gear, weaponry, ammo, food, and water to carry.

Captain Conner ordered everybody to "saddle up, we move out in five." We marched out in single file. Our platoon accompanied the command group, as usual, and we followed in trail formation. The sky was a crystalline blue as we departed, and the bright orange sun was high and hot enough to set the knee-high grass to steaming the night's moisture up and away.

We started up the hill. It wasn't really steep, but you still compensated for your heavy pack by leaning forward, and you rolled your shoulders around to find the most comfortable spot for the straps of your pack. The area was still open, and we should have been keeping a decent interval between each man, but inevitably we bunched up. "One round will get you all," the instructors had yelled in training. It was true, but I think there was some psychology at play. I think the closer you are to someone the easier it is to handle the fear.

We entered the tree line and immediately felt relief from the sun; it was cooler by a few degrees and a lot darker. A couple layers of vegetation in the form of tall trees and taller trees provided lots of shade. Aerial reconnaissance had somehow spotted the base camp under the dense vegetation, and we were headed toward the co-ordinates they provided. Not long after entering the jungle we intersected a trail and proceeded to follow it further up the hill. It wasn't too physically demanding, but it was wearing on me mentally. We were seeing signs of the enemy's presence such as the trail itself—who else would be using it out here? Also, we were coming across old bunkers and fighting positions and zig-zag trenches along the trail. You could tell they were old and not kept up: the edges of the trenches were falling in and there were no longer foot paths between the bunkers. But they were definitely here.

I was stressed, no doubt about it. I had been successfully suppressing my anxiety the last few weeks after our initial foray into the jungle. Even though the offensive was going on all around us, and they kept moving us into new positions to counter suspected attacks on the big bases, I was able to keep any undue strain at bay. But this time it just felt different. Before, I always realized that something could happen; but this time, I was sure it would happen. Lord only knows why I felt that way. Intel had been wrong way more than they had been right about these things in the past, but that was no comfort to me this time. I guess my countenance didn't hide the gloom and doom I was feeling because my old antagonist, Paul Randle, felt compelled to comment on it in some wise-ass way. This was the one day I didn't want to hear any crap from him, so I told him, "Another word, I'm knocking your fucking teeth out." Whether I could or not was questionable; point was, I was ready to try. It was out of character for me, to be sure, but it reflected the tension I was feeling. Not only was I sure that something was going to happen, but I was increasingly troubled as to my own fate. This was the first time I felt that way since arriving in-country, and it was unnerving.

We continued on, still upward, till we came to a fork in the trail. We took the one to the left and forged ahead. At some point a small observation plane arrived on the scene. He was doing some aerial scouting for us and asked us for our position and compass heading. After we informed him, he told us that we were not headed in the right direction and that we should backtrack and take the fork to the right. Being on a single track, it was easier for everyone to just do a 180 and return back from whence we came. All well and good, only now we were in the lead. It had given me some minor comfort when our platoon was in the rear; you were a bit less vulnerable in an ambush situation. Not anymore.

The scout pilot radioed again to report that enemy troops were definitely spotted ahead of our direction of travel. That news amped everybody up. All our senses were on high alert. Sgt. Trout was on the point. He carried a shotgun, a good quick reaction weapon. I was 8 or 9 troops back from the lead. I no longer was just carrying my M-16, I had it at the ready. We continued moving forward, more deliberately now, aware we were at a disadvantage. They had to know we were coming: the big

Chinooks landing the day before and spotter planes flying overhead today could leave no doubt we were in the area and on the move. We would never see them first—unless they wanted us to.

We had been on the move for about 5 hours when the trail split again. We had crested the hill and the terrain on top was nearly flat. The paths looked well-used. We were entering the base camp area. Sgt. Trout wanted to know which fork to take. Lt. Stockman told him to take the first eight guys to the right. I was number nine. The lieutenant told me to take the trail to the left.

Captain Conner told the second platoon, which was trailing us since we did the 180, to bear off further to our left to cover our flank.

Damn! I found myself on the point, the last place I wanted to be on that day. There was nothing to be done about it, it was what it was. But damn, it seemed like fate had it in for me this day. A wrong turn and the random chance of my position in the line had conspired to place me in this spot at this time. I had no time to dwell on it, but my premonitions seemed to be fulfilling themselves in some preordained fashion. Nevertheless, I had to clear my head and get on with the job at hand.

Sgt. Trout and I started forward together, him on the right me on the left. I flicked my selector switch on my M-16 from safe to auto as there was no longer anyone in front of me. The trails started to diverge, and I eventually lost visual contact with John.

I was moving slowly, a step at a time, straining to see through the brush. I was feeling vulnerable and more exposed than a Vegas showgirl. There was no doubt we were in an enemy camp. There were more paths visible now, interconnecting, all well-worn. We saw evidence of recent cooking fires and spotted sleeping hammocks hanging in place.

I moved ahead a few more paces, hoping the enemy had taken off. I didn't want this experience. This was far different than the one I half hoped for back in the bunker by the railroad tracks. Adrenaline was stoking my senses, and the flavor of fear flooded my mouth with the bloody taste of copper. There was a breeze brushing the hilltop, and every creak of a bending tree trunk sent my heart racing. I was crouched down, and every step taken was measured with caution so as not to snap a twig or crunch a leaf. I kept each stride short and paused to scan the area after each one. My eyes were straining. I saw nothing—but felt certain that there were eyes on me. I was tense, my muscles were taut, I was expecting to feel the impact of a slug at any second.

Suddenly, John yelled out, "**CHARLIE!!!!**" I stopped dead in my tracks, then all hell broke loose. Brrraaattt, Brrraaattt, Brrraaattt. I dove for the ground. Bursts of automatic weapon fire were zipping over my head. Shredded leaves, severed branches, and chunks of bark were falling on me. **FUCK!!! GOD DAMN IT!! I KNEW IT! I KNEW IT!! I KNEW IT!!!**

I went from being scared, to being pissed, to a state of unexpected calm in a manner of seconds. It was actually happening, no longer any need for apprehension, and being angry wasn't going to help. Quickly, my focus zeroed in on keeping my butt alive.

Apparently, an enemy soldier had purposely shown himself to John for a fleeting second, wanting us to follow him down the trail that he was on. This was an enemy tactic to lure American troops into a trap. But somebody jumped the gun and started firing before we could move further down that trail. The 2nd platoon on our left flank took the brunt of the initial fire. Vanderwall, who narrowly escaped drowning a couple weeks earlier, was shot in the head and died instantly.

I wanted to find some cover. The terrain of base camp was flat, and I had no trees close by with trunks wide enough to afford protection. I had noticed some trenches off to my right a few minutes earlier and decided to head that way. I hadn't twitched a muscle since I hit the ground. I was hesitant to move but didn't want to stay where I was, either. I wanted to ditch my rucksack: I sure didn't need it now, it only increased my profile and hampered my movement. I very slowly and deliberately undid my straps and proceeded to squirm out from underneath it like a snake shedding its skin. I had my helmet and flak jacket on and kept my web gear with ammo, grenades, and water attached.

I began a slow slither toward the trench that would have made any reptile proud. It seemed to take forever; however, I was unwilling to elevate myself even an inch off the ground to go any faster. Gunfire was sporadic now and seemed to be coming from more than one direction. A lot of our guys were firing as well. It was mayhem at first. Initially, I held my fire; I wasn't sure where everyone was. (I knew 2nd platoon was on our left flank, and some of the fire was coming from that direction.) Also, I wanted some cover; I didn't want to be out in the open, firing from an exposed position.

It probably wasn't any further than 15 yards or so, but it seemed to take forever until I finally made it to the trench. I slid over the edge and dropped in: it was only 2 feet deep, but it felt like salvation—heaven couldn't have felt better. A couple of guys were already there and we were soon joined by more. I felt more comfortable about firing now even though we had no real target, just a general idea of where to aim.

There was a group us: Lt. Stockman, Sgt. Browning, Sgt. Trout, Lonnie Brassly, Harry Dodson, Frank Jordon, Roy Farley, Jim Martin, my buddy Byrdy, and me. There was mass confusion in the beginning: a lot of hollering going on before we could better understand the situation. In due time it was established that the 2nd platoon was pinned down to the degree that they could not move at all. Any attempt to maneuver on their part brought volumes of AK-47 and machine gun fire. After assessing the situation, Captain Conner ordered Lt. Stockman to take his men and try to get around behind the enemy bunkers.

We used the trench that encircled the perimeter for our maneuver to the back of the bunker complex. Lt. Stockman, Frank, Lonnie, and Harry stopped first while rest of us continued along maybe 10 yards or so. Roy and I stayed there while the rest of the group moved 10 yards more down the trench. Sgt. Browning, Sgt. Trout, Byrdy, and Jim were in that group. The situation hadn't changed during our move to the rear. The 2nd was still pinned down and took fire every time an attempt was made to move. Enemy fire was coming our way, but we had the trench for cover.

We stayed in the trench for some time while Lt. Stockman was scoping out our next move. Roy was all fired-up and seemed anxious to move forward. He kept yelling at the enemy—obscenities and such. Then he started yelling that when we got to them we were going to cut their balls off. I was thinking, "Damn it Roy! What if, God forbid, one of them knows English? They would never chance a surrender." I wanted to call out "chou hoi" (which means to rally to the government side), but unlike Roy I didn't want to call attention to myself. That worry would prove ironic a little later.

The lieutenant decided it was time for all of us to leave the safety of the trench and move forward to the bunker line. We had yet to get a clear look at a bunker (they were too well camouflaged with the vegetation), but we knew where the fire was coming from. Before climbing out, we laid down some fire which immediately evoked a panicked vocal response from the 2nd platoon. We were firing too close to their position. The bunkers were evidently between us and the 2nd, causing even more problems than we already had. The sound and cyclic rate that a M-16 makes is markedly different than that of an AK-47. That's how the 2nd knew right away that it was us firing in their direction and not the enemy. It was time to move. Roy couldn't wait; he was up and out at the order. But for me, to be honest, climbing out of the security of that trench with bullets flying overhead was the hardest thing I'd ever done. The only thing harder would have been not to.

The lieutenant, who was off to my left, had maneuvered himself behind a bunker. He was on a blind side of it; there were no firing ports. He climbed on top, then quickly stood up to fire into the bunker entrance. His M-16 jammed and he instantly jumped off the bunker. He had barely hit the dirt when a grenade tossed from another bunker rolled out on the ground in his vicinity. Lt. Stockman later said he heard the pin pop on the grenade and thought he was dead. The grenade exploded, wounding the lieutenant and momentarily knocking him unconscious. Meanwhile, Sgt. Trout and Roy, along with Byrdy, crawled forward to position themselves around the back of another bunker when they came under fire. Roy was struck in the foot and had to pull back. I was moving forward at the same time, and we passed each other on the foot path. He did not appear to be in a lot of discomfort; indeed, he almost seemed "high." He greeted me with a smile and a "Go get em, Chuck." In the meantime, Sgt. Trout had one of his teeth struck, probably by a grenade fragment. I could see Frank with Sgt. Browning; they were looking up in the trees. Frank thought he saw something and started raking the trees with his M-16. I didn't see anything.

Byrdy and I hooked up and tried to move forward up the footpath. The track was wide and hard-packed; we were able to move side by side, progressing slowly I slid my rifle out in front of me as we crawled along, finger ever ready on the trigger. Slightly off to our left was a mound that looked like it might be a bunker. It was hard to tell because it was so well-camouflaged. Suddenly, I noticed something out of the corner of my eye. It was a grenade in flight. It hit the trail and bounced twice. Byrdy and I were about 20 feet away from it at that point. I began a backward low crawl, wanting to put as much distance as possible between me and the grenade before it exploded.

It's funny how your mind works at times. As I was moving backwards, I saw Byrdy kind of levitate and do a 180 degree turn in mid-air, and I was thinking: "Wow! How can he do that?" Ordinarily, you wouldn't think your mind would stop to admire a circus move when you just might have two seconds left before the fuse runs out. With just an educated guess as to when it might blow, I stopped moving and buried my face in the dirt. It went off, but neither Byrdy nor I were hit. It was an old-style "pineapple" grenade of Chinese communist origin. It breaks into larger chunks than our "lemon" grenades, so there's a better chance of not being hit by some metal. Byrdy and I retreated back down the path a way to re-evaluate our situation.

A little later, the lieutenant, having recovered somewhat from the knock- out blow he suffered, once again began an approach to a bunker. Frank, Harry and Lonnie were with him. Harry had been slightly wounded by grenade fragments a little earlier but was still able to function effectively.

At this point we were probably 3 hours into this firefight. It wasn't constant shooting, there were lulls in the action. During one of the lulls I heard a jet high overhead. I looked up and saw a Braniff Airlines 707 in bright orange livery climbing for altitude. Braniff was one of the airlines that the US government had contracted to fly troops to Vietnam and home again. Though we were in thick jungle, seemingly in the middle of nowhere, we were actually only 10 miles or so from Binh Hoa Air Force Base. So, seeing a jet on departure from where we were was not that unusual. What was surreal was seeing that "Freedom Bird" headed back to "The World" while we were in the midst of a firefight. I was imagining what the troops in that plane must be feeling: all ecstatic, probably hootin' and hollerin' with joy for getting out of Nam alive while we were in the fight of our lives thousands of feet below. They were in a different world already: their thoughts were projecting 10,000 miles eastward to homes many of them thought they would never see again and wives and girlfriends they thought they might never hold again. Their awareness of what was happening to us was no greater than that of the ants crawling past my eyeballs while my face was planted in the dirt.

Captain Conner was concerned that we were well into the afternoon and the 2nd platoon was still unable to maneuver. He wanted something done—NOW!! He wanted the situation resolved before the sun went down. Unfairly, I thought, he yelled at Lt. Stockman: "You better get moving and do your fucking job!" Shortly thereafter, the lieutenant positioned himself to charge the bunker that had the 2nd pinned down. He yelled to Frank to roll him a grenade. Harry, Frank, and Lonnie laid down suppressive fire to cover the lieutenant. At that point, Lt. Stockman jumped up, raced to the enemy bunker, and threw a grenade inside, killing three enemy soldiers. This relieved pressure on the 2nd. Firing erupted for some time before settling down again. Once again, we were in a lull.

Lt. Stockman called over to Sgt. Browning, saying that he needed someone to move forward and purposely draw enemy fire to get a better fix on the remaining communist positions. Once again, the fickle finger of fate pointed to me. I just happened to be right next to Sgt. Browning at that particular moment; naturally, he selected me for the job. I instinctively gave him my best "are you out of your fucking mind" look. He was not swayed.

I began to move forward, my mind was racing now. Too much had been happening for me to actually stop and think about what was going down. Up until now, I was just reacting to events. But this felt different. I was by myself. I had escaped the initial hail of bullets, I had made it into (and out of) the trench unscathed. I watched a grenade bounce just a few yards away and explode without result. Guys were wounded in front of me and on both sides. How much luck do I have left? Now, THIS? DAMN!! I kept in close contact with the ground as I moved closer in. There were troops all around; I wasn't sure of all their locations. I didn't know what I was going to do just yet but I knew I wouldn't put anyone else at risk.

I headed for an area that appeared to have a slight depression in the ground. Maybe two inches lower than that surrounding it. Doesn't sound like much, but you'll take anything you can get and be happy for it. There was a small sapling at the head of the depression that I decided to use. Its trunk was small enough that I could grasp it with one hand. Its height was maybe 3 or 4 feet. It kind of surprises me when I look back on it now— how I thought it through. Maybe I watched too many cowboys and Indians on TV when I was a kid. On those shows, in this type of situation, if you made it a little too obvious that you were trying to draw the enemy's attention, they would be on to the ruse and not take the bait. With that in mind, I intended to be subtle, as if someone was just brushing the sapling as he moved by it. I oriented myself to present the smallest cross-section to the direction I expected the fire to come from. Being right-handed I took my right arm and slid it under my body. I extended my left arm out in front and grasped the base of the sapling. Then I put my face into the dirt. My last thought before I moved the sapling was, "What is this going to feel like?"—assuming there was a good chance of being hit.

I very slowly twisted my wrist, first one way ever so slightly, then in the opposite direction. The movement produced the desired results: automatic weapons fire ripped through the air. Whether this was beneficial to anyone, I really don't know. After the firing stopped I looked up and saw my tiny tree lying on its side. The small trunk of the sapling had been hit at a level I approximated to be about 3 inches higher than that of my helmet. Relieved to be unhurt, I crept backwards to where Sgt. Browning was located. Not too long after this, the second platoon initiated an attack on the remaining bunker. Since we were on the opposite side, I didn't see anything that took place but can only go by what I heard, most of which was the results.

The second platoon advanced to the point where some guys were able to toss grenades into the remaining bunkers. Then all was quiet. Bill Archer went forward to check the bunker out. He peered into the opening and was shot in the head with a burst of AK-47 fire. He died instantly. More grenades were thrown, two more men were wounded, then it was over.

I stayed on the ground for some time, reluctant to give up the security of the earth. I had been hugging it for hours, practically intimate: so familiar was I with its smell, its feel, its contour. In due time I arose, seeing now what I could only imagine from ground level: how the bunkers were laid out, how they could cover each other, how we were in a cross-fire. The bunkers were dug deep in the ground, topped with logs, and covered with dirt for a roof that gave them a low profile. Vegetation growing on the roof enabled them to blend in with the surroundings. It was a smart set-up. I think I kept expecting something to happen, unable to accept that anything that intense for that long could that suddenly be finished.

It was real quiet for a while. I think most of us were trying to digest what had just happened, reflecting on the past few hours, probably in a near trance- like state. Soon enough, guys started to move around, talking and comparing notes. I walked over to one of the bunkers and looked in. There was a jumble of bodies inside— I could not even tell how many. Not all the parts were attached. On top of one pile, disconnected from its body, was a man's head. Perfectly upright, pristine, not a mark on it. He looked about 25 years of age, he had jet black hair cut short. His dark eyes were wide open, his complexion pallid and waxen, but his face held no expression that might have revealed his last thought. The flies were already at work.

I noticed a red and gold pin attached to the uniform of one of the dead soldiers in the bunker; it had the words Dien Bien Phu on it. Dien Bien Phu was the battle that caused France's defeat in their war in Vietnam, 14 years earlier. I wanted that pin, but early on in my tour I made a promise to myself that I would not take any unnecessary risks. If I climbed down in there, I might disturb some ordnance that was ready to go off. For as much as I wanted that pin, I was able to restrain myself. But damn, all these years later, I still want it!

I talked to a guy in the second platoon who had his helmet struck by a bullet. It struck at an upward angle about a third of the way up on the side directly above his face. The helmet, steel of course, has a liner made of a plastic type material that keeps the headband and suspension in place. The bullet, after penetrating the helmet, was slightly deflected by the liner and traveled up and over his forehead, trapped between the two. He was, as you can imagine, quite emotional over the close call. He said he was going to send the helmet home.

Captain Conner wanted a quick search of the camp for weapons, ammo, and supplies. We found a lot of supplies, medicine, food (in the now familiar US AID sacks), documents, mortar parts, and recoilless rifle rounds. We had to hurry. In addition to the 4 dead the company had suffered, we had 6 wounded to medevac. The forest was too thick and too tall to affect a dust-off at our present location. We had to find a suitable area where the helicopters could land. Time was starting to be a real issue now. We had to carry the four dead troops to a suitable landing zone. Out of the six wounded only Roy needed to be carried. We hurriedly collected the captured supplies and placed them all together. Explosives were set under the pile and timed to go off after we left the camp. The second platoon carried their own dead. Sgt. Jackson carried Roy piggyback style. We split up all our dead and wounded men's gear to carry between the rest of us.

We headed out of the base camp in search of an open area. I think we traveled a kilometer, maybe two, before we reached a suitable site. It wasn't perfect; we had to blow a couple of trees. But afterward, you would be able to fit a 2-chopper lift into the LZ (landing zone). Det cord was wrapped around the trees, set off, and in short order they were down. The choppers had already been called and coordinates given, but it wasn't always easy for the flight crews to find us. We would usually "pop smoke" for the pilots to make it easier to spot us. We always carried a variety of smoke grenade colors: red, purple, green, and yellow come to mind. Once you pulled the pin on the grenade and tossed it on the ground, quite a large volume of smoke was produced. The pilot then authenticated the color. If you popped purple smoke, the pilot might come back with, "I have goofy grape at my 10 o'clock." Then we verified it, and the flight crew felt safe that they were flying into the correct location. Our LZ was nestled basin-like, surrounded by hills, necessitating steeper approach and departure angles for the choppers.

Between the 2 platoons there were maybe 40 to 50 of us, which meant we would not be all leaving at once. We had only two choppers available to us, so we had to be shuttled 10 or 12 at a time to a base across the Dong Nai river. We settled into a defensive perimeter around the LZ, the threat of a counter attack not far from our thoughts.

The first helicopters picked up the wounded and the dead. The 2nd platoon followed. As time went by I was starting to get a little nervous. You could see that this was going to be a close call in getting us out before night fell. I didn't want to be stuck there in the dark waiting for the choppers to find us in what would be an inky black jungle valley. The pilots were not too keen on maneuvering close to tall trees, let alone with very limited visibility.

The way things worked out I was destined for the final group—no surprise there. On a day when I wanted to be last, I was first; now, when I wanted to be first, I was last. There were 10 or 11 of us waiting for the two choppers to return for their last lift. The sky wasn't dark yet, but the sun was low enough that the valley floor was in deep shadow from the encircling hills. I was sweating it out that they wouldn't make it back in time to land safely. I did not want to be stuck out there overnight with only 10 guys in an enemy stronghold.

As usual, we heard the low-pitched slap of the rotor blades before we saw the outline of the two Hueys approaching our position. It was already too dark for popping smoke, so Lt. Stockman used a strobe light to mark our location. The slicks (troop-carrying helicopters) landed just fine and we all scrambled aboard. The pilots pulled pitch, the rotors dug into the air, and we lifted off. The nose dropped to gather some forward momentum, and we began to climb out of the valley. As we crested the hill I could see the bottom of the sun resting on the distant horizon. It was like a sign indicating Hey! I made it! I was elated at the sight of it. Gradually, I perceived a growing physical sensation like a current traveling throughout my whole body. It was unlike anything I had ever experienced before. It felt like the tension of that day was being drawn out of my body and was being replaced by a sensation bordering on euphoria.

My perceptions felt supercharged; I was aware of everything. The colors seemed more vibrant, the solar disc sitting on the dividing line between day and night was impossibly orange. I felt the coolness of the atmosphere change as we gained altitude. It seemed like I could feel every molecule of air I was breathing enter my lungs. I felt the texture and temperature of the chopper floor, its movements, and every vibration. I could hear the wind rush over the uneven surfaces of the helicopter. I could smell the jungle below. I was in tune with everything. Every sensory nerve in my body was on high alert. I was relishing the very idea that yes, I was ALIVE!! I've never come close to experiencing anything like it ever again. I know it had to do with the day's events and my anxiety that the day would not turn out well for me. Scientifically, I presume the sudden release of tension triggered a flood of endorphins to rush through my body, fueling the feeling of euphoria. Or maybe it's as simple as what Winston Churchill once said: "Nothing in life is so exhilarating as to be shot at without result." Regardless of the reason, after the feeling passed I felt extremely guilty for having felt so good. After all, 4 people were dead and 6 were wounded. I never mentioned the experience to anyone.

It has been nearly 50 years since that firefight. After all these years, I can still see some of it as plain as day. The well-worn footpaths and brilliant blue sky. The bouncing grenade and dead enemy soldier's head, eyes open but unseeing. But it would take a long, long time before I would get to the point where I could actually feel the emotional toll that took place that day. At the time, I took what happened and added it to the place in the far recesses of my mind where I hid what killed my buddy Dan Morris and what happened to the unlucky new guys who lost their lives to the booby-trap and those desperate radio transmissions from the embattled lieutenant from D company. I locked them all away in a safe place where they couldn't bother me. I didn't have time to ponder over them; I had tomorrow to worry about.

In retrospect, I imagine that for most people being in a firefight is a life-changing event. I guess that is stating the obvious: some lives are taken, some lives are forever altered— physically, mentally or both. Having said that, I guess that I, too, was affected in some way. It's just hard for me to quantify in what way or even if to the good or to the bad. In my own mind, I don't think it changed me in any fundamental way. Whether this was because of my ability to conceal things away in the back of my mind, I do not know. However, that same ability would cause me some distress as time went on.

In my case, it may not have been life-changing but it certainly was the experience of a lifetime. My emotions ran the gamut from anxiety to fear to exhilaration. The fear came in many forms; fear of the unknown led the list. Not knowing what to expect preys on your psyche. The uncertainty ties knots in your stomach, and it becomes a struggle to manage the worry. Strangely, I had no great fear of death. My phobia had to do with being wounded. I was scared of being maimed, disfigured, or crippled for life— not to mention the pain that would come with it. Then there is the fear of not pulling your weight, of not being able to do what you have to do, fear of letting your buddies down, fear of cowardice. These last fears are what keep you going. They enable you to climb out of that trench when you don't really want to. There is a saying that goes: You only have to die once, but you have to live with being a coward forever.

When all is said and done, that fight that day came down to your survival and your buddies' survival. Your country put you in this situation, but in the heat of that moment, whatever the nation's motivation, it doesn't feel relevant. You did what you had to do, but ideology and politics played no role.

I think it was hard for the average GI to grasp how what we were doing in Vietnam was helping America. This was no war of payback; there was no Pearl Harbor to avenge. We had no symbol of evil incarnate, aka Adolf Hitler, for moral justification. While it's true that the aforementioned reasons are legitimate grounds for war, and more importantly tangible to those who do the fighting, you aren't thinking about them in the middle of a fight— whether it's Normandy, Iwo Jima, or a skirmish in the Mekong Delta. I do think, though, that they help you get through the in-between times. The Vietnam War was missing that basic need: a clearly defined goal that made sense to the soldiers. You need an objective that can be seen and is attainable. And one where the sacrifices that are made result in real progress toward that end.

I think that our firefight in the jungle of War Zone D on June 2nd 1968 was a microcosm of the whole war. We started out with no real mission other than to get into a fight. Historically, wars are about territory. Land is fought for, bled into, won, and kept. Not this one. Our war was a war of attrition. Just kill as many of the other guys as you can.

The "body count" became the be all and end all; it was the standard of success for commanders in the field. The count was everything. For a career officer a good count might be the difference between being promoted or not. A good count could mean a fast track to the top. The system was ripe for abuse. It corrupted the integrity of the Army. For instance, in our firefight the official record lists 16 enemy dead. I personally think that number was a little high. But since we had 4 dead, any less than 16 enemy dead would reflect a poor "kill ratio." The kill ratio (How many of ours were lost to kill how many of them) was second only to the body count in importance. A bad number reflects poorly on the commander, so the manipulation of numbers occurred regularly.

Hiram Walker, a US senator, once said, "The first casualty of war is truth."

Philip Caputo, author and Vietnam Veteran, said it best, "In Vietnam the only measure of victory was one of the most hideous, morally corrupting ideas ever conceived by the military mind, the body count."

And Ho Chi Minh once said, "You will kill ten of my men and we will kill one of yours, and in the end, it will be you who tire of it."

I think these quotes do a good job of summing up the situation we found ourselves in. My heart told me that things weren't right, my head was struggling to maintain a positive attitude. My heart would win in the end, but it took a while to get there, and I felt no satisfaction in the final resolution.

But back on June the 2nd 1968 I was still conflicted. Did the guys die for any real purpose? And how did I evaluate my own role in the fight? The day was an emotional roller coaster. I sure didn't want to be in a firefight, but I sure got a real high by surviving it. And having made it through, I was rather glad it finally happened. That anxiety of the wait was over, it was a rite of passage in a way. I was no hero but I could function, and I was able to do what was asked of me.

CHAPTER EIGHT
STAND-DOWN

We crossed over to the south bank of the Dong Nai river in near darkness. The choppers made a wide turn into the wind to land at a base camp. I noticed a road hugging the water's edge and a village a couple of hundred yards east of the bunker line before we flared and touched down. The "combat high" I experienced on cresting the hill as we flew out of the valley had ebbed, and the stark reality of what happened that day was settling in. We were unexpected guests at the base camp; it already had a full complement of defenders. We were assigned bunkers for the night. Our addition meant that everybody needed to serve only one guard stint through the night.

Sunrise the next morning found me still experiencing a deep sense of relief at having survived the previous day's activities. Twenty-four hours earlier I had serious doubts about my future. I was good at emotionally distancing myself from the events, but I was all too ready to dissect them in a clinical way. I didn't have a clue why we did what we did. I was only a private first class, but to me the whole operation seemed tactically unsound. First off, we were flying into the enemy's backyard in big Chinook helicopters. There was no way they could not know that we were coming: an American rifle company in the bush is anything but stealthy. Our movements could be easily tracked. If that wasn't enough, we had a spotter plane flying low over us guiding our way.

I don't know the enemy's intentions but I can speculate. Their base camp was large; it obviously held a great many troops. Once the Viet Cong were sure we were headed their way, the bulk of them skedaddled, leaving a smaller force to lure us into an ambush. That's what the enemy troop was doing when he let Sgt. Trout see a flash of him on that trail; he was the bait. They wanted us to follow him down that particular trail. Thankfully, they sprung the trap before we were entirely in it.

All the advantages that we had over the enemy were negated by our tactical position. We were in heavy jungle, close-in, and partially pinned down. Airstrikes were out: helicopter gunships wouldn't be able to see where the enemy was, and due to our proximity to the enemy, artillery would be just as deadly to us as to them. They were dug in and protected by well- camouflaged bunkers. In fact, we were so close that even our grenade launchers were of no use. The grenade round of a M-79 grenade launcher has to travel about 30 yards before it arms itself. Some rounds were fired at bunkers, but they didn't go off. They didn't travel far enough to explode on impact. It came down to raw courage like Lt. Stockman had that day to get us out of that mess. Even when it was over, it wasn't over: we had wounded to evacuate and no way to do it. The cover was too thick and the trees way too tall for a dust-off from that location, forcing a long hike to a suitable spot.

I wondered why they didn't use B-52 bombers. Their intelligence was obviously spot-on: they told us we were going into an enemy base camp, and we did. But why invest troops when you could have bombed the place from 30,000 feet with complete surprise? That way most of the enemy would not have escaped. The B-52's were used a lot in the war. The large 8 engine jet bombers could haul a massive bomb load of up to 108 bombs, each weighing in at 500 pounds. The code name for the bombing missions was "arc light." The bombers usually flew in a group of three, dropping over 300 bombs on the target. They lay a path of destruction hundreds of feet long. Craters 15ft. deep and 30ft. wide pockmarked the earth, and trees were felled, their trunks and limbs broken like twigs. Yes, this was a perfect situation for the bombers; however, that wouldn't put a feather in the cap of a commander who is out to "prove his stuff" by closing with the enemy.

For certain career army officers, Vietnam was "the only war we had." A combat command was highly desired, and when some of them got that command they wanted to make a name for themselves. A successful combat tour could make a career. Unfortunately, decisions made to enhance that career often were not in the best interests of the troops on the ground. My thoughts on this were reinforced only days after the firefight when one of our platoons was sent out on a BDA (bomb damage assessment). They were flown into an area that was just hit by an "arc light" mission. They counted close to 20 dead soldiers, and none of our troops were lost in the process.

While ruminating on how well or not so well our brigade staff was running the war, rumors were flying that we would soon have a stand-down. A stand-down in military parlance is a temporary suspension of offensive operations. That sounded good to me: a few days back at BMB (brigade main base) at Long Binh was overdue. But it was still just a rumor. Meanwhile, things went on as usual.

We continued making sweeps of the area and found quite a few enemy bunkers loaded with supplies that we blew up. The base had the 4.2 (four-deuce) mortar platoon on hand. It was the battalions in-house fire support, just as our 81mm mortars were for our company. The 4.2 stood for 4.2 inch diameter round. There was a fire mission one night in support of one of the line platoons. They sent out a lot of rounds, but I didn't hear about any results from the activity.

The guy who was burned by the phosphorous from a trip flare came back to the unit. He was a black guy and it looked like the phosphorous burned all the melanin in his skin and left him with bright pink splotches all over his face.

One evening we discovered one of the men in the company was missing. His name was Archer, same name as one of the troops we lost in the firefight a few days earlier. Word was he hopped onto a Vietnamese bus that was traveling on the road not far from our position and headed for Saigon. Maybe he was freaked out by having someone with the same name as his get killed. I don't know what was the truth; one thing was sure, he was AWOL. There was talk of GIs hiding out in Saigon and dealing drugs to get by. But then again, the military runs on rumors so who knows? One rumor that turned out to be true was our stand-down back at the BMB. Trucks were sent out to pick us up. We loaded everything onto the deuce and a halves and climbed aboard for the bumpy ride back to Long Binh.

Upon our arrival, back at our tent city, we heard the news that Robert Kennedy was assassinated. Wow, Vietnam was nuts, but it seemed that things back in "The World" were no less so. First, the day before we left for Vietnam we heard that President Johnson wouldn't run for re-election because of the war. Then just after we arrived in Nam we heard of Martin Luther King's assassination and all of the riots that followed. Then news of all the war protests going on, and now this—RFK was killed after winning the California primary for the democratic nomination for president. Crazy!

When you are out in the boonies, you live in a bit of a vacuum. You are in your own little world where all that really concerns you is surviving. You couldn't really say that about the big bases in Vietnam. What was happening back in the states was reflected in the attitudes of the troops who lived and worked on them. Nowhere was this more apparent than the obvious racial divide that was taking place at an ever faster rate since Martin Luther King's assassination. There was racial tension before MLK's death, but afterward it was no longer simmering under the surface, it was flat out in your face.

We saw this first-hand when we all went down to the enlisted men's club on the first night of our stand-down. All the blacks sat in one area and all the whites in another, and it looked as if both groups liked it that way. This put the black guys in the unit in an uncomfortable position. As mentioned earlier, there was not much of a race problem out in the bush because everybody depended on each other. That wasn't the case so much on base. Loyalties were tested when the grunts came in from the field.

For many blacks, Martin Luther King's mission of social change by non-violent protest died along with him. In the states reversing social injustice was taking on a more militant tone, and that attitude was showing itself in Vietnam as well. "Black Power" and "I'm Black and I'm Proud" were becoming part of the protester's lexicon. Many blacks who were drafted felt they were fighting a "white man's war." Why should they be fighting for something that they didn't have at home for themselves?

Soon a lot of blacks on the bases only socialized among themselves. They started growing their hair as long as they could get away with, wanting the "afro" look. They wore "Black Power Bracelets" and developed specialized greetings known as dapping. The "dap" occurred when a couple of men met each other. It was an elaborate sequence of fist pumps, handshakes, palm slaps, and grips, usually ending with arms crossed across their chests. It was to show solidarity.

To be sure, not everybody took part in the racial animosity on the bases. There were lots of black and white friendships. I even saw whites dapping with black guys. Nevertheless, the tension was real at times. Part of that tension was between the older and younger blacks. A lot of the Army's NCO (non-commissioned officer) corps were black. The Army at that time was a good career for a lot of black men who could not get jobs with similar pay and benefits in the civilian world because of discrimination. The Army was their lives and their livelihood, and they represented the Army to the young black draftees who hated it.

This generational gap was not limited just to the blacks. The divide between the career soldiers and the young draftees was wide no matter what color you were. The newest troops, fresh from the states, arrived with an anti- war attitude, mirroring what was happening back in America. They were anti- establishment, and the older career soldiers represented the status quo. Clash was inevitable. The twenty-year men, the careerists, the "lifers" in Army lingo, had a hard time adjusting to this new wave of soldiers who were questioning, rebellious, and not inclined to follow in lockstep to the sometimes inflexible, unbending rules and authority. Our platoon sergeant, Sgt. Browning, and the company first sergeant fit this lifer category. Neither of them adjusted to the new realities of this war. The term lifer as used by the troops was a pejorative. To call someone a lifer was to denigrate them.

One divide that was felt by almost everybody who humped the boonies was the differences in what was asked of the infantry troops compared to those who lived on the bases. While not entirely fair to the "REMFs," it was hard not to feel a little resentment when you compared your life in the field with theirs on base. I hadn't had a real shower in almost two months, wore the same filthy clothes night and day for weeks, slept on the ground, and stayed up half the night on guard. Not to mention eating most of my meals out of a can, carrying 50 or more pounds of gear on all-day patrols and dealing with monsoon rains two days out of three. In addition, there were any number of insects ready to bite and mosquitoes and leeches to suck your blood out. They, the REMFs, had showers, clean clothes, three hot meals a day, a roof overhead, a real bed, and a space to call their own. For a few bucks a month they could hire a Vietnamese housemaid who polished their shoes, did their laundry, and cleaned up their area. The REMF's had fans, stereos, and mini refrigerators. They could go to air-conditioned clubs at night and see live entertainment and grab a couple of beers. The bigger bases had PXs, libraries, movie theaters, and even swimming pools.

To be fair, a lot of REMFs worked long, hard hours on the bases, particularly those in the supply and maintenance fields. They were subject to rocket and mortar fire at any time. The truck drivers and MPs who ran convoys through dangerous areas were vulnerable to ambushes. REMFs— or more politely, support troops—made up the vast majority of soldiers in Vietnam. Figures vary, but in general it takes 6, 7, or 8 support troops for every grunt in the field. At the height of the war when there were 550,000 servicemen in Vietnam, only 75,000 were out in the boonies. The support troops did a good job. Sure, they were "in the rear with the gear" (or less generously, "in the rear with the beer"), but we did need them.

Having said that, it still left a bad taste in your mouth when you saw some REMFs get perturbed at the grunts for coming in out of the field, taking over their club for a few days and breaking up the REMFs normal routines. Or when some administrative type REMF lieutenant chewed you out for wearing your bush hat on the base. Wearing your bush hat was a point of pride for a lot of grunts, and it was really Mickey Mouse to prevent us from wearing them in the rear areas. You were supposed to wear the official fatigue cap while on base. Basically, it was a baseball cap. It had to have been designed by someone with a vicious sense of humor. It was made with a high crown, shaped to make whomever was wearing it look like a mini cone-head. Practically everybody resisted wearing them and bought hats with a more traditional baseball cap look from the local Vietnamese.

There was no saluting out in the boonies, no standing at attention, no inspections, and no Mickey Mouse regulations to follow. To turn into a garrison troop the second you walk through the gate, after two months in the bush, was too much to expect—and it didn't happen. Fairly or unfairly, most guys begrudged the REMFs comparatively cushy standard of living, and to be sure, would have traded places with any one of them in a second.

But none of that was on my mind when we first got back to the base. What I really wanted was a shower. We didn't have hot showers back at our tent city, but we did have water tanks mounted on towers. The sun would heat the water just a little, but it felt great compared to a cold rain out in the jungle. I scrubbed weeks of dirt out of my pores; what I thought was a great tan was washed down the drain. I walked out of the shower feeling lighter, my spirits high. I donned some fresh fatigues and felt like a new man. I headed to the mess hall for a hot meal and sat down at a table to eat it. Having something that was actually cold to drink was heaven. I was really enjoying some of the small, everyday things that we so take for granted.

One thing really felt strange: walking around without a weapon. All our M-16s were put away in the armory when we arrived on base. I had mixed feelings about this. On one hand, it felt great to be rid of that constant reminder about what you were doing over here. But on the other hand, I felt a certain uneasiness not having it close at hand. After all, I just spent two months without it ever being beyond arms reach.

In the evening, we went down to the enlisted men's club. It was air-conditioned, and the cool air felt invigorating. The beer was cheap, and they had live entertainment (in the form of a Filipino band) that played mostly Top 40 Pop songs. It was a fun evening and it ended with the band singing an iconic song of the Vietnam War. The music was originally recorded by a British rock band called The Animals. "We Gotta Get Out of This Place" was the title, and the theme was actually about a young couple escaping the ghetto. No matter, the chorus resonated with the feelings of thousands of young draftees who wanted to be anywhere but Vietnam. It became an anthem for the disillusioned troops who just wanted to go home.

The song was probably sung every night in every enlisted men's club—from the Mekong Delta to the DMZ. Everyone joined in at the chorus. It was the last song of the night and everyone was fairly tuned up by that time, so it was always sung loudly and with great enthusiasm.

We walked back to our tents. I was looking forward to sleeping on a cot. Jim Martin, one of the guys in the Fire Direction Center of the platoon, was on the next cot over. Jim, nicknamed "flea", felt like talking, mostly about the firefight on June the 2nd. He was really disturbed about how it all went down and kept me up till the wee hours rehashing that day. He was emotionally distraught, and I felt bad about not being able to connect with him. But it was not in the cards for me at that time and place. I was still in protective mode.

Day two of stand-down was party day. We had a big barbecue in the afternoon with steaks for everyone and all the beer or coke you wanted. Colonel Behm was there to award everybody their Combat Infantry Badges. The badge is silver and infantry-blue in color. The main part of the badge is a rectangular bar about three inches in width that has a replica of a 1795 Springfield Arsenal Musket (like those used in the War of Independence) superimposed on its blue background. A silver oak leaf wreath partially surrounds the bar. Criteria for the badge to be awarded is as follows: "A recipient must be personally present and under hostile fire while serving in an assigned Infantry primary duty, in a unit actively engaged in ground combat with the enemy."

The dichotomy of Vietnam service was reflected in the troops' acceptance of their Combat Infantry Badge awards. As much as many of them didn't want to be there, as much as many of them felt it was an unjust war, as much as many of them would trade jobs with a REMF without looking back, most felt pride in wearing it. Whether sewn on your fatigues as a patch or pinning the badge on your dress greens, it said something.

In addition to the CIBs, we all received a Zippo cigarette lighter. The lighter had my name engraved on it, as well as our unit crest and name. It also had Vietnam engraved on one side and a small CIB attached to the cover. I still have mine.

Entertainment was scheduled for the evening. It was held outside in our battalion area. They rigged up a flatbed trailer for a stage. A band played a couple sets and the night ended with a strip show.

Day 3 of stand-down was a downer. The party was over and word was we were leaving for War Zone D the next morning. The day was spent getting ready for the trip north. Our company, B, was going to help build a new base from scratch further north from where we were before. I didn't like the idea of going back to War Zone D, but I had no sense of foreboding this time, no metallic taste in my mouth, and no fear of never seeing another sunset. Captain Conner stopped by the company area while we were preparing for our trip north and asked if anyone was interested in taking training for mine detectors or flame throwers. He got no takers. No surprise there!

The next morning, we retraced our steps from our first trip two months earlier down to the helipad. Nobody was carrying too much weight this time. We were all a little more seasoned, the fear of the unknown somewhat abated. We took off from the BMB midmorning and headed northeast.

CHAPTER NINE
A O LEHIGH WAR ZONE D

We were flying at 1500 feet above the jungle when I spotted the Dong Nai River up ahead. Upon reaching it, the pilots banked slightly and began to follow its trace through the heavily forested land below. The river was swollen with monsoon rains and seemed barely contained by its banks. The vegetation on either side seemed endless and was unbroken by anything remotely resembling human habitation. I was thinking, Damn, this really is the boonies.

The river looked beautiful as it meandered its way through the jungle. Its source was the Central Highlands, and it coursed its way over 300 miles, much of it through the forest primeval below us to the South China Sea.

Eventually a clearing in the jungle appeared. What might have been a road at one time headed toward the river. It was our destination, and the choppers formed up in trail formation and descended to land on what was left of the road. We hopped out and got blasted by the dirt and grit churned up by the rotor blades. The choppers departed, and we started looking around at our new digs. There were no tall trees in the area, just some scrub brush plants and scraggly grass. It was obvious that someone was here once doing something, but there was no evidence of what that might have been. The road was a mystery as well: it seemed to disappear into the jungle on one end and submerged itself into the river at the other.

Our new base was called Melinda. A lot of bases were named after commander's wives or girlfriends, but there were no strict rules in that regard. Some of our bases were named after Indian tribes as our battalion's heritage involved fighting on the frontier. Our crest depicted an Indian teepee on it to represent battles fought on the Great Plains in the late eighteen hundreds. In keeping with that, the companies in the battalion were named Apache, Blackfoot (ours), Comanche, Dakota, and Erie.

Blackfoot company was chosen to build and provide security for FSB Melinda. It meant a lot of work for us in the coming days, but it was better than being out on patrols like the other companies of the battalion. With any luck, we might have a hot meal flown to the base camp some nights.

Our mortars provided first response fire if any of the other companies requested it. So, the first order of business for the mortar platoon was to dig our mortar pits, ammo bunkers, and personal fighting positions. We hadn't had the mortar tubes with us since our first week in the field when it was realized that carrying them was not going to be practical in the jungle environment. In fact, we hadn't fired them since we arrived in-country, so we were going to be a little rusty in the event of a fire mission. The platoon had 3 squads, each with their own mortar. We also had a FDC (fire direction center) which took fire mission request calls from the forward observers out in the field.

The pits were about 8 feet in diameter and dug into the dirt about 18 inches deep. Then we added 2 or 3 rows of sandbags atop the edge of the circumference. The mortar baseplate was centered in the pit, the tube inserted and the bipod attached, then the sight was installed. Aiming stakes were stuck in the ground some yards away from the pits to sight in on. This was a reference point to orient the mortars on the map. The FDC received location information from the FO's (forward observers) then used a plotting board to figure out the direction of fire. There were a lot of variables to account for to get the mortar rounds in the right place. The tubes could be adjusted for elevation: from nearly straight up for extremely close fire support, to lower levels for distance. Direction was called deflection, and this was changed by turning a traversing screw. Each mortar round came with 9 cloth bags of powder that provided the thrust to propel the round. Once the distance was figured out, the correct elevation and the number of powder charges needed were found on a chart.

The first round sent out was usually a marker round that the FO could make adjustments to. Once the marker round went off, the FO could request an adjustment which usually sounded like "drop 50, right 50" or something similar to that. The gunner then adjusted the elevation of the tube so the round dropped 50 yards closer. 50 right required the gunner to adjust the deflection by using the traversing screw to change the direction. I was hoping we wouldn't have to use the tubes because we were all a bit rusty.

We were all dug in well before nightfall with some rounds ready to be dropped in short order but most still in their wooden shipping boxes. The first night by the river was uneventful, and the next morning we started helping to build the rest of the camp.

The first choppers arrived shortly after first light. They were the Army's big ones: Chinooks and Skycranes. They hauled their loads by slinging them underneath with ropes or cables. It made for fast deliveries. The chopper would fly in, settle over the drop-off area in a hover, slowly lower till the load touched down then release the ropes, and off it went for another load. They brought in lumber, PSP (perforated steel planking), tents, generators, ammunition, and untold numbers of sandbags yet to be filled.

The base needed a TOC (tactical operations center) first thing. The TOC was the communications center for the battalion as well as the command and control center. All field operations were coordinated through the TOC. Requests for artillery or air support were funneled through the TOC, so it was important to get it up and running. One quick way the Army did that was by using shipping containers called Conex boxes (steel boxes). We used them to pack all our equipment in back at Fort Lewis for overseas shipment to Vietnam. They were made out of a fairly heavy gauge steel and measured 8 feet long by 6 feet wide and 6 and one-half feet high. By arranging 3 of them in a U shape with a blast wall on the open end of the U, you had the basics of your TOC in a short amount of time. The sides were covered with stacked sandbags to the top. PSP would be laid down for a roof and sandbags layered on them for overhead protection. Soon the TOC was bristling with antennas and ready for operations. We put up tents for a medical unit, built bunkers, and did just about anything else that needed done.

Toward the end of the third day the camp was just about done. It was close to sunset, and I was just finishing up the last few sandbags that we needed at the ammo bunker. Lonnie asked me, "Hey Chuck, what is that brown stuff on your back?" I had no idea what he was talking about. He told me I had some brown splotches on the upper half of my back. I didn't feel anything, but I figured I'd go see the medic when I had the chance. I wrapped up for the day and was already looking forward to going down to the river the following morning to get cleaned up after 3 days of sweat and dirt accumulation.

I was awakened about 2:30 AM by someone yelling, "Up, Up, Up!!" I was instantly awake and alert (deep sleep was a luxury that not many field troops experienced) and wondering what was going on. I heard Lt. Stockman on the radio; he was talking with somebody from Delta company. Delta had been hit by enemy mortar fire and was requesting counter-mortar fire from us. It looked like we were going to have our first live fire mission in support of troops. Everybody was a little tense: we hadn't fired our mortars since Fort Lewis three months earlier. Nobody wanted to make a mistake and be responsible for a "friendly fire" incident.

Troops being hit by their own fire support happened far more often than you would think.

Lt. Stockman gave the coordinates of Delta company to Sgt. Trout and Jim Martin who were the FDC. Then he told them where Delta wanted us to place the mortar fire. They used the plotting board and charge charts to figure the elevation, deflection, and amount of powder bags for each round. It probably took a little longer to get that first round down the tube than it should have, but everybody was double-checking everything. The first round was a marker round, and someone from Delta made corrections from its impact point. We all kind of held our breath until we heard from them on the radio. Thankfully, we were in the ballpark, and they gave us some adjustments and called for fire for effect. We then began to use all three tubes.

I was in the first squad. We no longer had a full complement of men since Roy and Lenny were wounded on June 2nd and would not be returning. You can go through a lot of mortar rounds in a short amount of time, and what rounds were ready and on hand were gone in no time. Lonnie, Byrdy, and myself were hard-pressed to keep up with demand. We used our entrenching tools to break the metal bands holding the ammo boxes closed. Each box held three rounds, each in a cardboard tube, impregnated with some kind of moisture-proof substance and sealed with heavy-duty tape. We were working furiously hauling boxes, breaking the bands, un-taping the tubes, setting the fuses, and counting the proper number of powder charges.

I was exhausted when the fire mission was over. It might have been the middle of the night, but I was drenched in sweat. The area around our pit looked like one of the rounds went off there: empty wooden boxes littered the ground; cardboard tubes were scattered everywhere; strips of tape and excess powder charges were strewn about—all evidence of the non-stop effort that took place.

The guys might have been hating the war, but they still gave 100% when it came to supporting their fellow soldiers. I sat there on the sandbagged pit wall and felt good about the effort, enjoying a sense of satisfaction that we were able to help out. Delta company, who we were supporting with mortar fire, had one soldier killed that night, and two were wounded by the enemy mortar fire. The adrenaline was still flowing for some time after the fire mission, and I only fell back to sleep shortly before the sun announced the new day.

I was just finishing my cookies and cocoa when Lt. Stockman, just back from the TOC, announced that the whole battalion had to move to a new AO (area of operation) just south of Saigon. Then he added, "by tomorrow!" Saigon was being rocketed every night, and intelligence was worried about a new ground attack. The brigade commander was sending our battalion to guard and patrol the southeast approaches to Saigon. We had to be in place by the 20th of June; that gave us one day. We'd been here all of three.

The lieutenant said we had to pack up the essentials and burn everything else. We all had to be back to the Brigade Main Base at Long Binh by nightfall as we were going to leave for Saigon the following morning. We started immediately to tear down the mortars and collect all the shells for transport back to base. We took the tents down and at least partially destroyed the bunkers we'd just built by removing the PSP roofing. We started a fire and threw all the lumber on it and anything else they said we wouldn't have time to take with us.

The TOC had to be taken back because of all the communication equipment inside. A Sikorsky Skycrane was flying in for the Conex containers that made up the TOC. We knocked the sandbags down and attached cables to the corners of the boxes. When the Skycrane hovered over the box, one of us stood on top of the box and reached up to slip the cables over a hook that hung below the chopper. The Skycrane was huge and very powerful. Its 6 main rotor blades created quite a whirlwind, and if you were the one trying to hook up the cables, you inevitably got a good sandblasting for your efforts. Since you were already hot and sweaty, the dirt and grit stuck to you and you just felt as grungy as could be.

We worked hard throughout the day and managed to get all the essentials flown out. We were next. A flight of Hueys descended and landed along the road. We hopped aboard, took off, and left what remained of FSB Melinda behind. I could not wait to get back to Long Binh. I was hoping for a hot meal, a cot to sleep on, and most of all a shower.

I wasn't the only one with those priorities: we had to wait in line to get our few minutes under the water tank. I got something to eat and then returned to the company area where I stashed my stuff under a cot in one of the tents. Captain Conner was there and laid out the agenda for the next day. Lt. Stockman's platoon was going to leave first in the morning. So much for sleeping in! Each member of the platoon was to be stationed on different street corners to guide the convoy that was transporting the battalion to the south of Saigon. It was all "Hurry, hurry, we have to get there." It seemed like they really knew something big was going to happen. This time I felt more excited than anxious; for some unknown reason, I wasn't really worried. I was dead tired from working all day and being up half the night on the fire mission. All I wanted to do was lie down on my cot and get a good night's sleep. I skipped going to the club that night, even though I had no idea when I might get the opportunity to go again.

We got up early and walked to the mess hall while it was still dark.

Having a hot breakfast was a nice treat. Afterwards, our platoon loaded up in a deuce and a half (A truck in the 2½ ton weight class) and headed toward the base main gate to get on the road to Saigon. As we made the turn onto the main road, I saw a sign next to a wooden platform that held the remains of a crumpled army jeep. The sign read: "WARNING, you are about to enter one of the most dangerous combat areas in Vietnam—A PUBLIC HIGHWAY. PLEASE DRIVE CAREFULLY."

We headed south toward Saigon about 20 miles away. The further south we traveled I noticed the land was gradually changing from small rolling hills to a flatter landscape. At one point, we passed the Vietnamese National Military Cemetery, the equivalent of our Arlington. We intersected with Vietnam's Highway 1 and soon after approached the Newport Bridge that crossed over the Saigon River. At that juncture we could see the city ahead, about two miles in the distance. Once we reached the city, the truck driver stopped at each intersection that required the following convoy to make a turn. Our job was to spot the convoy as it approached and wave the lead driver in the correct direction.

In short order, I was dropped off and given my directions to pass on. It felt odd to be standing on that corner somewhere in the middle of Saigon, suddenly alone, albeit in a sea of Vietnamese. Before the war, Saigon was a city of 500,000 residents but now was swollen to 3 million, mostly refugees from the countryside trying to escape the war.

At first the assignment didn't seem too difficult. But I didn't count on all the military traffic that constantly passed through the city, not to mention all the bikes, motorbikes, cyclos, scooters, cabs, civilian trucks, and cars transiting the streets. It was exciting being in all that chaos, but I was nervous about not seeing the correct trucks in all that streaming traffic, so I couldn't really enjoy it.

I was checking out all the bumpers on any approaching deuce and a halfs to see if I could see the 199th unit designation stenciled on the right front corner in white paint. Finally, I saw a column of trucks coming my way. I spotted the 199th and started waving at them to make the turn. I'm sure the driver was told to look for us, but I still felt relieved when he started turning in the right direction. It was like a funeral procession in a way: the convoy was stopping for nothing. Once the first truck went through the intersection, it didn't matter what the traffic light said, everybody was going through. It underscored the impression that the command really wanted us in our new AO—like yesterday!! The last deuce and a half in the line was tasked with picking up all of us "street corner directors." The driver didn't want to lose touch with the tail end of the line and barely came to a stop for each of us. Half the time guys already in the truck were grabbing us and pulling us up over the tailgate as the driver was taking off. We passed through the rest of the city over a couple of bridges that spanned canals and were soon on the southern outskirts of the city. The city ended rather abruptly, going from urban to rural in a flash. Our battalion was based in that narrow transition.

Our new AO was called Laura, the battalion base camp was called Blackfoot, and our new mission was called "*Toan Thang*" (I have no idea). But the official mission order was: "To provide ground, mortar, and rocket defense for Saigon from the Viet Cong and North Vietnamese Army and to interdict infiltration and attack routes and resupply havens."

CHAPTER TEN
AO LAURA (A SWEETHEART)

We hung a right, pulling off the pavement and onto a dirt road that was barely a lane wide. Thatched huts hugged the side of the road for a hundred yards or so before the landscape opened up. The truck pulled into a large grassy area about the size of a football field. We were going to set up shop in the middle of it. To our north was a marshy area with waist-high grasses and tall bulrushes alongside a canal. To the east and west were small villages. To the south across the road we drove in on were rice paddies that stretched out as far as I could see. We were only thirty miles from yesterday, but the landscape had changed dramatically. The wrinkled topography of War Zone D was replaced by an alluvial plain made dead flat by millennia of monsoon rains.

It looked like the sun was going to be a constant companion down here, no more triple canopy jungle providing shade and temps a few degrees cooler. Nonetheless, I was ready to put the confines of the jungle behind me. I didn't know what awaited me on this northern edge of the Mekong Delta, but I felt it had to be better. Just being able to see a horizon gave me a feeling of freedom. The jungle was claustrophobic: there was no change in scenery, and it was green in every direction, even up. You saw no civilians. You had no time to yourself. There was nothing to do but the numbing all-day patrol, the every evening fox hole dig, half the night on guard duty, and do it all over again the next day. To me, leaving the jungle was analogous to getting out of prison.

Another truck showed up with bunker building supplies, sandbags, PSP, and culvert (pipe) halves. Lt. Stockman had us filling the bags with dirt minutes after they were dropped off. He wanted the bunkers completed by sunset in case the anticipated attack came that night. For some reason I was not overly concerned about making contact with the VC that night. I just didn't think it was going to happen. I had no rational excuse for believing that. I just did.

We worked hard all that day and got our defensive positions completed before sunset. It was a rain-free day and I watched a golden sun cross the sky and settle below the horizon, bringing on darkness in short order. Twilight in the tropics gives barely a warning that night is about to fall. The heavens were clear that night enabling light from a crescent moon and starlight to reach us. Having the city practically at our backs gave us enough ambient light to let us see pretty well. It brightened my spirits.

Our bunkers were basically above ground level. The water table in the area was too close to the surface to allow digging: any hole in the ground soon filled with water. Consequently, there was no hiding our presence. You couldn't miss us; we were out in the open and elevated. Every Vietnamese in the area watched us set up camp. There was no doubt the VC knew our location.

Tactically, that is not a very good situation, but it did have its benefits on a personal level. For one thing, I could smoke on guard duty. For another, we could stay up and BS into the night. Noise security was no longer much of an issue, and we had good fields of fire. With all that light, peering through the starlight scopes presented a brightly illuminated picture of the rice paddies to our front.

I think most of us were enjoying our new situation, the danger of imminent ground, rocket, and mortar attacks notwithstanding. However, there was a threat that was casting a pall over our platoon. Rumors of an impending "infusion" had been floating around since we started building FSB Melinda up in War Zone D. Word was that it was inevitable; we just didn't know when. Infusion in the Army's case meant the introduction of troops from one unit into another. The reason we were susceptible to this action was because we had all arrived in-country on the same date, and the Army didn't want too many troops rotating home from the same unit at the same time. We were lucky to have arrived as a unit, but because of the individual rotation policy, we would not be able to maintain our unit integrity.

A newly drafted inductee in the army typically needed about five months of training before he was ready to be deployed overseas. When you factor transportation time and leave time, he would have about 17 months left out of the 24. Early on in the war there was a proposal for a 15-month tour of duty in Vietnam, but the idea was axed by the Commander of Vietnam Forces, General William Westmoreland. The general felt that a 12-month tour was more acceptable. He stated: "the harsh conditions provided one of the strongest arguments for a one-year tour of duty." The die was cast: 365 days was the obligation of any draftee. This one-year tour of duty, coupled with the social, generational, political, racial, and anti-war divisions that were rocking America and were carried to Vietnam by the newly conscripted GI's, nearly destroyed the Army.

The first casualty of the Individual Rotation Policy was unit cohesion. Shared experience is the glue that binds any group together. The IRP ensured that continuity was always being compromised by the constant movement of troops both into and out of a unit. There is nothing quite as bonding as sharing combat with your fellow troops. Therefore, a natural division occurred between those who had been under fire and those who had not. It wasn't overt or mean-spirited, but the new guys represented an inexperience that could compromise the veteran troops' chances of survival. In addition, in units that suffered heavy casualties, some troops weren't really interested in making new friends only to lose them.

Compounding the problem was the Army's policy of having officers spend only 6-month tours in the field instead of the 12 that the enlisted men had to serve. The Army wanted to give as many officers as possible a chance at a combat command. This created an easy to understand antipathy amongst the troops toward the officer corps. Being exposed to possible death or crippling wounds for twice as long as the officers seemed patently unfair.

What was even worse were officers who looked on their combat command as a rung on their career ladder. Having a combat command was a sure-fire way to get promoted, so they looked on their time in the field as getting their "Ticket Punched." Vietnam was "the only war they had," and they wanted to take advantage of it. Unfortunately, some of these officers wanted to make a name for themselves and sometimes put their troops in jeopardy to accomplish this.

For all of these reasons a typical infantry unit in Vietnam was in a constant state of flux. Experienced troops were leaving the country about the time they were really getting a handle on things, only to be replaced by complete rookies who had to learn the ropes from scratch. John Paul Vann, senior advisor for all military advisors in the III Corps Tactical Zone, summed up the results of the Individual Rotation Policy and One Year Tour Obligation by stating: "The US Army has not been in Vietnam for nine years, but for one year nine times." In essence, lessons learned had to be re-learned and re-learned—again and again.

For the average post-Tet drafted GI who was sent to Vietnam, completing the one-year tour was THE goal. Winning wasn't really relevant to these new troops, having arrived in-country from an America that had lost faith in the purpose of the war and confidence in those leading it. Their personal mission was to do their time, stay alive, and return home in one piece.

CHAPTER ELEVEN
FIRST NIGHTS

Our new AO was completely different from our last couple of AOs up in War Zone D. For starters, AO Laura was heavily populated on its northern edge and had many small villages throughout the rest of the area. War Zone D, devoid of civilians, was a free-fire zone: if you spotted someone, he was considered the enemy, and you could engage him without authorization. AO Laura was the opposite: unless fired upon, you needed Provincial authority from Vietnamese officials for offensive operations. There were no secrets down here. There were civilians everywhere; any of them could be Viet Cong or VC sympathizers. There was no way to tell; the VC didn't wear uniforms. Farmers by day could be Viet Cong ambushers, rocket launchers, or booby- trap setters by night.

The fact that we had to clear all our missions through the province chief just about guaranteed that the local VC always knew what we were doing. Just like when we were up in the Rocket Belt and we came out of the jungle onto a road, only to be greeted by Vietnamese ready to sell us their wares. I didn't think this was a matter of lucky guesses or coincidences. They had to know, and if they knew, it was a good bet the VC did as well.

There was no high ground down here: in every direction, it was table top flat. The only break on the horizon were the nipa palms that grew along the banks of the many streams and canals that crisscrossed the area. We were just about two months into the rainy season now, so all the rice paddies were filled with water. Mud, along with a blazing sun, tortured us on many a day to come.

Our first night in the AO passed uneventfully. There were some explosions in the city, probably from rockets, but they didn't originate in our sector.

There was barely a hint of light on the horizon when the villagers began to move out onto the road out to our front. There was a dusk to dawn curfew in effect, and it looked like they didn't want to waste a minute of the day. Farmers were headed to the rice paddies on foot and workers to the city on bicycles and small motorcycles for their day's work. The farmers wore mostly the traditional garb of loose fitting black trousers and a shirt of the same color. They also wore the classic conical straw hat that was practically a national symbol of Vietnam. It was ideal for protection against the brutal tropical sun and the torrential downpours of the monsoon. It wasn't long before boats and sampans (a flat bottom Asian skiff usually propelled by one or two oars) began to navigate the canal to our rear. The area was abuzz with activity. I was really liking this change from the isolation of the jungle.

Our battalion was initially positioned on the northern edge of AO Laura, barely outside the city limits of Saigon. Our battalion Fire Support Base was set up in a cement factory about a mile down the paved road from our position. Its official name was FSB Blackfoot, but no one ever called it that. It was always referred to as what it was, a cement factory. Lt. Stockman left for the cement factory to attend a morning briefing on our new mission. The rest of us spent the morning constructing our mortar pits and making our bunkers a little more comfortable. Hopefully, we'd be here long enough to make the effort worthwhile.

The lieutenant returned to our location early in the afternoon. He called us all around him and said he had some news to share. First off, he said, "effective immediately, Captain Conner no longer will be your company commander." He was assigned to the battalion operations staff and was not returning to the company. We got a new captain within a week. Then he told us that he, too, was leaving. He was being reassigned as an advisor to the Vietnamese Army. However, he would be staying around until our new lieutenant arrived.

I was ambivalent about Captain Conner leaving, but that wasn't the case with Lt. Stockman. I was sad to hear the lieutenant was being transferred, not because we had any sort of personal ties, he kept a professional distance in that regard, but because I respected him for his competency and courage. I think the majority of the platoon felt the same way. The disassembly of our company had begun. It wouldn't be long before the rest of us found out whether we were staying or moving on.

Our first full day in the new AO was June the 21st, the summer solstice. Back home, it was the longest day of the year. In the tropics, due to the proximity of the equator, daylight hours don't vary much throughout the year. The ratio of daytime to nighttime hours doesn't stray too far from 12 and 12. Saigon's first day of summer's light faded into darkness around 6:15. Such a contrast to back home when the first day of summer meant the stars wouldn't start to show up till past 9:30. I was only a few years removed from the adolescent joys of summer that those long hours of daylight provided: getting my new summer sneakers; softball late into the evening; playing release out in front of our house; "apples, peaches, punkin pie, who's not ready holler I." Now here I was, 10,000 miles from home, in the dark, with parachute flares instead of street lamps and wearing combat boots instead of a new pair of Keds—and where all the games were played for keeps!

Some kids showed up that afternoon. A few of them spoke very passable English. I got to talking to one young lad, probably 11 or 12 years old. He was selling cokes kept cold in Styrofoam containers (fashioned from discarded military medical supply shipping packaging). I purchased a bottle of coke from him. We had a nice chat. He asked me how long I'd been in Vietnam and how long it would be before I went home. Apparently, even the kids knew that the most important thing on a troop's mind was how many days left he had to go. He generously gave me some ice for my canteen before he left.

I was feeling pretty content with the present situation: a defensive position, no humping the boonies, hot chow, new sights, and interaction with the locals. The satisfaction was bittersweet, though. With the infusion coming, I could find myself back in the jungle in no time. Not only the jungle but with a bunch of guys I wouldn't know. I wasn't looking forward to that. If I had to go, I was hoping to go with at least a couple of other guys from the unit.

Activity on the road in front and the canal behind us diminished as dusk approached and the curfew was in effect. It rained that afternoon for a short while, but the skies cleared to greet the stars and a crescent moon rising in the east.

Back in the jungle we began our guard shifts shortly after dark for several reasons. First, there was absolutely nothing else to do but pull guard or sleep because you had to maintain noise and light discipline. You couldn't talk with anyone or even have a smoke to pass the time. Besides that, we were all fairly tuckered out after a full day on patrol and digging in for the night, so we could use the rest.

But down here was different: we hadn't been on a sweep and hadn't expended all that much energy building our camp. There was no need for noise or light discipline as we were all out in the open for everyone to see. We found ourselves BS'ing the evening away, smoking, and even listening to the radio. Lee had brought one down from Long Binh. We wouldn't start the guard shifts till 9:00 PM.

We rotated guard shifts every day to give everyone a chance for a first or last shift. They were desirable because you could spend the majority of the night undisturbed. It wasn't always feasible, though. I had been on two-man LPs (listening posts) where you pulled alternating one or two hour shifts all night long. Neither was ideal: one-hour shifts left you feeling unrested the following day, and two-hour shifts made it difficult to maintain focus for that long. Two hours in the jungle, in the wee hours, staring out into nothingness on an overcast, starless, moonless night seemed interminable. Invariably, your mind drifted off only to be brought back with a jolt of adrenaline when some nocturnal creature made a noise. Was the creature from the human or animal family?

I was going to pull the first shift that night. I settled into my sandbag easy chair atop the bunker. I had the starlight scope at the ready. I scanned the rice paddies every few minutes. Because there was so much light that the scope could amplify, the landscape became bright enough that it would be very difficult for someone to escape my notice. That was a comfort.

I eased back, lit up a smoke and listened to Sam Cooke singing "Cupid" on the radio. Now this was the way to pull guard! I was about halfway through my shift when my mellow mood was interrupted by two rockets streaking upward from the ground, maybe a few miles distant. They were headed our way, and the bright orange/white blaze thrusting them forward made it easy to follow their path as they arched over our position on their way to Saigon. I turned to watch and waited for their impact. They probably fell into the city center. I saw two bright flashes that lit the sky and then seconds later a couple of loud booms.

Saigon had been rocketed almost daily since mid-May; it was the reason we were there. The rockets weighed about 100 pounds, total, with a 40 pound warhead. They had a six or seven mile range. They weren't especially accurate even when used with a launcher but were even less so the way the VC used them, propped them up on bamboo poles or even rice paddy dikes. In this way, they were basically terror weapons. Aim them at the city and you were bound to hit something—more than likely innocent civilians. The blasts resulted in deaths and wounds to the residents and also caused fires that left scores homeless in the densely populated, refugee-filled city. The communists were trying to show the populace that the government was incapable of protecting them.

The normal MO for a rocket launch by the VC had them hightailing it immediately after the missile was on its way. This was because we had radar that could pick up mortar and rocket launches, triangulate their positions, and have counter-fire on the way within minutes. We had the radar set up on a tower at the cement factory. Sure enough, in a matter of minutes, artillery rounds started peppering the area the rockets came from. Flashes from the artillery rounds impacts were popping up on the horizon and their rumble carried across the paddies. Helicopter gunships flew overhead dropping flares, lighting up the fields of rice, and occasionally firing their mini guns, spitting bullets out so fast that you could not distinguish individual rounds, just an ungodly growl that accompanied the red laser beam of tracer rounds—thousands a minute.

It was quite a sight and sound show, and the action was gravitating north toward our position. The flares were floating down leaving smoke trails that caught the amber glow and reflected the light, crosshatching the sky in eerie patterns. The whup-whup of the rotor blades, the growl of the guns, the rumble of the artillery, the bright flashes of the shells impacting the earth, and the otherworldly shimmering glow of the flares reflecting their amber light off the canal and rice paddy water conjured up a surreal scene. It was made more so while listening to Martha Reeves and the Vandellas singing "Dancing in the Streets" on the radio. It was strange, it was unreal and all too real—at once both beautiful and horrific.

Everyone was awake by now, my guard time was over, and JP officially was on watch. Sleep wasn't really an option with all that was going on, so I decided to write Mom and Dad a letter. The flares provided plenty of light so I put pen to paper and set out to describe this unreal night and the hectic days preceding it. Finally got to sleep sometime after midnight; at least I didn't have to get up during the night. The next couple of days passed with us staying in place and following the same routine. Saigon was hit again, 12 nights in a row now. We saw some more rockets fly over but weren't entertained by the likes of the fireworks show we had a few nights ago.

Lt. Stockman came back from the morning briefing with some sad news. He told us that Captain Conner was in a helicopter flying over the Saigon River when it lost power and crashed into the water. He did not survive. He died on his birthday.

I guess the pattern was set by now in regards to my reactions to this kind of news. It was a matter of acceptance without much emotion. While I was ambivalent about him as our company commander, I did think he was a good man. I felt bad for his family, in a clinical kind of way. I pondered the random fates that we all were subject to and then secured those thoughts in my mental lock box before the questioning of my own destiny could take me places I didn't want to go.

CHAPTER TWELVE
SAIGON

After about a week of remaining stationary at our little bunker complex, the threat of the anticipated ground offensive seemed to wane. While the duty was easy and we were getting one hot meal a day, the troops were getting antsy. We were well-rested, relatively well-fed, and mostly healed up from the cuts, scratches, insect bites, leech lesions, and the fungal infections endemic to the jungle. The lure of Saigon, practically in our back yard, proved too powerful to a group of re-energized 19 and 20 year olds itching for some relief from the boredom of our present assignment. The officers decided to let a few of us at a time go into the city during the daylight hours.

In the colonial era Saigon was known as the "Paris of the Orient" or the "Pearl of the Orient." The French had laid the city out with wide boulevards lined with trees, open parks, and buildings in the architectural style of the south of France: cream-hued stucco walls, brightly painted shutters of blue or green, and burnt orange colored tile roofs. By the time I got to see Saigon in the summer of 1968 only vestiges of its once quaint colonial charm were left. Nobody would mistake it for a pearl now.

Jim Martin and I got the ok from Lt. Stockman to go into the city one morning. As usual, a few rockets had hit the city overnight. That seemed to be the norm and did little to break the patterns of the populace, except to those directly affected. We were directed to leave our weapons behind as the Vietnamese prohibited soldiers from carrying rifles or pistols in the city center. So, we stashed our M-16's in our bunker and headed down the dirt road toward the highway. It was only about a half-mile walk, and we mingled in among the locals headed in the same direction. It felt good to be rid of the guns and grenades and liberating to actually have a day to yourself to go and do as you please.

Upon reaching the paved road, we flagged down a cyclo for a ride into the downtown area. A cyclo is like a motorized rickshaw. It has three wheels, two in front separated by the seat. Behind the seat is basically a motorcycle from the handlebars back. Our driver was an older gent with a craggy, weathered face, and a smile filled with blackened teeth. He wore the usual loose-fitting pajama type clothes, flip-flops, and a pith helmet. We began to negotiate a fee. We had some idea of the amount we should pay from guys who had gone into town before us. It was a ritual, this haggling process that went on for every good or service purchased. We made an offer for the fare and the old guy rolled his eyes, yelled *"Choi oi,"* and *"nebba hoppin GI,"*—and on it went from there. A compromise was soon reached, and we were on our way. We were still getting ripped off by local economic standards, but for us it wasn't all that much money.

The road into Saigon was packed with traffic of all sorts: pedestrians along the sides, motorcycles, scooters, bicycles, cars, trucks, buses, military equipment, and even horse drawn carts—all vying for space. It was a chaotic, frenetic ride that our cyclo chauffeur seemed to take in stride as he weaved in and out of traffic at a frenzied pace. Frankly, Jim and I feared for our lives. Our pleas for him to slow down were only met with exaggerated nods and slightly maniacal black-toothed grins.

It was a custom among older Vietnamese to chew the leaves of the betel nut plant, just like people who use chewing tobacco. The leaf chewing provides the effects of a mild narcotic but over time leaves your teeth darkly stained. I couldn't help but think our driver had overdosed himself that morning, but with the way people drove over there, apparently, he wasn't alone. I was beginning to give more credence to that sign we saw when we left Long Binh about public highways being the most dangerous places in Vietnam. During my first trip through the city I was in a deuce and a half, but your perspective on the validity of the sign changes markedly when you contrast the view from the relative safety of riding in the back of a $2\frac{1}{2}$ ton truck to essentially being the front bumper of a cyclo.

We crossed over two canals that connected to the Saigon River and brought agricultural products into the city from the countryside. We turned onto a road that hugged the bank of the river and passed the docks where ocean-going freighters were being offloaded. Saigon, even though it was 37 miles upriver from the South China Sea, was a major port facility and many, many thousands of tons of war materials were destined for delivery there.

Our destination was Tu Do Street; remarkably, we arrived unscathed. Tu Do Street had everything a GI trying to escape the terror, drudgery, and boredom of the boonies could want. The street, once called Rue Catinat in French colonial days, started at the Basilica of Our Lady of Peace mid-town and threaded its way through bars, brothels, black markets, and drug dealers to the waterfront.

Jim and I stepped out of the cyclo and into a world almost as foreign as the jungle. There was a buzz about the place, to be sure. The atmosphere was charged with "anything and everything goes" possibilities. I was just taking it all in: new sights, sounds, and smells. There were people everywhere. The sidewalks were packed with pedestrians, and the street traffic never stopped. Thousands of little two-cycle motorbikes and Lambretta motorized carts spewed out noxious fumes, and diesel truck engines well past their overhauls sent plumes of black exhaust into the air. During the heat of the day, the sun seemed to exacerbate the problem to the point that your eyes stung and watered from the foul air.

I was both amazed and discomforted by the sights on the sidewalks: black market street vendors were everywhere; street food was cooking on the sidewalks; orphans were begging and Vietnamese Army veterans were, too. Homeless people housed in cardboard shelters populated the alleyways. Drug dealers sold openly on the sidewalks, apparently with no worries of getting caught. So, too, the prostitutes corralling customers.

All of these were the byproducts of the war. In the last few years, the population of Saigon had ballooned to 6 times its pre-war population to three million. Most were refugees from the countryside trying to escape the war. The local economy could not support them, and the government surely could not. It was easy to turn to activities that the burgeoning numbers of GIs looked for. Compared to the locals, the American troops were flush with money, and the Vietnamese offered them plenty of opportunities to spend it.

One thing that my naive 19-year-old mind found incredible was the black marketers selling US military equipment on the sidewalks of Saigon. There were poncho liners, jungle boots, fatigues, boonie hats, and air mattresses. All items in short supply somehow made their way onto the street corners of the capital city. I found out later that truckloads of war material were routinely hijacked from the docks. Not only military equipment, but also consumer goods bound for Post Exchanges were purloined from the US government. Why this was seemingly allowed to go on in plain sight was a mystery to me. Corruption was rampant and tons of money ended up in the wrong hands.

GIs also contributed to the black market. We all had ration cards that allowed us to buy a certain number of consumer items from the PX. The cards were issued to prevent the troops from buying items then reselling them to the Vietnamese for resale. The card had boxes outlined with a product item printed in the block. Your card had two blocks that said camera. If you purchased a camera from the PX they punched a hole in that block preventing you from buying another one. At that time, most of the goods were made in Japan and relatively cheap by stateside standards, and

Uncle Sam shipped them home for you. Some items on the card were: the aforementioned still cameras, movie cameras, tape decks, stereos, radios, turn tables, amplifiers, TV's, watches, and even small refrigerators. All these items helped combat the boredom endemic to those living on the main bases. For us in the field, however, the ration card didn't mean much. First off, we rarely saw a PX. Secondly, you couldn't have most of that stuff in the boonies. And lastly, we had no place to keep it back at the base that was secure from theft.

Another disturbing sight were the disabled Vietnamese Army veterans you saw on the sidewalks looking for handouts. They might be missing an arm or a leg and had no prosthetics to take their place. They weren't the only ones looking for a donation; the streets were filled with kids begging for food or cash, and if you gave to some you were swamped in minutes by others looking for the same.

There were lots of food vendors on the street. Some were cooking up pork or chicken with noodles right there on the sidewalk. You could buy a bowl of whatever it was and sit down on a chair or stool and eat your lunch on the sidewalk. They had a couple of buckets there to wash and rinse off the bowls and spoons when you were done. I decided not to try any Vietnamese food that day, more out of concerns for cleanliness and microbes in the water that everyone warned us not to drink. Some of it did smell good, but who knew if you might be eating a dog or monkey meat mixed up in all those noodles and vegetables. And, then again, some of it looked kind of disgusting. They had this slimy stuff laid out on trays that looked like, maybe... I don't know... snakes, snails and salamander parts. There was no danger in me sampling *that* plate.

As we walked along, we passed bar after bar that catered to GIs. They had American names like the Pink Pussy Cat, New York Club, Florida Bar, Bunny Bar, Olympia Bar, and so on and so on. Rock and roll music was emanating from them. Many had Filipino bands singing western pop, top 40 music. Inside, hostess girls awaited young troops seeking some female companionship.

Speaking of the brothels, there seemed to be no end to the young girls trying to entice soldiers to step inside those establishments. Outside the doorways pretty girls dressed in mini-skirts and sporting American hairstyles and makeup called out to passersby: "*Hey GI, you want short-time love?*" or "*I give you beaucoup love...ti ti (little) money.*" No doubt they were as cute as could be, but frankly, they evoked more pity than passion in me. I felt sorry for the position they were in: probably refugees, supporting a family or two. My reluctance to pay for artificial affection hadn't wavered.

Drugs were everywhere and cheap. Marijuana could be purchased as cigarette packs. The dealers removed all the tobacco from, say, a pack of Marlboros and replaced it with marijuana. They left a little unfilled at the end to fill in with some tobacco. Looking at the cigarette with the filter on one end and the tobacco at the other you would never know it was really a joint. There was more potent stuff if a guy was interested, but while I was there in 68-69 it was mostly marijuana the troops were into. Later in the war, when things really fell apart, some troops were doing heroin, but I never saw or heard of any guys doing that.

All of this vice was going on right in front of the Vietnamese police with absolutely no attempt to hide any of it. Pimps, prostitutes, and drug dealers paid them no more heed than Saigon drivers did their traffic directions at intersections. The police were dressed in white shirts, hats, and gloves and were called, derogatorily, "White Mice." Not necessarily entirely because of their white clothing but because of their timid manner involving the Viet Cong and the way they turned a blind eye to everything going on around them, including the "Saigon Cowboys". The "Cowboys" were mostly draft dodgers turned hoodlums. They preyed on unaware GIs walking the city's streets. They rode small motorcycles, two up: one the driver and one the snatcher. They would speed by an unwary GI walking too close to the curb and snatch a camera off his shoulder, rip a watch off his wrist, or even snag his sunglasses before he knew what happened. We had been forewarned to be on the lookout for them, and I kept my eyes peeled. I thought I spotted a couple of them once when one caught me staring and returned my gaze with a devious look that seemed to say "next time." Too much money was being made to upset the applecart. Saigon was sin city, and it stayed that way as long as the money flowed. They didn't get much from me, though, except for a couple beers at a bar just to sample the atmosphere. I was fairly vice- challenged except for cigarettes, and I got those for free.

Jim and I decided to visit the USO for some lunch. I heard you could get a real cheeseburger and a milkshake there, and I hadn't had either for months. The rumors proved true, and we both enjoyed an all-American lunch.

We were surprised to see some all-American girls there as well. I had heard about "Donut Dollies" being in Vietnam but had never seen any before now. Donut Dollies were young girls, for the most part, hired by the Red Cross to be recreational workers. They wore a uniform of sorts: powder blue tunic blouses and knee length skirts with Red Cross pins and patches and name tags. They worked in USOs and also went out to bases in the field when it was safe to visit the troops. They usually brought along some word game to play, but mostly it was just to stop by and chat with the guys. The girls got their nickname, Donut Dollies, during the Korean War when part of the morale-building exercises they provided were distributing thousands upon thousands of donuts and coffee to the troops. As could be expected, the "round eyes" drew a lot of attention wherever they went.

After lunch, we continued walking down Tu Do Street toward the center of town. The closer we got to the Basilica, the less seedy our surroundings became. There were more government buildings and more conventional business establishments. The pace of the place didn't vary, though: the steady hum of hyperactivity was pervasive and reflected the sense that the city was under a siege mentality. The capital had been hit by over 400 rockets in the last couple of months. During the Tet offensive, Viet Cong troops had entered the city and that was still fresh in everyone's mind. The recent May offensive, at least for American troops, had been the bloodiest of the war to date. Evidence that the city was on edge was everywhere. Government buildings were sandbagged around the first floors, and entrances were guarded by military police. Checkpoints were set up around the city to check traffic for booby-trapped vehicles. Guards opened doors and trunks, stopped trucks to check cargos, and looked underneath them all with mirrors. Barricades and barbed wire were ready to be put in place at night. No military vehicles were left unguarded: the Viet Cong were known to remove the pins from hand grenades, slip rubber bands over the handles, and drop them in gas tanks. The gas eventually dissolved the rubber band, the handle flew off, and the grenade exploded. I think the filler caps on M151 utility vehicles (military jeeps) were large enough to slip a grenade in, so I think the stories could well have been true.

Military vehicles were ever present, and I didn't envy the drivers having to negotiate their way through throngs of pedestrians, bikes, motorcycles, cars, and trucks that seemed to obey traffic rules as if they were merely suggestions. It was scary. I'm sure that quite a few city dwellers fell victim to the large trucks transiting across town. You saw entire families on quite small motorcycles weaving in and out of traffic. Dad was driving, a small child would be half on his lap and half on the gas tank. Mom was behind Dad cradling an infant in one arm and holding onto Dad with the other. Then, there would be another kid sitting on a small luggage rack holding onto Mom, and a couple chickens hanging upside down off the rack as well. Nuts!!

If you could manage to ignore the traffic, sandbags and barbed wire, you could see that Saigon must have been a beautiful town in the past. There were some wide avenues lined with mature trees, many grassy areas, and park-like open areas. The colonial architecture conjured up images of a bygone era. It was probably a great place to be if you were French. If you were Vietnamese, it wasn't such a good deal. The French used the Vietnamese for workers in the paddies, fields, and plantations and compensated them with barely above slave labor rates.

I recognized some of the places we were seeing from news reports on television back home. The Continental Palace Hotel was one; newsmen often used it as a backdrop for reports from Saigon. The National Assembly Building was another landmark often seen on TV news. In fact, I'd bet big money that it probably was front and center on the newscasts of June 21, 1968. The same night we had the big light and sound show a rocket hit the National Assembly Building. It may have been one of them that went directly over our heads.

We spent the rest of the day sight-seeing around the town. It was really interesting and exciting for me, having never experienced anything quite like it before. It was cool to see some of the Vietnamese girls in the country's traditional dress, called an ao dai. The dress was made up of a full length tight-fitting silk tunic that was split on the sides up to the waist and worn over pantaloons. School girls and unmarried women wore all-white outfits while married women wore different combinations of colors.

Another unusual sight was seeing men walking down the street hand-in-hand. We saw this a few times during the day, one time it was two soldiers. We later learned that it was not uncommon for Vietnamese male friends to do this, and it did not invite speculation that they might be homosexuals.

It finally came time for us to head back to our position, and we hitched a ride in a Lambretta three-wheeled truck that was headed out of the city. I was sorry to see the day end. It had felt great to be out on our own with the ability to come and go as you please.

I got a nice surprise when we got back: a package full of peanut butter cookies and Heath bars had arrived from home—the candy bars courtesy of my sister Mary Kay.

After getting something to eat and setting up for the night, we started shooting the breeze with some of the other guys in the platoon about our day in the city and comparing it to what other guys had experienced in town. I passed the cookies around. It was customary to share goodie packages from home with the other guys, and most guys followed the practice. It was nice because everybody could get excited when any one person got a package. Night was soon upon us and Lonnie turned his radio on so we could listen to some music. Those early evening hours under the stars, BSing with the guys, having a coke, and sharing some goodies were the best part of the day. I relished them because of what our evenings had been like in the jungle, and also because I knew they could end at any time.

It still felt a little odd to be playing the radio, after all those nights of noise discipline in the jungle. I enjoyed it nonetheless. They played the same Top 40 format that I was used to listening to back home.

Just being able to play a radio anywhere you wanted to was a relatively new convenience in the early sixties, thanks to the invention of the transistor. The word transistor isn't heard much in everyday conversation anymore, but back in the day it was a revelation and electronic manufacturers used to brag about how many transistors their products had. Until the transistor, radios relied on vacuum tubes to amplify the radio waves in the air to audible levels. The tubes were large, consumed a lot of energy, generated a lot of heat, and were less than rugged. The transistor solved all those problems in one fell swoop and enabled the truly portable radio to be born. A portable vacuum tube radio, at best, was the size of a toaster. Now, you could slide a transistor radio into your shirt pocket.

I had gotten one for Christmas one year when I was 12 or 13 years old. I thought it was pretty neat, and I listened to it outside on summer evenings. On some nights, I could pick up stations from distant cities and listened to WLS from Chicago. They actually played the same kind of music the local stations did, but somehow it was way cooler coming from far away Chicago.

Chicago didn't seem all that far away anymore, now that I was halfway around the world. But the music was all the same: The Beatles, The Rolling Stones. The Doors, The Bee Gees, The Supremes, Aretha Franklin, James Brown, Otis Redding, Stevie Wonder, and Simon and Garfunkel.

While the music that AFVN played could carry you back home, their "public service" announcements brought you back with harsh doses of reality. Such as: "Listen Up!—you troops out in the boonies. If you get bitten by a snake, try to kill it and bring it back so the medical staff will know what kind of anti-venom to give you." Or: "Let's keep those shot records up to date and get your cholera, yellow fever, and plague boosters before it's too late." And: "Don't forget to take your malaria pills," or "Always keep your weapon clean and use LSA (lubricant, small arms) to keep it well oiled, and keep that ammo clean to prevent your weapon from jamming." Another: "Don't let Immersion Foot keep you out of the action. Try to dry your feet at least once a day, and change those soggy socks frequently."

Sometimes they played a verse of a song as a lead in to their announcements, such as Marty Robbins singing "Cool Clear Water." Then a voice said, "Yes, that's what we all want, but sometimes when you are out in the boonies it becomes necessary to use what is at hand. When filling your canteen with relatively clean water use two halazone water purification tablets. If the water is muddy, use four tablets... wait 30 minutes..." Then you heard Marty singing once again, "Cool Clear Water."

The powers that be seemed to be fixated on venereal disease, so the radio station never let you forget it. One spot began with Bobby Vinton singing "I'm Coming Home," then the radio voice broke in... "Do you want to go home? Sure you do, so do I. While casualties inflicted by the enemy will be the first thing to stop you, do you know that VD is the second? Avoiding the source is the ideal way, but I know some of you won't listen to that. The only other way is immediate medical attention. If you are worried see your medic."

Another one started out with Shirley Ellis singing the "Clapping Song" song, mostly just the clap part, as "The Clap" is the non-medical term for Gonorrhea. The song is a perfect introduction to a spiel on the dangers of that sexually transmitted disease. Personally, I would have much rather just heard the song.

And like every other radio station in the world, there was news, sports, and weather. I wondered how anybody could get so excited about baseball scores during the sports segment. The juxtaposition of reports of heavy fighting in the Central Highlands, Saigon being rocketed, Bien Hoa Air Base mortared, and the Dodgers beating the Giants in extra innings was a bit surreal.

As for the weather forecast from the AFVN Weatherscope, it was delivered by someone sounding just a little too chipper while telling you that you will be miserable tomorrow. They could have shortened it considerably by just saying "95 x 3" for the rest of the month. 95 being the high temp, the relative humidity, and the possibility of rainfall. It didn't really matter; it wasn't like any plans were ever changed because of the weather.

Then back to the music, usually prefaced with this enthusiastically sung jingle, "AFVN...It's what's happening!!" Then: "Number 12 on the countdown this week is, 'Like to get to Know You' by Spanky & Our Gang."

I never heard Adrian Cronauer (played by Robin Williams in the movie "Good Morning Vietnam") while I was in Nam. He rotated home long before I got there. Pat Sajak, the host of "Wheel of Fortune," was a DJ in Vietnam around the same time I was there. I have no idea if I ever heard him.

During my first 3 months in Vietnam.....

April 4, 1968— Martin Luther King is assassinated in Memphis Tennessee. Race riots start in over 75 cities around the country, including Pittsburgh. The Hill, the North Side and Homewood suffer civil unrest for days after the assassination. Multiple fires are set, property is damaged, one man dies, and nearly a thousand arrests are made.

April 11, 1968— President Johnson signs the "Civil Rights Act of 1968."

April 23, 1968— Students at Columbia University protest the war in Vietnam by taking over the administration building on the campus and shutting the school down.

April 26, 1968— A million college and high school students cut classes to show their opposition to the war.

April 1968— US troop levels in Vietnam reach 530,000 men.

May 1968— "Mini-Tet," or "The May Offensive," takes place across Vietnam. Heavy fighting near Saigon occurs once again. The month of May would prove to be the most deadly of the war, costing America 2,412 soldiers. My unit, the 199th, lost 42.

May 1968— In response to President Johnson's bombing halt of North Vietnam, peace talks have been initiated in Paris.

May 17, 1968— A Catholic priest and 8 others steal a local draft board's records in Maryland and burn them.

June 2, 1968— Famous author of baby care book, Dr. Benjamin Spock, was convicted of counseling young men to avoid the draft.

June 6, 1968— Robert F. Kennedy dies after being shot at a victory gathering at the Ambassador Hotel in Los Angeles following his win in the California Democratic primary for President.

June 1968— Valerie Solonas, who formed a society called "SCUM" (the Society for Cutting Up Men), shot Andy Warhol with a 32 automatic pistol in his New York film studio called "The Factory." He survived.

In Music— Johnny Cash performs live at Folsum Prison in California. Simon and Garfunkle release "Mrs. Robinson." And the theme song from "The Good the Bad and the Ugly" reaches #2.

At the movies— "2001 a Space Odyssey" "Rosemary's Baby" "The Graduate"

In Sports— Manchester United wins the European Cup Final, becoming the first English team to do so.

In Business— Gold prices soar to $41.37 an ounce.

Since I arrived in Vietnam 3,240 troops have died, bringing the total for the war to date to over 25,000.

CHAPTER THIRTEEN
THE PADDIES

While our position remained static, there was movement in the personnel of our company. Both our new company commander and platoon leader had joined us in the last couple of days. Captain Williams would be running the company and Lieutenant Anthony Russo was taking over as our new platoon leader.

Comparisons are inevitable when new people take the place of others with whom you are familiar. Captain Williams seemed to be cut from the same cloth as Captain Conner, so I didn't anticipate any great changes from the company command standpoint. Like Captain Conner, he seemed capable and competent but also like Cpt. Conner, he was well aware of the career implications of a combat command and what it could mean for advancement. For career soldiers, the successful completion of a combat mission always came first. For the enlisted men serving under their command, success was measured by a different standard—getting home in one piece. There was bound to be conflict.

This was not the case at the platoon level. Lieutenant Stockman wasn't aiming for a career in the Army and, at first glance, Lt. Russo didn't look the part of a 20-year man, either. Other than that, the contrasts between Lt. Stockman and Lt. Russo were stark. Whereas Paul Stockman seemed comfortable with authority and carried himself in a way that produced an innate respect among the men, Tony Russo lacked that natural command presence. Unfortunately for the new lieutenant, he was replacing someone known to be capable and courageous. A tough act to follow. In his favor he seemed congenial, wasn't pretentious, and was eager to learn.

Intelligence reports continued to stress the possibility of ground attacks against the city. Saigon, once considered the most secure spot in the country, felt like a city under siege. The nightly rocket attacks, the Tet offensive, and the recent May offensive had laid to rest the illusion of safety that the capital city might offer.

It was thought that 15,000 or more enemy troops lay in wait within a 48-hour march of the city. These troops, hiding in villages in groups of only 3 or 4, dressed like farmers. Possessing fake or authentic documents they were nearly impossible to detect. They could mingle with the locals during the day, hiding in plain sight.

The US military wanted to: 1. interdict enemy troops attempting to infiltrate into the city, 2. search for buried arms caches, 3. stop the rocketing of the city with a presence out in the expanse of rice paddies, and 4. stop the VC before they could enter the capital, should the call come to form batallions for an attack on the city.

With this in mind the higher-ups decided that our time on "easy street" was coming to an end. Starting soon we were heading out into the paddies on daylight patrols and setting up nighttime ambushes and observation posts. One good thing, though, we were staying at AO Laura and maintained our bunker positions at night unless we were picked for an ambush or OP. The daylight patrols meant we only had to carry weapons, ammo, food, and water for the day. And normally, if you were selected for a night ambush or OP you wouldn't have to go out during the day. All and all, not too bad a deal.

Before we began our forays into the paddies we celebrated the 4th of July by shooting star clusters up into the night sky. It was a clear night for the holiday, and Lord knows who started it off, but soon star clusters were shooting skyward at every American position around the city. Star clusters came in various colors and were used for signaling or marking positions. They came in aluminum tubes and were set off, after removing the cap, by hitting the bottom of the tube on the palm of your hand. The cluster shot up into the sky and 4 or 5 separate "stars" ignited and burned brightly while falling back to the ground. It was a nice show, and I wondered what the heck the Viet Cong might be thinking out there in the paddies.

Our AO Laura was bordered on the north by the city itself, on the east by the Saigon River, by Highway 5 to the west, and the Van Co river to the south. It was a rectangle roughly 5 miles east to west and 10 miles north to south covering about 50 square miles of rice paddies, streams, canals, and villages. It proved to be far different than anything that we had experienced.

Our first day in the paddies started with a truck ride. Shortly after daybreak several Deuce and a Halfs showed up at our position, ready to transport us a few miles to a drop-off point where we began our patrol. Our new lieutenant told us to saddle up and climb aboard the trucks. The trucks were multi-use vehicles. Unfortunately for us, the troop transport benches along the sides of the truck bed had been removed. That left you with two options: sit directly on the stiffly sprung 2½ ton truck bed and get bounced around like a Mexican jumping bean on the rutted roads, or risk falling off the truck by sitting on the narrow steel side walls that ran the length of the truck bed.

We had ridden the trucks many times by now, so experience dictated choosing the latter method because you could really get knocked silly on a washboard road. If you chose the side wall method you had to take your back pack off because the extra weight tended to pull you backwards off the side rail. To cushion the bumps and mitigate the possibility of being knocked over the side, you sat down on the rail and leaned toward the center of the truck bed, so if a large bump occurred you were more likely to fall inside the truck instead of out. Also, you wanted to just barely put weight on your butt. To accomplish this, you placed each hand on the rail alongside your hips and slightly raise up so that your arms bore some of your weight and could act as shock absorbers. Your bent knees served this function as well. Not the best way to travel but better than walking.

We traveled south for a few miles before turning onto a dirt road barely wide enough for the trucks to proceed. We passed through a few villages of thatched huts that clung to either side of the road. Surrounding all the villages were a sea of rice paddies as far as the eye could see. The paddies were sectioned by dirt dikes that looked to be 18 to 24 inches tall and wide enough to walk on. They kept the water in the paddies and provided paths for the farmers to transit the fields. The only breaks in the flat horizon were stands of nipa palms that lined the many streams and canals that cut through the area.

We finally reached the drop-off point and dismounted the trucks. Lt. Russo told us we would be traversing the paddies to our south to gain access to the tall nipa palms long the banks of some irrigation canals. The thick vegetation provided good cover for Viet Cong and were logical places to bury arms caches. They were also used as staging areas for the nightly rocket attacks on Saigon.

We couldn't walk across the dikes—many of them had been booby-trapped. The first time you walk in a rice paddy is a memorable event, not so much because of the mud, which was expected, but for the smell that emanates from them. Just traveling by them they are kind of stinky, but I don't think anybody was prepared for the stench that assaulted our olfactory senses after pulling a foot up out of the muck. The odious slime that soon covered our pants was an amalgam of water buffalo dung, human waste, and rotting vegetation. It was so foul that involuntary sounds of disgust were pouring out of the guys' mouths. Man, it was bad.

But like many things in life, there is always some humor mixed in with the misery. Buck, in particular, had the look of ultimate repulsion and recoiled in horror after his first whiff. He was going to loathe the paddies. Buck was a guy who took two showers a day in college just on general principles. He had made admirable strides in coping with weeks without showers, filthy clothes, and dirt ground deep into all his pores. But I could see by the look on his face that this new challenge to personal hygiene was not going to be easy for him. Something about human nature makes a person feel better when they can share hardships, and Buck's utter revulsion unknowingly helped lighten my mood.

Day after day, we headed out into the paddies and back. I don't think any of us believed it at first, but if you are exposed to a constant smell long enough your mind actually starts to ignore it. What we found out about the paddies, that we could *not* ignore, was just how hard it was to walk for any distance in them. Your boots sank into the ooze with every step, and the water muck mixture snared your foot in some kind of suction trap. This created a herky jerky movement, just one step at a time. Eventually, we got a bit better at traversing the paddies; the key to success was being light. That wasn't always possible, but if you just had your rifle and a few ammo magazines you could, if you moved fast enough, keep your feet from sinking as far as they usually did. This was a good option if you had a short distance to cover, but it was impossible to keep that pace up for long. Regardless, most times we never traveled that light. Even though they were just day patrols, we still carried a rifle, 21 magazines, 4 fragmentation grenades, 4 canteens of water, food for the day, a helmet, a flak jacket, and stuff for the squad like extra ammo, rope, mines, LAW's, and smoke grenades. Yes, it was lighter than the loads we carried up in War Zone D, but walking in the paddies was far worse than our days up north.

The paddies just about killed my buddy Byrdy. He was heavier than I was and the paddy mud just sucked all the strength right out of him. The harsh heat and high humidity were torture on him. It was hard on all the heavier guys, and it seemed as though they could never carry enough water to compensate for the sweat pouring off of them.

One issue that exacerbated the heat was the helmets and flak jackets we wore. The open paddies provided no shelter from the sun's rays, and that steel pot we wore on our heads worked like an oven. The nylon flak jacket could not breathe, and it wouldn't take long before the sweat was running heavy and the jacket clung to your fatigue shirt that was clinging to your skin, thus losing any cooling effect the evaporating perspiration might provide. Those early days were long and hard. Over time we learned to cope with our new environment, and just like the jungle, we adapted. We carried extra water, we ditched our flak jackets and helmets on low risk operations and generally learned how to navigate the paddies a little smarter. It never became easy, but it did become routine. That wouldn't be the case for everybody, however.

One new addition to the company was not well acclimated to the heat and humidity before going out in the paddies. I didn't know his name, but he was heavier than most of us and had red hair and a fair complexion; not the best attributes for pounding the paddies under a relentless midday sun. We had our normal early morning start and by afternoon had covered a lot of ground. We had no rain to cool things off for the hump back to the pick-up point. All of us were tired but this new guy was really suffering. He probably had drunk all his water and, being new and not knowing anyone, was reluctant to ask anybody for any.

The high sun combined with the muggy air can brutally sap your energy. Each step in the unending muck turns into a challenge. Too much of one, apparently, for our new replacement. I heard this splash off to my right, and I looked over to see the newbie down on his hands and knees, crawling through the paddy, dragging his rifle through the slop. His face was bright red, he looked completely out of it and was mumbling incoherently. The medics attended to him and determined he needed a medevac chopper to take him to a field hospital. I don't know if he had heat exhaustion, heat stroke, or what—but his brain seemed fried. We never saw him again. Here and gone in a matter of days.

Each day, after our platoon finally made it to the nipa palm-lined canal, we began our search for hidden caches of arms or rice along the banks. The silt that made up the river, stream, and canal banks was even harder to walk in than the mud of the paddies. The waterways were everywhere in the delta. The main one was the Mekong, the one responsible for 15,000 square miles of alluvial plain that was perfect for growing rice. The river begins in the highlands of Tibet and courses its way 2,700 miles to the South China Sea. After its waters enter Vietnam, the river branches out into 9 separate channels like your fingers do from your hand. From this geographical feature, the river gets its Vietnamese name of Song Cuu Long, which means "Nine Dragons River." The water provides irrigation, drainage, and transportation for the inhabitants of the delta. It is the heart and soul of the area, and all daily life revolves around it.

Canals were built during the French colonial period to connect the various waterways of the delta—providing water to the paddies and transport for the rice to get to market. The area ended up with hundreds of miles of navigable waterways, most of which were bordered with the nipa palms. The nipa palm is a bit of an oddity: it has a short trunk that grows horizontally under the ground, and the stalks grow into giant palm fronds 30 feet in height. They grow right up to the water's edge and are densely packed on the banks of streams and canals.

Different species of mangrove trees also lined the waterways.

Mangroves and nipa can survive in brackish water. The salinity comes from the twice daily inrush of the tidal flow. Even though our position was 30 miles in from the sea, the water levels in some areas could vary up to ten feet from high to low tide.

The waterway's banks and bottoms were made up of a fine silt that gave little support, and more often than not you were up to your knees in it. Searching the river banks was tiring, time consuming, and tedious. Crossing these stream and canal banks from one side to the other presented problems at both high tide and low tide. Crossing at high tide carried the risk of drowning, low tide the certainty of drudgery.

The water carried so much silt that the streams looked like chocolate milk, and it was hard to tell how deep they were. One guy would take all his equipment off, take one end of a rope, and start across to the far bank. If he could walk the whole way, the rest of us followed. But if it was over his head and he had to swim for it, once on the other side he tied the rope off and the rest of us used it as a safety line.

We blew up air mattresses to use as rafts for our equipment. Nobody wanted to be in deep water with 50 pounds of gear on. In the first 5 weeks after moving into the paddies, the brigade lost 3 men in the murky waterways. One troop, an RTO (radio telephone operator), fell off a boat with a radio strapped on his back and never surfaced. Another soldier drowned crossing a canal. The crossings were the scariest when the water was neck high and you had all your gear on.

I was carrying a radio the day I went under. I had both arms extended over my head to keep both my M-16 and the handset for the radio dry. I probably drifted off the line and slipped into a hole in the stream bed. I barely had time to close my mouth before the thick brown water was over my head. I couldn't see two inches in front of me and had no other option than to keep walking. When I slipped under, my helmet came off and landed open end up, so it was floating downstream when I came back up. I was greeted by laughter when I reappeared. To be honest, I'm sure it looked funny; I probably would have laughed, myself. But in reality, it was quite scary. Nobody can swim with a radio strapped on their back and combat boots on their feet. Luckily, the only casualty was a pack of smokes I had tucked into the band on my helmet.

Crossing at low tide meant slogging through tidal flats that sloped down from the stream's banks. In some places, there was barely a rivulet of water where a few hours earlier it may have been six feet deep. You sank much further into this river silt than you did in the paddy muck. It was common to get stuck to the point that you couldn't move, and we used ropes to pull each other out of the slime.

Another element to the delta were the villages. They lined the streams, canals, and the few roads that traversed the paddies. The homes were usually thatched, made from the fronds of the nipa palms that were endemic to the waterways. Most were primitive: dirt floors and no plumbing. A lot of the cooking was done outside.

Every day, for weeks, we searched the canal bank for arms caches or food stockpiles buried in the mud. The first day, we found nothing for our efforts and finished our patrol in a teeming rain. It was a pattern that we repeated often in the coming weeks.

CHAPTER FOURTEEN
CAMP DAVIES

A few days after our first forays into the paddies, we got word that we were going to Camp Davies for a few days. Camp Davies was an Army logistical base positioned on the Saigon River adjacent to the Port of Saigon's loading docks. From the looks of it, the base must have been one of the first ones completed in the war zone. We were all really impressed at first sight. Row after row of metal warehouses, all built along paved streets. We passed a large mess hall, a club, and a movie theater. We found out we would be billeted in single-story barracks complete with electric lights, real beds, and hot showers. We thought we were in heaven.

The night after we moved in I had my first real hot shower in three and a half months. I didn't want it to end. We ate a hot supper inside on real tables, and the drinks were cold. It was an experience to savor and I did. We had no guard duty that night and were free to go to a club or movie. Afterward, we all slept on an actual mattress. We couldn't believe the REMFs had it *this* good... EVERY DAY!!!

Being an infantryman is living a life of uncertainty, which breeds distrust. We never seemed to find out what we were doing or where we were going until the last minute. We were always the last to know and so it was with the long-rumored infusion. It was finally on, and it would happen the following day. It figured; we got posted to paradise and it was going to be yanked away from most of us before another good night's sleep could be had.

I was nervous about it. I didn't know where I might go or who might go with me. I didn't want to leave at all but at the same time I didn't want to stay if all my friends were going. We got the news after a hot breakfast, which I would have enjoyed more if it wasn't for the uneasiness I was feeling about my chances of being assigned to a new unit.

The lists went up a little later and were eagerly scanned by everyone anxious to find out their fate. I was relieved to not find my name on any list but saddened to see many of my friends were. Two of my best friends, Byrdy and JP, were going to other battalions within our brigade. That wouldn't really matter, I'd probably never get a chance to see them. In fact, most of those infused stayed within the brigade, but a couple were going to the 101st Airmobile Division who were up north at the time. I didn't envy them at all as things were a lot hotter (combat wise, not temperature) up there. As it turned out, the majority of the platoon were going elsewhere. Luckily, Lonnie, a good friend, was not one of them.

That afternoon, troops from the other battalions in the brigade began to show up at our barracks at Camp Davies. They weren't any happier about having to move to a different unit than our guys had been. All of them had been in-country longer than all of us and thus would be going home sooner. Of course, that was the point of the infusion: not to have everybody in a single unit rotate home at the same time. In that regard, the Army had accomplished its mission, but in doing so it destroyed the unit's cohesion, hurt morale, and diminished effectiveness for weeks.

We had a few more days at Camp Davies to sort out what platoons the new guys were assigned to and what duties they would have. Sgt. Krotine, my squad leader, escaped the infusion along with Lonnie, but we still needed three new guys.

A lot of the platoon's new guy's names have escaped me after all these years, even ones in my own squad, but I do remember some. We got a couple southern boys named Jerry, one was Ames and the other Adams. We got a new sergeant named Ralston who proved to be a really class act. Carl Roberts was from the Lone Star state so naturally he was "Tex." A native Hawaiian joined us and inevitably was cursed with "Pineapple" as a moniker. We got two black guys, Gary Meinert, and the other, a really cool dude with a cool name, Thornton Maxwell III. I had never met a "third" before. All and all things went pretty smoothly and we soon sadly said goodbye to Camp Davies.

The good thing was we were staying in AO Laura, who was continuing to be a sweetheart. Other than the rocket attacks on Saigon and a few mortar rounds dropped into our battalion base camp at the cement factory, a mile down the road, nothing much was happening in our area of operations.

We continued our sweeps through the paddies, but we got some other assignments as well. One was guarding bridges in the district, and another was staying with the Vietnamese Regional Forces and Popular Forces in their little forts that dotted our AO. And lastly, we had to stop and inspect boats and sampans traveling the canals for smuggled weapons before they entered Saigon. All these jobs were better than slogging through the paddies, but the bridges and forts were the best.

Our platoon was assigned to a small bridge that crossed a stream that entered the Kenh Te Canal. This canal connected to others to the south and west that provided a water highway for goods to be brought to the city. The canal emptied into the Saigon River. There was a major highway bridge across the canal about 300 yards downstream from our small one over the stream. Our bridge was no more than 50 feet long and just wide enough for a single lane. It was of simple truss construction with a wooden plank deck that rippled like piano keys when a vehicle rolled over it. We built sandbag bunkers at each end and attempted to make ourselves comfortable by scrounging this and that whenever the opportunity arose. The road both coming to and going away from the bridge was dirt and it hugged the bank of the canal. During the day it was fairly busy with bikes, carts, motorcycles, and the occasional truck. The canal also saw constant traffic with sampans, junks, and a sampling of military vessels.

This bridge proved to be a fine assignment. In the daytime, there was a constant flow of pedestrians to and fro, and kids from the neighborhood hung out with us. We had no real duties at the bridge during the day other than our very presence on the site. At night after curfew we did pull guard shifts, but we had enough guys that lack of sleep was never an issue. It had a very relaxed atmosphere: we had no officers or senior sergeants around, and the enemy seemed to be taking the month off with the exception of the rocket attacks. For those interested, the "working girls" showed up a couple hours after sundown; exceptions to the curfew were readily extended to them. Also, for those inclined, marijuana was easily and cheaply obtained.

I have very fond memories of the bridge, especially in the evenings after the sun went down and the temperatures cooled and freshened the air. I'd turn on the radio and lie back on the sandbags, listen to some tunes, light up a smoke, and look at the lights of the city reflecting off the canal. The girls showed up and often stuck around after "business hours." Since the same basic group of us returned to the bridge again and again, we got to know the girls a bit and I developed a nice friendship with one even though I wasn't a "customer."

We constantly had people showing up at the bridge trying to sell us stuff. I had learned that I was going out to the boonies for a couple of nights of observation post-duty at a Vietnamese fort. It's nice to have a watch for nighttime guard duty, but I hadn't had a chance to get to a PX since I lost my Timex and smashed Byrdy's on the bunker opening. This old lady used to drop by the bridge selling watches from a wooden case she carried around. Her face was weathered from too many years outside in the sun, and she had cataracts so bad that her eyes were a cloudy gray. Her teeth were black from chewing betel nut, but that never kept her from smiling. I was tired of borrowing watches so I decided to buy one from the ancient street vendor.

I told the *mamasan* I was interested in one of her watches, so she opened her wooden display box to let me see what she had. She had a nice display of Seiko watches, and I picked one out that had radium on the hands and numbers. I thought the glow-in-the-dark feature would be handy for checking the time on those pitch-black nights when the rain clouds were hanging low and thick. The watch had a lot of other features as well, some of which are now outdated: 23-jewel movement, self-winding, unbreakable main spring, and anti- magnetic second hand. It was waterproof and had a stainless-steel case that was ideal for the hot humid climate, not to mention all the creek and canal crossings. I was pleased with my purchase and felt I had the perfect watch for my needs.

My first night in the boonies with my new watch proved how well the radium worked—*too* well, actually. I think you could see that watch face glowing from 25 yards away. Not exactly what you want on your wrist if you are out on an ambush. I could not believe how bright it was: it should have come with a warning from the Atomic Energy Commission as a radiation hazard. As nice as it was, it clearly was unsuitable for night operations in the boonies. As it turned out, the sixties would be the last decade radium was used on watches. First chance I got to see the old *mamasan*, I asked her if I could trade in the radioactive watch for another one that was less attention- getting.

We settled into a rhythm, rotating between 3 small bridges and 3 Vietnamese Popular Forces forts in the AO. Though some days still found us sweeping paddies and river banks where enemy war material might be hidden. Other than the physical demands of these missions, they tended to be fairly relaxed. It appeared that the Viet Cong were avoiding contact with our forces, and very little was happening throughout our brigade. Every now and then we were reminded that they were still out there waiting and the situation could turn deadly at any time. As usual, it would be up to them when it happened.

Our platoon was conducting a sweep along a canal in a dense stand of nipa palm when our point element came across a chicom (Chinese communist) claymore mine in our path. Like ours, the chicom can be command detonated as well as booby-trapped. If command detonated, they would have blown it by now before anyone could spot it. We could have had men killed and maimed in a millisecond after a detonation that would have sent hundreds of steel balls slamming into our point squad. Luckily, that didn't happen so we thought it was probably booby-trapped. The lieutenant said to check it out. It was a nerve-wracking few minutes for the men clearing the mine. They found out that it wasn't booby-trapped; it was command detonated. The firing wire was traced back to a bunker. We must have caught them off guard and they took off in a hurry, leaving the mine in place.

This little episode reintroduced the anxiety that I had not been feeling as of late because of how quiet things were. The guys up front that day knew if the VC had decided to stay and blow the mine, instead of hightailing it, their lives would have been over or irreparably changed. That's the sort of thing that will run through your mind for days. They are the kind of thoughts that germinate into the "what ifs" and "how comes." Why didn't they blow it? Maybe they tried and it malfunctioned. How lucky was I? Would it have killed me, or would I have ended up preferring to be dead? I know I had those kinds of thoughts; I assume other guys did as well, although no one spoke of them. Fortunately, I wasn't preoccupied with them, but they were never too far away, always lingering, waiting for a trigger to bring them to life. A fear of being gut shot, falling into putrid paddy water and having the nasty liquid slosh into my wound was one that revisited me often.

About a week later we came across some punji pits on a trail we were following. They were long past being functional: they were no longer camouflaged and the stakes were rotted. In the early days of the war, before the Viet Cong were supplied by the North, they used a lot of primitive but effective methods to fight the government. The punji pit was one. Punji pits came in all manner of shapes and sizes, but the ones we encountered were about two feet square and an equal measure deep. Sharpened bamboo stakes were implanted into the bottom of the pit pointed straight up, or they could be implanted in the sides of the pit at a 45- degree angle, pointed downward. In the case of the latter, the unfortunate troop walking down the trail doesn't notice the camouflaged pit and steps into it, slightly spreading the angled stakes as his foot passes through them. Instinctively, he yanks his foot back up, impaling his lower leg on the stakes. The harder you pull, the deeper the stakes go into the flesh. The Viet Cong also smeared the ends of the stakes with feces to increase the odds of infection. In the early years, American advisors fell victim to these traps often enough that the Army developed a steel insert to be placed under the leather insole of their new tropical jungle boots to negate the threat. These boots provided protection from a vertical spike but did not provide protection from the angled ones. At any rate, by the summer of 1968 the Viet Cong had enough conventional weapons that they no longer had to bother digging pits.

On another day, we came across a sign with a skull and cross bones crudely painted on it along with some Vietnamese words. We thought it was probably a warning about mines in the area. We didn't know if it was a warning to the villagers to stay out of the area or a false warning to us so we skirted the area. If it was the latter, they succeeded since no one wanted to tempt fate to find out.

Most of the new guys who joined us from the other units after the infusion were of the same mindset—let's just get out of here alive!!! While just getting out of Vietnam alive was my first priority, I was still trying to rationalize the war, to find something of value in it. If I could believe we were doing some good, I was able to handle things a lot better psychologically.

Doing good or not, I was feeling a lot better mentally since we moved into AO Laura. I liked having occasional access to the city, interacting with the locals, having a place to come back to after a day in the paddies, the freedom that working in small groups provided, and most of all, I liked that the Viet Cong decided to take some time off from the war, rocket attacks excepted.

CHAPTER FIFTEEN
RUFF-PUFF DAYS

We traveled around our AO by many different means. When traveling in large groups we used Army trucks, LCM's (landing crafts) on the waterways, airboats (like those used in the everglades), APC's (armored personnel carriers), and helicopters. But when in groups of two or three we sometimes had to make our own way. Not just when going somewhere on our own but occasionally when we were assigned a mission and location but not given any means to get there.

During one particular mission, Thornton and I were told by Lt. Russo to find our way out to a Vietnamese Popular Forces fort that was accessible only by water. We were to man an observation post for a few days at the fort. We stocked up some C- rations for a few days and packed some extras to use as payment for rides from the Vietnamese. We started our trip by flagging down a Lambretta, a three wheeled, motorized, utility cart, and asking the driver to take us down the dirt road that paralleled the canal. We got to the point where a bridge had been blown off the piers by the Viet Cong and had fallen into the stream. Unable to proceed any further we paid off the driver with rations and started looking for some water transportation to take us upstream to the fort. An old man came along in a sampan, and we waved him over to the bank. With some pidgin English and some hand gestures we were able to get him to agree to take us to the fort. Thornton and I climbed into the sampan and handed him some C-rations. He then handed Thorn and me 2 open-ended tin cans. Their purpose became readily apparent as our added weight dropped the sampan deeper in the water, exposing some less watertight sections of the sampan to the stream.

This particular sampan was about the size of a canoe, but it was made of wood and had less freeboard (distance between the water and deck), especially now with me and Thornton in it. With water now seeping through the seams, Thorn and I needed no encouragement to bail, but the old man seemed so unfazed by the situation that my immediate fears about sinking were allayed. *Papasan* stood in the back of the sampan on a small deck and rowed from a standing position. The oarlock was on a vertical wooden support about two feet off the deck. Picture gondoliers in Venice, only the rowing action was more toward the back than along the side.

We soon found out how much bailing it took to keep the water at bay and were able to take some time to watch life along the waterway. We passed thatched houses along the banks with sampans tied up at the water's edge. Kids were running alongside the stream checking out the Americans in the sampan. Larger sampans loaded with fruits and vegetables were headed downstream toward Saigon to sell at the markets. *Papasan* stayed close to the bank to stay out of their way. The larger ones were motorized, and the waves from their wake rocked our little sampan to the point I was concerned with being swamped. Another concern was feeling vulnerable when we passed through some densely packed nipa palms— forming a wall of green on either side of us. Perfect concealment for anyone wanting to take a potshot at us. Nonetheless, I was having fun. It was cool to be out on our own experiencing the culture and being able to interact with the locals, notwithstanding having to bail our way to the fort.

Papasan dropped us off at the fort. It wasn't actually a structure but a triangular earth embankment topped with concertina wire. Think of a barbed wire expanded slinky, only 3 feet in diameter instead of 3 inches. Each corner of the triangle had a guard tower. Inside the fort were some small structures we called hooches, where the Popular Forces and their families lived. These Popular Force troops were tasked with the defense of their own villages. Their counterparts, the Regional Forces, had slightly broader responsibilities. Neither group was known for aggressiveness or competence. Most Americans referred to them by the less than intimidating name of "Ruff Puffs."

We set up shop inside the fort under a thatched roof that provided some shade from the sun and kept us dry in the rain— but it had no walls. There was a table about the size of a picnic table where we kept the radio. We had to call in sitreps (situation reports) several times a day and on the hour at night. This meant that one of us had to be up at any given time the whole night through.

It was interesting watching the goings-on in the fort, the everyday life of families, the rhythms of the day. Much of life centered around the water. All comings and goings were done on the water; there were no roads nearby. The troops took sampans out to fish. The *mamasans* washed their clothes in the stream as well as their pots and pans. Somewhat disconcerting was the fact that the stream also served as a lavatory. Two planks set on stilts extending out over the water served as the facility;

privacy was not an option. Small children, not yet potty trained, just walked around sans pants—no diapers to wash that way. Mothers of infants breastfed in front of us without any concern for modesty. It was definitely a different world but fascinating to me.

Our first evening there some of the folks invited us to eat supper with them. We had been warned by the Army that it was not a good idea to eat the local food, and having witnessed that the kitchen and bath were in the same general location at this fort, I could understand why. However, most of us had already broken that rule and lived to tell about it and I was hoping that if what I was eating was thoroughly cooked it was safe enough to eat. So as not to be impolite, we joined our hosts for supper. The main course was a stew of some sort: rice and vegetables, and small chunks of meat. We contributed some C-rations to the meal and we all had a nice time, particularly when trying to communicate in each other's language, usually butchering the pronunciations and evoking lots of laughter.

Thornton and I started our guard shifts around 10:00 PM, and alternated every two hours. The night passed uneventfully. We called in our sitreps on the hour with a simple "sitrep negative," meaning nothing of any note was worth mentioning. The new day dawned draped in a haze that made the rising sun appear reddish and larger than normal. The promise of a hot muggy morning followed by torrential afternoon rains seemed likely.

The first radio call of the morning informed us that we were to start searching the sampans transiting the waterway beside the fort for smuggled weapons. Concerns were still high that another full-blown offensive was in the works and that the Viet Cong was again attempting to conceal weapons caches in the city. I woke Thorn, told him what was up, then fixed my cocoa and cookies for breakfast before the first sampans started to show up.

We stood on the bank and waited. Soon a medium-sized sampan appeared, loaded with fruit and vegetables. Thorn and I began yelling toward the boat, "*dung lai, dung lai*," which means stop. Then we extended our arms and flicked our hands up and down. It looked like we were waving goodbye, but in Vietnam it means come here. We were also yelling, "*lai day, lai day*," which also means come here. The sampan pulled over and we searched it without results. We repeated this several times in the early morning hours when the most traffic headed toward the city. At the end of the day, all we accomplished was ticking off the boat crews by messing up their carefully stacked produce.

The rain came as expected. The tide was low that afternoon, so boat traffic came to a standstill except for small sampans like the one we rode in on. With nothing to do, I went exploring around the fort and ran across a guy hanging rat skins up on a line. I asked him what he was doing, and he managed to convey to me that rats were #1 *chop chop* (food). I was scared to ask but had to know, *"Is that what we had to eat last night?"*

"Oh Yeah! #1, #1." Well, how about that—rat stew! I felt ok so I guess it didn't hurt me any, but I decided to make sure I knew what was in my next Vietnamese meal before I ate it.

The skies had cleared by evening, and it looked like a nice night was before us. A few of the Vietnamese troops came over to see me and Thornton with thoughts of doing a little partying. They brought some rice wine with them and were willing to share. I had seen a pot of rice earlier in the day that seemed to be "active" in some manner. I didn't know if it was fermenting or brewing or what, but it was obvious they were making some sort of alcoholic beverage out of it. At any rate, the guys were ready to share some of their finished product. Thornton was all for that, but I thought the liquid had the look and smell of lethality to it, and I passed on their generous offering.

Well, soon enough, all the guys were having a rousing good time, including Thorn. Several hours passed and I began my guard duty stint from one of the guard towers and called in the hourly sitreps. I went back to the hooch to get Thornton since he had not shown up at midnight for his turn. I found him lying on the table, quite the worse for wear. I tried to arouse him but he was toast; no way was he pulling his guard duty. I was pretty annoyed over this as now I had to pull a double shift. I came back at 2:00 AM to see if the rest had revived him, but he seemed no better at all. He just lay there, capable of nothing much more than breathing. I shook him, slapped him on the face, and yelled at him. It didn't matter, he just lay there. Now I was more concerned than ticked off. Does the guy have alcohol poisoning? Should I call for a medevac? If I do, Thorn is going to be in big trouble. This wasn't like getting blasted back on the base. We were on duty, there was no end to the charges the army could come up with, starting with dereliction. And, no doubt, there would be some spill over; I would be in trouble too. Trouble loomed both ways: trouble for sure if I called for a night time dust-off, and more trouble for me if Thorn has alcohol poisoning, goes into a coma and dies, and I hadn't acted. I wasn't sure what to do. When you don't know what to do, when it's fifty-fifty, it's always easier to do nothing than something, and that is what I did. But I spent the whole night worrying if it was the right decision. All my hourly "sitrep negatives" were hardly truthful; my situation sucked.

I went back to check on Thad when the horizon began to lighten. I had been up all night but I wasn't tired; the stress of the situation had forestalled fatigue. I was immensely relieved to see Thorn sitting up on the table. I felt lighter with the weight of uncertainty off of my shoulders. I was so happy to see him alive that I wasn't as mad at him as I should have been.

Besides, he was a pretty cool guy and I liked him enough to let things slide. He looked pitiful, though, and he was paying a heavy price for the night's festivities. The morning sun was not kind to his eyes, and anything above a whisper hurt. Clearly, he wasn't going to be much help for a while. After he recovered somewhat, Thorn was very apologetic. I was ok with that. He had just wanted to escape the war for a while. Thad was with the 4th Battalion 12th Infantry before the infusion brought him to us and was involved in heavy fighting during the May Offensive.

After a couple more days at the fort we were replaced by some other guys, and we made our way back to the bridge. Once there, we were told to report to the cement factory where our battalion headquarters were located. It was our company's turn to provide security for the base.

Instead of waiting around for some military transportation we decided to head out on our own. That was one of the great things about this new AO: we were spread out all over the place in small groups without much supervision, so we had the freedom of making our own decisions. Lonnie and I walked out to the main highway and flagged down a Shell Oil tanker truck that was returning to Nha Be for another load of gasoline. Nha Be had the largest storage facilities for gasoline in the country. It was located along the Saigon River about 5 miles south of our position. The cement factory was along the way. I don't know if carrying a gun had anything to do with it, but the tanker drivers always stopped for us. The big yellow trucks with the Shell emblem on the sides were like a shuttle service for us between the bridge, Camp Davies, and the cement factory. We never bothered getting into the hot cab of the truck. We slung our rifles over our shoulders, picked a side, stepped up onto the running board, slid one arm through the window, hooked an elbow inside the door and grabbed onto the side door mirror with the other arm, and away we went. It's actually a bit of a thrill to ride the running board at forty miles per hour, and as an added bonus our sweat evaporated in the rush of air, cooling us off as we sped down the road. It was just a small pleasure felt in the midst of hot sticky days, but those rides remain fresh in my mind.

The cement factory grounds covered about five acres with a large warehouse in the center. There was a cement wall (what else) on three sides and a canal in the back. All the battalion headquarters staff were in the warehouse. Large bunkers were placed along the perimeter wall; that's where we were staying.

Security for the cement factory wasn't bad duty and compared to humping the boonies in the jungle it was great duty. But I had quickly gotten spoiled guarding the bridge and manning an observation post at the fort. I was ready to go back to that after a couple of days of bumping into officers every time you turned around and dealing with the regimentation of a battalion base camp.

I was manning a bunker in a far corner of the base camp one morning when one of the guys told me that Lt. Russo wanted to see me at the company headquarters. The lieutenant told me that I was going to be his RTO (radio telephone operator) whenever the platoon went out on a mission. I said ok (not that you have a choice) and asked him what I needed to do.

I had mixed emotions about this new development. There were good points and bad points about the job, but I was thinking mostly about the bad ones, and they weren't inconsequential. To start with, there was the extra weight to carry. Slogging through rice paddies and tidal flats was tough enough. I wasn't relishing having the extra weight sinking my feet that much further into the muck. It wasn't just the radio I had to carry. I also had to carry a spare battery, several smoke grenades, hand flares, and the long whip antenna. Maybe 30 pounds altogether.

Another issue I had with being an RTO was the fact that it made you a target. As an RTO, your job was to shadow your lieutenant at all times. You had to be right there whenever he needed communication. The Viet Cong knew this, of course. That radio could call in artillery, air strikes, and gunships on them. Eliminate the radio and you disrupt command and control of the unit.

With all that in mind, I'd heard it said that the antenna sticking up in the air off of your back was sending out a signal that said "shoot me first." Some RTOs tried to conceal the fact that they were carrying one. They put the body of the radio in a rucksack. Then if they could use the short flex antenna they bent it at 90 degrees at the base so the antenna was more horizontal than vertical—thus reducing their profile. If you needed the ten foot whip antenna you were out of luck; there was no hiding it.

So, it looked like I was going to have another constant companion in addition to my M-16. I'd be attached to a AN/PRC-25 for the foreseeable future. The letters meant Army Navy/Portable Radio Communication model 25. To the guys, it was a "prick 25."

It wasn't all bad, though. Having the radio and sticking by the lieutenant all the time meant you were always in the know. Also, whenever Lt. Russo was on the mission, it meant I wouldn't have to walk point. He wasn't always with us, and at times I was sent out with other platoons, in which case I reverted to being a rifleman. But for the most part, in the coming months I would be humping the radio unless I was on a bridge or at a fort.

My first day with the radio was a search mission of the houses along the main canal into Saigon. The intelligence guys still felt that an offensive was coming, that the Viet Cong were keeping a low profile while preparing for another attack on the capital. The fear was that weapons were being smuggled into the city and being hidden in people's homes. We would be searching homes in the area alongside the canal.

We cordoned an area about 500 yards long and began to search the homes for weapons. It felt strange to just walk into folk's homes and start looking for hidden arms caches. The homes were small, many with just one large room, and made of whatever material they could find. It was obviously a poor neighborhood. Inside there might be a table and a few chairs and hammocks for sleeping. It looked like most of the cooking was done outside on small stoves in front of the houses. The stoves may have been charcoal.

The homes were right next to each other. Some were on stilts and hung out over the canal. It was a whole different world: tons of people all crowded together, refugees everywhere, some living in cardboard boxes. It was early morning when we started to look for contraband, the time of the day when the markets were open for folks buying food for the day. There was no refrigeration in the homes, so if someone wanted meat for dinner they bought it that day. Watching the women haggle over the price of a piece of meat was an eye-opening experience. The sellers lay mats out on the ground and then lay their fruit, vegetables, bread, and meat out on plates resting on the mats. Nothing was covered, not even the meat. Flies crawled over the meat while the *mamasans* were settling on a price. The buyer picked a piece of meat up off the platter and flipped it over to check both sides. If she didn't like the looks of it, she'd put it down and the next person picked it up to look at. For all of us used to going to the super market and picking up meat that was chilled, lying on a Styrofoam plate and wrapped in plastic, the process looked revolting.

We had some ARVN (government) troops with us and some Vietnamese interpreters to help us interrogate anyone deemed suspicious. The residents, for the most part, took our intrusions in stride; there wasn't much they could do about it anyway. Some were downright friendly. I had one old man give me bread and chunks of pineapple to eat. I wasn't sure what his motivation was; at first, I thought it might be to distract me from my search. I didn't let that divert my attention, but I didn't find anything anyway. Usually the people were asking us for stuff, so I felt a little bad that I was suspecting the old man of ulterior motives. The bread was really quite good. It was a different shape than I was used to. It was long and slender and probably prepared early that morning. It was light and moist with a crunchy crust. Other than a baked in bug or two that needed to be plucked out, it was great. The pineapple chunks were sweet and juicy and tasted refreshing in the rising heat of the morning. My impromptu breakfast was an unexpected treat; we normally never had fresh bread or fruit. I told the old man, "*cam on ban*" (thank you) several times before I moved on.

Sgt. Trout was another beneficiary of a local's largesse. I walked into a hut and saw a Vietnamese man pouring a clear liquid into John's canteen. I asked John what was up, and he told me the man was giving him some sort of liquor. I asked him if I could have a whiff of it. It smelled like the same stuff that damn near killed Thornton. Once we left the man's home, I warned John he was dealing with dangerous stuff.

We were supposed to check the papers (ID's) of all the people, and we did, but I had no idea what I was looking at. Naturally, the info was in Vietnamese. I could have been looking at a Mickey Mouse Club membership card for all I knew. No one told us what to look for ahead of time, so what are you going to do? I don't recall any of us finding anything of note that day, but the ARVN's picked up fourteen suspects and took them away to be interrogated. Later, we found out that five of them were Viet Cong.

CHAPTER SIXTEEN
IDYLLIC DAYS

I spent a few more pleasant days at the bridge and then got a new assignment to man an observation post at another bridge a few miles to the south. Tex, who had joined our unit along with Thornton during the infusion, was with me.

Our new bridge was of the same plank and truss construction as our original bridge by the canal. A stream ran under this one, and like the other, the deck was only about three feet above the water line at high tide. The bridge connected two halves of a village. The thatched homes belonged to farmers who tended to the rice paddies that stretched out on all sides of the village. Unlike America where farmers live on the land they work, the Vietnamese live together in small villages and walk out to the fields every day.

There was no electricity in the village or running water or any of the other things we take for granted. But by Vietnamese standards the village seemed middle class: the homes were neat, no rotting thatch, some were wood with corrugated metal roofs, they weren't butted up against each other, and the villagers looked healthy.

Bunkers had already been built so we didn't have that task to deal with. Like at the other bridge, our main job was just to be there. In reality, we were just a tripwire. The two of us weren't enough to stop any anticipated offensive that might choose this road and bridge to head north to the capital. We were there to radio in and let them know the Viet Cong were on their way. There were small groups of us scattered all over the AO for just this purpose.

I felt no concern about being a tripwire because for some reason, I just didn't feel like anything was going to happen—despite all the intelligence guys saying different. It was the exact opposite of what I was feeling up in War Zone D where I was dead sure something bad was going to happen.

Down here I was feeling calm and relaxed; frankly, I was enjoying myself. The new bridge did nothing to change how I felt. All the folks were super friendly. They had cast their lot with the government side so were glad to have us around. We had plenty of time on our hands and we got to know the locals pretty well, especially those living on either side of the bridge and the Ruff Puff village defense force.

We also had plenty of time to observe the daily life of the village and its environment. We'd see the market open every morning, the *mamasans* haggling over prices, the kids going to school, the fishermen casting nets off of their sampans, and the farmers heading off to the fields. But even before all that human activity began, if I had the last guard shift I'd get to see the sun seemingly jump off the horizon so fast that the day should be over in 6 hours instead of 12. Then it appeared to slow and get down to the business of baking the earth, the rice, and the people. I'd watch the tide roll in and make the stream flow backward, then hours later ease back out to uncover the fine silt of the stream bed and the mudskippers.

I really enjoyed watching the mudskippers skitter across the tidal flats at low tide from one tidal pool to another. The mudskippers looked like evolution interrupted. Like they didn't know what they wanted to be. They're fish, but amphibious. When the tide flows out leaving mud flats of silty slime the fun starts. They squirm out of the slime and use their pectoral fins as walking appendages to skip across the mud flats, using mouths that open as wide as their bodies to skim nutrients off the mud surface. They have eyes that rest on the top of their head and look out 180 degrees from each other. They are territorial and rush to defend their territory from other skippers, and sometimes end up in a mud wrestling match. When alarmed, foldable fins rise up off their back. Their color is a grayish-green with white spots speckled all over. They would never win a beauty contest, but I did enjoy watching their antics.

I really started feeling in sync with nature. Being outside all the time with nothing to do you start to observe little things that went unnoticed before. Things like how the moon rose slightly later every night and how the times of the tides reflected that. How much higher in the sky the sun was here compared to back home. I'd notice slight shifts in the wind direction and a temperature drop of a degree or two that foretold the arrival of rain. In the afternoons I'd watch the bright white cumulus clouds building and billowing upwards of 20,000 feet, then turn dark and lift higher still before releasing torrents of cold rain that peppered the stream's surface into thousands of tiny geysers.

Unlike the other bridge that edged the city, this bridge's setting was rural. Though not untouched by the war, it seemed to have maintained its traditional way of life. It was quiet, not much traffic passed our way. There were no refugees huddled in cardboard boxes like in the capital. There was no sign of prostitutes, drug dealers, or scammers trying to make a buck off of every GI they saw.

It was easy to like the villagers. It was fun to play with the kids, and you could easily let yourself forget why you were there. Tex and I thought it was as idyllic a situation as we could ever have found ourselves in. We thought it couldn't last, but it did. Every day or two a jeep showed up with the supplies we needed. Our only duties were being there, keeping an eye out, and reporting nightly on the radio. We settled into the good life.

We got to know the villagers better all the time, and Tex ended up becoming emotionally attached to a young boy who was orphaned by the war. His name was Cuong and he was around ten years of age. He was very bright and spoke a lot of English. He started hanging out with us in the evenings. Tex kept telling me that he wished there was something he could do to help Cuong. He wanted to adopt Cuong and take him back to the states. I knew Tex was sincere, but he was also delusional; there was no way that was going to happen.

I had heard stories of GIs wanting to marry their Vietnamese girlfriends and take them back home with them. They ran into miles of red tape and bureaucratic land mines set to derail even the most dogged pursuers of that dream. I think adopting would be that hard and more. Unfortunately, Tex told Cuong of his plans. I don't know what he was thinking. We could have been pulled off the bridge and miles away before the next hour was up. Just the logistics of it would be impossible. I didn't feel it was fair to let Cuong think that the idea was very probable. He was very excited by the prospect of going to America. I told Cuong that Tex would try very hard, but there were many, many obstacles in the way and it was more likely not to happen than happen.

I ended up making a friend of my own while on the bridge. He was a member of the village self-defense force, a Ruff Puff by the name of Trang. Trang was older than me, but for whatever reason we hit it off and had a lot of fun with each other. He knew more English than I knew Vietnamese, but that wasn't saying much. It was really nice because the friendship was genuine. Many times, your guard was up because there were so many Vietnamese trying to take advantage of you for your money. Trang, however, never asked for anything. In fact, he was generous to me in several ways that I appreciated dearly.

One of the first things he did was lend me a hammock. At night Tex and I stayed with the Ruff Puffs in their little fort. They had a shelter, just a roof really, no walls, but it kept the rain off of you. Anyway, we all stayed there overnight, six Ruff Puffs and us. Trang asked me if I wanted to try a hammock instead of the air mattress I was using. I said sure, not really expecting much, but to my surprise it felt great to sleep in and had other advantages as well. You didn't have to blow it up; it kept you up off the ground away from the rats; it was 2-ply and sewn on 3 sides so you could slip in between the plies and have a cover over you to keep the insects at bay. As long as you had a place to hang it, it was great. I decided to get one of my own first chance I got.

Another time he took me to a thatched hut in the village that served as a tavern of sorts. It wasn't much in the way of ambiance, one table and some chairs. Nevertheless, it was nice. Trang ordered two beers; I offered to pay but he refused to let me. The girl set down two bottles of Tiger Beer (brand name) on the table. The bottles were the usual brown color, and they had a tiger painted on their sides. GIs referred to this brand as tiger piss, but it wasn't that bad. (Wasn't all that great either.)

As any smoker knows, you can't drink beer without a cigarette, so Trang pulled out a pack of smokes called Ruby Queens. Ruby Queens were short and unfiltered like a Camel or Lucky Strike. He offered me one, and I felt like I couldn't refuse his generosity. These Ruff Puffs make very little money so the gesture was meaningful. I lit up and took a draw, expecting it to be like a Lucky or Camel. No way, it was tantamount to smoking a stick. I think I covered the urge to hack fairly well, but was sure this would be my first and last Ruby Queen.

My fondest memory of Trang, though, was of a late night fishing excursion we shared. I was nearing the end of a 12 to 2 AM guard shift one night when Trang asked me if I was hungry. I said sure, and he said let's go catch some chop chop. So, as soon as my shift was over we walked down to the stream and got into a small sampan. Trang pushed us off the shore. High tide had been reached and the stream was in a slack water state when the water is nearly still before it begins to recede. It was a cloudless, moonless night that brought the magnificence of the whole Milky Way into sight. Trang lit a small candle and placed it on the bow, then cast his net and let us ever so slowly drift downstream. I lay back in the boat and just gazed skyward at the heavens, floating lazily in the dark and quiet night. It was the very definition of tranquility. At that point I could have cared less if we caught any fish. I was lost in the moment, but serenity wasn't Trang's main goal. My reverie was broken when he nudged me when it came time to pull in the fish.

The fish were small but there were enough of them for a meal. We headed back to the bridge. Trang had a small stove that he fired up to start boiling some water while he cleaned the fish and I chopped up some vegetables. I guess what he made could be called fish stew, for lack of a real name. He added rice, some vegetables, then the fish—and let it cook for some time.

Then it was time for our early, early breakfast. I can't say my taste buds were treated to a wonderful meal, but I must say I've never had a breakfast quite as memorable as that one. It was a special night sharing those late hours with my new friend. Trang and I knew at the most 25 words we both could understand. We used hand gestures, body language, and facial expressions to communicate with each other. It was fun and we had a lot of laughs trying to get a point across. It was an improbable friendship; other than being soldiers, we had nothing in common. However, it did happen, and it made my stay in the village, which was pretty darn good by itself, immeasurably better.

Knowing Trang made me want to rationalize the war as being a good thing, and at times I managed to do just that, at least for a while. Getting to know the folks in the village, playing with the kids, and palling around with the Ruff Puffs at the bridges, forts, and outposts added to this desire to have the war really mean something. I vacillated about the war, mostly because of these personal relationships, for a little more than half of my tour, but I could never sustain a positive attitude for long. By the end, I could find nothing of redeeming value. Regardless of that, the time I spent in AO Laura was easily the best experience I had during my year in Vietnam, thanks to Trang and others like him.

The next day, Tex and I got word that we were reporting back to the bridge by the canal. I knew I was going to miss everybody at the village but going back to the other bridge was hardly a hardship. Besides, I'd get to see Anh, one of the "working girls" with whom I had started an unorthodox friendship.

Unfortunately, going back to the canal bridge turned out to be short-lived. We got word that we would soon begin riverine missions in the delta and the Rung Sat Special Zone. I wasn't aware that the Army had a navy, but they did, and I soon found myself aboard a variety of vessels dedicated to transporting infantry troops to and fro along the myriad streams, canals, and rivers of the delta. In the months to come I would also find myself aboard US Navy vessels that provided the same service only in far more formidable boats.

The boat I was on most often was called an LCM-8. The letters stood for: Landing Craft, Mechanized. Their original purpose was to land heavy mechanized equipment on beaches. The Army, faced with operational areas that could not be reached by land, decided to use the LCM-8's as troop transports.

The landing craft were 73 feet long and 24 feet wide and probably stood 10 feet above the water line at their highest point. They were powered by 4 GMC diesel engines putting out a combined 660 horsepower. Since the boat weighed in at 135,000 pounds, it had a hard time getting out of its own way. I think they traveled at about 9 miles per hour, which meant if you got ambushed along a river or canal you were not going to speed out of the kill zone. While doing some research on the specifications of these boats I came across a quote from a crew member on one that stated "the LCM's moved at the speed of dark." Most of the Army crewmen of these craft called their vessels "mike boats." All the boats that transported us came from the 1099th Transportation Company. They called themselves the "River Rats.

CHAPTER SEVENTEEN
LONG DAY IN THE RUNG SAT

We found out that we would be taking the mike boats down the river to the Rung Sat Special Zone. I don't know who named it, but it was far from special in any positive way. After my first mission there, I wrote home to report that I had been in "the most miserable place in Vietnam." The Rung Sat was four or five hundred square miles of mangrove swamps, salt marshes, nipa palms, and brushwood interlaced by hundreds of miles of streams, canals, and rivers.

I stumbled across a U. S. government intelligence report on the Rung Sat that was on an internet site. I'll paraphrase some highlights: "foreboding and desolate"... "no dry land in wet season"... "much of the land is covered with water at high tide"... "poisonous snakes, mosquitoes, stinging and biting insects, red ants and leeches"... "combat loaded troops sink up to knees in mud"... "ground operations are very slow moving"... "some mangrove swamps are impenetrable"... "heavy thunderstorms"... "humidity almost always at least 80%"... "tide levels of 10 feet between low and high"... "at low tide, streams have steep muddy banks that are difficult to negotiate"... "when tides are coming in or going out, the water current can be as high as 8 miles per hour, making crossings very dangerous"... "immersion foot is probable after 48 hours"... "cuts and scratches are easily infected due to wet conditions."

A person might understandably ask why on earth would we go there, let the enemy have the wretched place if he wants it. That would probably be the case except for one thing, the Rung Sat sits astride the Long Tau shipping channel. The shipping channel connected Saigon with the South China Sea. Saigon was the major port of entry for war supplies for the southern portion of the country, but it was 35 miles inland. Ocean-going freighters had to transit the shipping channel to get there, and it ran through the heart of the Rung Sat. Mangrove forests lined the banks of the meandering channel and provided perfect cover for Viet Cong intent on sinking a freighter and blocking the channel. This was of main concern to our military and provided the reason for us to go there.

As noted earlier, the LCMs we were using to travel to the Rung Sat were slow, so we all had to get up about 3:30 in the morning to board the mike boats to get to the zone for a full-day sweep. I had little idea when I walked up the ramp how full a day it would be. We were underway by 4:30 AM. I think we had about 75 troops aboard as we backed out into the Saigon River and turned south. It was still dark so I tried to get comfortable on the steel floor of the well deck and catch a few z's before the sun came up.

The top of the orange-red globe broke the horizon around 6:00 AM, providing the light for my first good view of the shipping channel. The Saigon river at that point was very wide. I'd guess $\frac{3}{4}$ to a mile across, and we were navigating down the center of it. It was more than a river, though; it was an estuary, which accounted for much of its width and depth. An estuary is a partially enclosed body of water where fresh water from rivers and streams mixes with salt water from the ocean.

We weren't alone on this trip: there were other landing craft full of troops from the other companies in the battalion. All the companies in the battalion (A, B, C, and D) were represented. I didn't know it then, but the brigade commanding general was in the company of Colonel Behm, our battalion commander, for the trip down river. We had a convoy.

It was kind of neat traveling by the boat: I was like a tourist taking in new sights. We passed the fuel depot at Nha Be where a couple dozen large cylindrical gas tanks sat next to the river. They were big enough to hold tens of thousands of gallons. Nha Be was the destination of the fuel trucks we caught rides on between the bridges and base. As the sun rose, the traffic on the river increased. We passed large junks and barges and spotted many small sampans hugging the shore. Navy PBRs sped up and down the river. They were speedy patrol boats that blasted by our lumbering LCMs so quickly it felt like we were stopped. Those patrol boats were made of fiberglass, were about 30 feet long, armed to the teeth, and exceeded 30 miles per hour. They always seemed to be going full speed and they looked like great fun.

Gradually, as we neared the mangrove forests of the Rung Sat, the river traffic disappeared and there were no longer any signs of village life along the banks. I wasn't the only one to notice this change: as we ventured deeper into this untamed swamp, the chatter among the troops waned and was replaced by a sense of foreboding. The river bank looked different now, all the mangrove trees had lost their leaves. They had been aerially sprayed with Agent Orange. It was eerie. The trees looked like they belonged along the Ohio river on a crisp January morning rather than along this overheated tropical waterway.

We turned off the main channel into a narrower branch of the river. The trees weren't sprayed along this stretch, and the mangroves looked impenetrable. Nonetheless, we would soon be beaching the boat and heading into it. Captain Williams, our new company commanding officer, gave us a little mission talk in the boat. Although he had been in command for quite a few weeks, this was my first opportunity to be with him on a mission. Other than platoon-sized rice paddy sweeps with our lieutenant in charge, I'd been having a good time. We were in small groups, guarding bridges and manning observation posts at Vietnamese forts all this while without any real supervision, so I wasn't quite sure what to expect from him in the field.

We gathered around him in the well deck to hear the mission plan. Captain Williams was pretty *gung ho* and was anxious to get things started. I guess he was trying to fire us up when he told us he wanted to see us run off the boat as soon as the ramp was dropped. We all kind of looked at each other with an "are you kidding me" look. The river banks were steep and muddy. If you hit that mud at full speed off the end of that ramp, you were begging for a face plant into the slime. I didn't expect to see anyone running.

When we arrived at our put in point, the crew nudged the LCM as far up the bank as they could, then, dropped the ramp. Nobody ran. We stepped off into the muck and struggled our way up the bank, only to reach a barrier made up of the root systems of the mangrove trees. The mangrove had root systems that begin above the ground level, which makes moving through them tedious and exhausting. Our mission was to sweep through an area between a back channel and the main channel looking for Viet Cong (who more than likely had hightailed it out of the area by now) and arms caches (a more probable expectation).

After extracting ourselves from the tangle of mangrove roots, we broke into an area that was a little more open but was in a depression. It was covered in water, but no matter, we started searching from that point. We slogged along for several hours, not finding much of anything. We crossed some streams using ropes and air mattresses. It was wearisome and fruitless thus far. It was hot and humid, and the thick air made for labored breathing when the mud was deep. Our direction took us into an area where Agent Orange had been laid on thick by Air Force spray planes. The Air Force used C-123 cargo planes outfitted with tanks and spray booms to lay down a thick mist of the plant-killing chemical. They flew low in a formation of three, laying down a broad swath of the destructive defoliant. The stuff did a heck of a job; it managed to turn an already spooky place into the "Twilight Zone." The denuded trees were eerie enough, but what really freaked me out were the giant fruit bats hanging from the bare limbs. They were a good foot long and had a three-foot wingspan. Their presence only added to the sinister feel that pervaded the swamp.

We finally hit an area that wasn't under water. It was past noon so we decided to stop for 15 minutes to grab a bite to eat. We formed a perimeter and in the process found an above ground bunker. We found nothing inside, but Captain Williams said we would blow it up after lunch before we continued on. We had a pretty demanding morning physically. I was starving: hungry enough to actually eat some cold meat slices out of the can, which I usually abhorred. The captain said we didn't have time to heat our food as we were behind schedule.

Lonnie, a fellow squad member and friend, and I were eating together. I asked him if he wanted to blow the bunker up before we left. I usually shied away from things like that if I could; I had promised myself to not expose myself to danger if I could avoid it. It's one thing to get messed up, it's entirely another to do it to yourself. But for some reason that day, I *really* felt like blowing something up. Lonnie said sure, so we were ready when the captain asked for somebody to blow it.

I hadn't used any explosives since training and neither had Lonnie, but we didn't want to look stupid so we didn't ask anybody how much we should use. We grabbed some C-4, some timing fuse, and an igniter and scoped our bunker out. We climbed inside and began to discuss where to place the explosive and how much to use. Figuring it was better to go bigger than risk not using enough, we overcompensated by a wide margin. Next, we had the same discussion over the timing fuse. We didn't want to look like rookies and have the fuse burn down forever before the explosion, so we under- compensated the fuse. This was not a good combination. We lit the fuse and ambled back toward the rest of the troops waiting for us to finish before moving on. We made it about halfway to where we should have been when it blew. When we looked back and noticed a chunk of earth the size of a clothes dryer arching up over our heads, we proceeded to run for our lives. Captain Williams welcomed us back with a scathing look but didn't say anything. Lesson learned!

We moved out again, continuing our search. The heat was scorching, and the humidity was as high as the temp was hot. The sweat rolled off us, stinging our eyes and attracting dirt like a magnet until you just felt gritty all over. It was easy to outpace your water supply. Soon after, we started to hear some gunfire in the distance, disproving my supposition that the Viet Cong would flee the area in the face of all the troops we put ashore. We didn't know what was going on, but there was no doubt somebody was in contact with the enemy. Unless we heard otherwise, though, we would continue on with our own mission. Knowing now that the Viet Cong hadn't fled the area diminished my concerns about snakes, red ants, leeches, and the oppressive heat. Not by much, they just weren't the first thing on my mind.

As the day wore on we heard reports on the radio that A company had a firefight and had sustained casualties. Other things were happening that we were not yet aware of. For one, the boat General Mitchell (the commanding general of our brigade), was aboard controlling the operation was hit by a rocket-propelled grenade. He and our battalion commanding officer, Colonel Behm, were both wounded and the boat disabled. Two other companies had made light contact with the enemy as well.

By late afternoon we had covered our area of responsibility and were headed for our pick- up point. Luckily, we had made no contact and experienced no casualties beyond insect bites and leeches, but nonetheless were pretty well beat. A lot of guys low on water finished off what they had, expecting to be back on a boat returning to base shortly. That wasn't to be the case. We got a radio message that our pick-up point had changed. The Army LCMs would not be coming to get us, but a Vietnamese Navy landing craft would be.

I surmised later that whoever was now running things designated the Army LCMs to pick up the companies that had been in contact that day and left *us*, because of the disabled boat, to be picked up later on by the Vietnamese Navy.

We set out for our new pick up point—tired, thirsty, and disgusted with the situation. We had to cross two streams, so the map said, to get to our destination. Only trouble was, it was low tide and nothing was left of the streams but the stream beds and a tiny thread of sluggishly moving water down their centers. Crossing these streams proved difficult and tiring. The stream beds were more like quicksand than mud, though they were actually silt. Silt is finely grained and light enough to be suspended in water. That's why the rivers in the delta are brown. When the tide recedes, what's left is silt and water slurry that holds little weight-bearing ability.

Regardless, we had to cross. We were up to our knees in it before we hit thicker ground. I could manage it, but it was tedious, one step at a time, hard work. I was lucky: I was light in weight and was blessed with strong legs, the best combination for traversing silty stream beds. Others were not, and we had to use ropes to help a lot of guys across. Twice done, we finally arrived at the pick-up point. There was no one waiting for us. Radio traffic ensued and inquiries were made about our situation. There had been a mistake, and we were told to go back to our original take out point. It was a good thing that the guy telling us this was doing it on the radio, or there may have been one more casualty that day. Everyone was thoroughly pissed, including the officers. Nobody wanted to cross the stream beds again, but we were left with no alternative. So off we went, once more.

Besides that, time was beginning to be an issue. This was planned as a one day mission: we had packed light, no gear for overnight, no extra food, and some guys were already out of water. A nighttime pick up at low tide was not a desirable situation. So off we went to beat the clock. There was no way we could negotiate mangrove roots in the dark. The thought of spending the night in the Rung Sat at high tide was a good motivator. We re-crossed the stream beds in the same fashion as before and arrived back at our original position as the sun was dipping down toward day's end. Relieved at seeing the Vietnamese landing craft approaching from down river, I headed out on the tidal flat. The tide was just starting to come in, so a lot of river bank was still uncovered. We all had to slog across the silty bottom to get to the boat when it arrived, and I couldn't wait to get on it and just lie down; I was beat. As I mentioned, I had strong legs and I got myself pretty far out, but my enthusiasm for getting on that boat got me in a bit of trouble. I sunk too deep in that slime and got myself stuck. Trying to extricate myself just seemed to make things worse. I gave up and decided to just wait things out. I'd probably need a rope to get me out, just like the guys crossing the streambeds needed.

Sgt. West and a guy named Garcia had also started out but hadn't gotten as far as I did before they got stuck as well. I looked back and saw them a little higher on the bank and a little off to my left. All three of us were immobile, and there was nothing to be done but wait.

The landing craft was nearing our position, the ramp was already partially down, and the boat seemed to pick up a little speed. It was headed straight for the three of us, and it soon became apparent that there was no way the landing craft was going to stop in time. I don't think the Vietnamese captain even saw us. The sun was low on the horizon and directly in his eyes. We were in olive drab fatigues that blended in with the dark brown river bank. He was probably looking at the troops high on the river's edge, backlit by the sun, and was trying to get up enough speed to run the boat as far as possible up the mud flat to get as near as possible to those troops.

It was nearly simultaneous; everyone started yelling, "*STOP, STOP,*" then "*DUNG LAI, DUNG LAI!!!*" I could not believe my eyes. Fuck, he's going to run me over. Again, I screamed at the top of my lungs, "*STOP, God damn it, stop!*" On it came, it was like watching your own death in slow motion. Suddenly, the captain must have realized we were there: the pitch of the engines changed and the front end of the boat skewed to the right. But landing craft don't stop on a dime and its momentum was carrying it forward. It was a close call, but the boat slid past my left shoulder with about 6 inches to spare. That last minute swerve, had saved me. The lowered ramp slid by, then the hull. I heard a yell and looked back over my left shoulder to see the lip of the ramp headed directly for Sgt. West and Garcia. The ramp had about a foot of clearance between it and the tidal flat. Sgt. West was a couple feet closer to the oncoming ramp than Garcia, and just as it reached him he ducked under and it slid over his head. Garcia, with an extra second, leaned back as far as he could then, arched his neck back for every inch he could gain. The steel grid of the ramp stopped just under his chin. I could not tell if Sgt. West was ok or not as he was under the ramp. Ever so slowly, the 50- ton, 50 foot-long craft slid backwards into the river uncovering Sgt. West. He looked fine, at least physically—Garcia, too. I was still nervous having that much boat that close. Any misstep by the crew would have me squished into the bottom silt. Finally, I was clear of it. Relief flooded through me. It's an actual physical sensation that's hard to describe but leaves you feeling weak. I think the aftermath is worse than the event. When you have a moment to visualize yourself being pressed down into that river bottom, struggling to breathe, it unnerves you.

The landing craft maneuvered itself into a better position for picking up the rest of the troops further up river. They told the three of us to stay where we were (like we had a choice), and one of the smaller patrol boats that were escorting the landing craft would come in and get us. That gun boat couldn't get there soon enough, as far as I was concerned. I'd been stuck there in the muck for a while, and now that the tide was rolling in, the water had crept up to my waist. I knew I had plenty of time before the rising water level would be of any real concern, but it was still disconcerting.

Finally, the patrol boat eased its way close in to our position. The operator of the boat nudged the bow into the mud of the river bank just below Sgt. West and Garcia. I was just off to the side of the boat when it came to rest. A couple of crewmen were at the bow and began to reach down to help pull Sgt. West and Garcia aboard. As I waited my turn, the boat began to slide backwards off of the bank a bit on account of the actions of pulling the other two aboard. It happened quickly: the boat free of the mud began to pivot into me, caught by the current of the incoming tide. I didn't even have time to yell. The boat was going to roll me over.

I had another one of those experiences when your actions outrace your thought process. I reached up and barely managed to wrap the fingers of my left hand around one of those rope cleats they use to tie the boat to the dock. At the same time, I reached back and threw my M-16 upward in an arc, hoping it would find its way into the boat. Then I grabbed the cleat with my right hand as well. I started to pull upward as hard as I possibly could and at the same time tried to kick my legs free of the mud. I was starting to get bent over backward by the hull of the boat when I began to feel my legs moving just a bit, and a moment later they broke out of the mud's hold.

I was momentarily elated at my escape from the river bottom when I realized the stern of the boat had caught more of the current and was swinging in toward the bank. If I lost my grip, I'd slide right under the hull and get squished between it and the river bank. I desperately needed on that boat, and once again I needed to pull up. I really don't know how I managed to get aboard; fear of death and a full dose of adrenaline surely helped. Somehow, I pulled myself up high enough to swing my leg up and hook it over the lip of the gunwale, then I rolled myself over onto the deck. The two maximum exertions within seconds of each other had left me totally spent. I just lay on the deck, my chest was heaving, and I was gasping for breath. I was truly at the limit; I could not have done anything more. Gradually my respirations returned to a normal state and I sat up. I was relieved to see my rifle; my toss had been good. I wouldn't have to explain why I didn't have it.

Our boat moved out to the center of the river and edged up close to the side of the landing craft, and the three of us transferred over to it. It was all but dark now as I climbed down into the well deck. With everybody now aboard, the captain revved up the engines, and we headed for the main channel and the route back to Saigon.

Most of the guys were lying on the bottom of the well deck, using their packs as pillows and quickly nodding off. Everybody was totally beat. We had been tapped out before the double stream crossings; now we were at a new low. Added to that was my own personal misadventure with the boats that put me in a state of physical depletion that I had never experienced. Conversely, my mind was wide awake. I just knew I wasn't going to fall asleep, not with all my senses keyed up into that super aware mode that I seem to enter after encountering high stress situations.

This time, though, I didn't have that "high" feeling that I had on the helicopter flying up out of the valley back in War Zone D. No, this time, even though I was every bit as aware of my surroundings as my last episode with the phenomenon, I just had a deep sense of gratitude for still being alive. I felt calm, relaxed and very mellow. I decided to climb up on the catwalk between the inner and outer hulls. It was only about 18 inches wide with a 5 foot drop to the steel floor of the well deck on one side and a 5 foot drop into the river on the other, but that wasn't going to bother me much after the day I just had. I was soaking everything in, just glad to be alive, I guess, and super appreciating just being able to feel. I lay back against my backpack, legs outstretched, and felt the warmth radiating from the steel hull that had been baking in the sun all day. I heard the thrumming pitch of the engines and felt their soothing vibrations in my fatigued muscles. I was enjoying the warm breeze; in my altered state, it felt more like a caress. The sky was clear and full of stars, and man, they seemed to be shining down on me that night. If that landing craft hadn't skewed to the right at the last second or if that cleat on the patrol boat had been an inch higher, I probably would not be here to tell you this story.

We probably had been in the channel for about an hour when the moon began to rise on the eastern horizon. It was nearly full and looked larger than normal. The bare trees along the river were backlit by the silvery orb, and the moon shine traced a rippled path across the river. Off to my left was a wall of cumulonimbus clouds that became visible, thanks to the lunar light beams shining on them. There must have been a high-pressure front sweeping in from Cambodia. The cooler air was displacing the warm, sending it upwards of 20,000 feet or so, creating a squall line of thunderstorms. The towering clouds were many miles away, but you could clearly see the lightning, incandescent and powerful. The thunderbolts rolled up and down the squall line like flashes going off along the red carpet at the Oscars. It was a beautiful scene on either side of the boat. The moon seemed incredibly bright. I pulled out a cigarette and lit up, my first one in many hours; it tasted great, and I could feel the nicotine course through my body. It was light enough that I saw a large crane or egret take off and gracefully fly along the river bank. I think that that night was the most sublime I had ever experienced, and it contributed greatly to the sense of serenity that had come over me. I was alive, I was breathing in not only air but all the beauty and majesty nature has to offer. I was in a state of utter contentment.

Unfortunately, contentment has a short shelf life in Vietnam. I spotted a hunter killer team of helicopter gunships working over an area about a mile away from the river. Their tracers stitched the night air with bursts of red laser-like streams of lead, impacting their targets on the jungle floor. I didn't know if they were supporting some of our troops or out looking for targets of opportunity. Regardless, someone might be dying out there. Suddenly, the spell was broken; I began my retreat back from reverie to reality. Sobered now, daydreams dashed, Louie Armstrong was no longer singing "What a Wonderful World." As if to hammer home the point, the wall of thunderstorms that had looked so mesmerizing in the distance was now looking ominous as it closed in on us. The wind had shifted and it was bringing that chill you feel before the storm reaches you. It feels refreshing at first, but you know what's coming. I climbed down off my catwalk perch as those first drops began to hit. They felt cold and they were big, leaving wet splotches the size of half dollars on my fatigues. We were soon enveloped by it. No more stars, no more moon, just a teeming downpour, crashing thunder, and brilliant flashes of lightning. There was no cover in the open well deck, and all of us were soaked to the bone in no time. Adding to the discomfort was the uneasiness that comes with being in a big steel boat in the middle of a river in the throes of a lightning storm.

Luckily, the storm was fast moving, and the worst was over in a half hour or so, leaving us to wait out our destination in a light rain. Finally, we pulled into the canal off the Saigon River that our little bridge was on. Our usual group was staying at the bridge. Trucks were there to take the rest back to the cement factory. The ramp was dropped, ending a long, long day. I walked up the road to the bridge. Because of the rain, I'd be sleeping in the bunker. I was wet, cold, hungry, and exhausted. The bunker was dank, musty, and smelled of rat droppings and urine. The vermin lived there while we were away and sometimes when we weren't. Either way, I was too tired to care.

CHAPTER EIGHTEEN
FNG'S

Several days after our excursion into the Rung Sat, we went out on a run-of-the-mill sweep of some paddies. They sat several miles south of an operating base alongside a dirt road that ran between a couple of the bridges we guarded. Our platoon was providing security for that base, and we spent our nights there.

When we returned from our mission, we found out that we had a few new guys ready to join us. They were fresh from the states, or from "The World." Everybody has been the new guy at one point or another in their lives: a new school, a new job, a new organization, what have you. Most people have experienced some of the worries of the new guy. Will I be accepted? Will I fit in? What role will I play? Being a new guy in Vietnam presented those problems and a whole lot more. For starters, FNGs (fuckin new guys) were considered problematic until they proved otherwise. How would they react if they came under fire? How well will they hold up humping the boonies or slogging through the paddies? Will they be reliable? Will we be able to count on them? Consequently, they were rarely met with open arms. In some units that incurred heavy casualties they might even be met with hostility. One reason for that is they could be taking the place of a popular platoon member who was killed or wounded badly enough that he would not return. Maybe the guy was a hero; who wants to try and take the place of a hero? Again, in units involved in heavy combat the guys already there didn't want to make any new friends. It was hard enough losing the ones you had; you didn't need to make new ones, only to lose them.

My unit didn't fit into the heavy combat category, and none of our new guys were met with hostility—more like indifference, at worst. Nevertheless, the aforementioned questions needed to be answered before they were fully accepted as one of the group. Until that day came, they remained the FNG (fuckin new guy), a cherry, or just "fresh meat." Two of the new guy's names that I remember were McDonald and Fuller, and they stuck out like sore thumbs: fresh-faced, wearing brand new jungle fatigues, and sporting shiny boots.

I was very fortunate to come over as a unit. It spared me a lot of the angst that the FNG's endured. I can well remember my first few days in the field, how stressful they were. The apprehension and the anxiety of suddenly being in a combat environment can be overwhelming. But at least I was with people I knew, and that was important. Being able to share that stress makes you feel stronger. The platoon was a support system that helped you through those first few days. Having a buddy with you bolstered your fortitude to deal with adversity.

The new guys didn't have that support system; they were on their own, they wouldn't know a soul in the unit. Can you imagine what that must have been like for a young kid, getting dropped off in a jungle clearing by the evening supply chopper and entering a completely foreign world?

He's standing there with the boxes of C-rations, plastic jugs of water, a case of smoke grenades, and extra batteries for the radios. He reports to the lieutenant who, not having time for anything other than "what's your name?" shuffles him off to the squad most in need of men.

He looks around at the leaden skies and feels the mist turn to drizzle. His new squad leader points out a spot on the perimeter and tells him to dig a foxhole there before he does anything else. Other guys are doing the same. Some are building lean-tos out of ponchos and sticks in an attempt to keep out of the rain. A few might be heating some C-rations or grabbing a last smoke before dark. One might be re-reading the letter— for the tenth time— that he got from his girlfriend. Everyone is tired, they humped all day under heavy packs, they have stuff to do. No one has the time or inclination to be the welcoming committee for the new guy.

It's hard to take it all in; it feels surreal. Less than a week ago he was saying goodbye to all his folks at a backyard picnic. Now he's standing in a small clearing, surrounded by jungle, in a cool rain, and 10,000 miles away from home. And if all that isn't bad enough, there are people out there in the jungle who would kill him if they got the chance. He pulls out his entrenching tool and using his foot plants the spade in the soft soil of the jungle floor. As he leans down to pry the first shovelful of dirt out of the ground, he gets a strong whiff of the moist earth. If he's anything like me, the first scent of that soil will stay with him forever, and every time he comes across it, it will remind him of that first night in the bush.

The squad leader checks on him, tells him his guard hours, and warns him not to fall asleep on his shifts. Not to worry, if there is one person who is not going to fall asleep that night, it's the new guy. He'll be lucky if he can go to sleep when he's *not* on guard. He's going to be peering out into the blackness of that jungle wall, not being able to see a thing, but he'll be hearing lots of things. The nocturnal comings and goings of the creatures of the night, the rain water dripping off the leaves, maybe even the obscene call of the foul- mouthed lizard. It will be a long scary night for the first-timer, and he'll relish the first hint of light cresting the treetops that will mark the end of it.

Mornings are as busy as evenings: getting something to eat, filling canteens, taking down your poncho hooch, and packing your rucksack for the day. Mostly, people are just telling the new guy what to do. "Saddle up, we move out in 5," the sergeant calls out, and the newbie begins his first day humping the boonies. His fatigues are still damp from the overnight rain, and they won't get a chance to dry because of the sweat that will soon be pouring out of his not quite acclimatized body. He'll soon be cursing that sun he was so happy to see a few hours ago. The straps from his backpack are digging into his skin and every so often he jerks his shoulders up, trying to reposition them. He'll learn quickly. Now he knows why he saw a lot of guys wearing towels around their necks before starting out in the morning. There are a lot of lessons to be learned, usually the hard way. You won't have to be told twice to be on the alert for red ants after you've been bitten by the fiery little pests. Add in the leeches, mosquitoes, centipedes, and snakes, and the new guy realizes it's just not the enemy he'll be fighting.

He'll probably spend a couple afternoons really thirsty because he drank up all his water. It's easy to do those first days when he isn't used to the heat and humidity and the effort it takes to hump the boonies under a blistering sun. Resisting the urge to drink is difficult at best, impossible at worst. But that desire to drink will ebb as the days pass. In a few weeks he'll start to look like everyone else: his fatigues will be bleached and faded by the sun, ground in dirt, and stiff and crusty with salt rings. The leather parts of his boots will have all the dye leeched out, leaving them more gray than black.

The other guys will eventually come around, *if* he's pulling his own weight. The sharing of hardships eventually brings people together, and the new guy will feel like a member of the group, but maybe not a full-fledged one. If the group he has joined had been in combat together a certain bond was created among them, and until the new guy experiences a similar situation along with them, he will always feel like he's not quite one of them.

CHAPTER NINETEEN
CORDONS AND SEARCHES

Our brigade lost 18 men in August, an uptick in action due to our excursions out of the AO into places like the Rung Sat. Of those fatalities, my battalion accounted for 3 of the KIA (Killed in Action). The battalion also had 21 wounded, mostly in A and D companies. My company B continued its run through the raindrops. Although things were happening all around us, we made it through the month unscathed.

September 1st saw the command of the brigade turned over to General Heyward because General Mitchell's wounds caused him to be evacuated back to the states for medical care. (As mentioned earlier, Mitchell and our battalion commander, Colonel Behm, were wounded when an RPG hit their command boat down in the Rung Sat.) AO Laura was a disappointment to the higher-ups who wanted more results than we were getting. Our sweeps of the area, while beneficial in the amount of enemy arms caches found, were not resulting in any contact with the enemy. Our many nightly ambushes were also fruitless. To try and change those dismal results a new strategy was employed beginning in September. We started a series of cordons & searches in AO Laura as well as points deeper in the delta.

In theory, a village thought to support Viet Cong activities would be surrounded and then thoroughly searched for weapons, with the hope of ensnaring some Viet Cong in the process. Several companies in the battalion would encircle a village during the middle of the night. Then in the morning another company would enter the village to begin the search. Any Viet Cong trying to escape would run into one of the units making up the cordon. Along with the search company was a contingent of Vietnamese interrogators and translators. Our company was involved in several of these new missions in the coming weeks, both as the search unit and the cordon unit. In between we continued our sweeps, bridge guarding, and observation activities at the Ruff Puff forts.

I have a lot of memories of this period but they are all jumbled together, and I'd be hard pressed to pinpoint their exact time and place. Generally speaking, it was September, October and November of 1968. Most of our time was spent in AO Laura but side trips were made to places like the Rung Sat, to areas south of our AO, and a new area for us called the "Pineapple." I'll cover the Pineapple separately, later.

We covered a lot of ground during those months: on foot, by truck, APCs (Armored Personnel Carriers), helicopters, and something new for us, the Navy's Mobile Riverine Force (less formally, the Brown Water Navy). They looked so menacing plowing through the murky water, one after the other, dark green and bristling with weaponry. They made the Army's LCMs look naked by comparison. They had multiple machine guns on either side, a twenty millimeter cannon and rapid-fire grenade launchers. Their crewmen were outfitted with flak jackets and a type of shorts made of the same material that I had never seen before. The shorts wouldn't have been practical to walk in, but the Navy didn't have to worry about that.

Their boats were called ATC's for Armored Troop Carrier, or "Tango" boats. These boats were escorted by gun boats called "Monitors" after the famous Civil War Ironclad of the same name. They had machine guns, two cannons, and flame throwers capable of sending liquid fire 150 yards. All together in a line, churning up the water, they looked very formidable. The sight of them made me nervous. Where were they sending us that we needed this kind of firepower?

The ATCs turned into the river bank and dropped their ramps so we could enter. The insides were quite different from the Army's boats. Whereas we sat on the metal floor of the well deck on the Army boats with no cover, the Navy boats had individual seats mounted on collapsible legs that would crush on impact if the boat hit a mine. They also had a cover over the troop area to keep out the sun and rain. We were traveling in style, but the fact that we were in this armada was unsettling.

We headed south on the Saigon River for about an hour before turning into a series of smaller and smaller canals. It got to the point where at most 10 feet separated us from the canal bank on either side. The nipa palms grew up along the banks and up and over the canal. From inside the well deck it looked like we were floating through a green tunnel.

We finally reached our destination and disembarked. We walked up from the canal bank where many sampans were pulled up out of the water and were lying haphazardly along the shore. As we approached the village, I sensed a difference about it than other villages we had been in. Maybe it was the quiet, no one was making any noise. That made me uneasy. It soon became obvious that this place was dirt poor. The thatched hutches were in need of repair; they looked shabby and gave the whole village a forlorn look. The villagers looked no better than their homes. Their clothes were well-worn and most of them were in their bare feet. But the biggest difference was in their demeanor. I'd been in friendly villages, mostly close to the capital. I'd been places where the people studiously avoided even looking at you, but this was the first time I'd encountered faces full of contempt for us. Depending on the individual, you might be seeing fear, hate, or disgust. This place had no kids rushing to greet us, flashing peace signs and asking for candy, cigarettes, or C-rations. The younger ones were clinging to their mother's legs, and you had to wonder what they had been told about us.

Not surprisingly, there were no males of fighting age about, just women, kids, and old men. We began a search of the village huts; it was sad how little they had of value inside of them. We found nothing in the way of hidden arms, and I left the village carrying no more than the images of all those accusing eyes.

That experience didn't help my mood much. I struggled to make sense of the war, and trips into villages like that didn't help. As I neared my 6th month in-country, I'd been feeling a little blue and on a number of occasions spent some days in the doldrums. Usually a stint on a bridge or fort snapped me out of it, but I slipped back into it easily when returning to the field. When you are 19, six months is a long time; add in a war zone and time slows to a crawl. I guess it was a combination of things that had me in a bad state of mind. I was tired of being wet all the time. I was tired of C-rations. I was longing to wake up in a bed with a roof over my head. I missed my 10 o'clock TV time when I'd make a batch of popcorn, mix up a glass of Tang and watch my favorite TV shows: Mission Impossible, I Spy, Run for Your Life, and the Dean Martin Show.

I knew that I had been incredibly lucky up to this point and was afraid that my good fortune couldn't possibly last. I kept having this recurring fear of being shot in the belly and falling into a rice paddy and having that putrid water rushing into the wound.

And then on some days it was just incredibly boring, especially when on a cordon. You went out in the middle of the night to surround some village. If nothing happened by 7 or 8 in the morning, nothing was going to. But you might spend many hours sitting on a rice paddy dike waiting to pull out. I used to carry paperback books in the waterproof pack used for my gas mask. I can recall on one occasion sitting on a paddy dike out in the middle of nowhere reading "Valley of the Dolls" by Jacqueline Susann. It was a massive best seller of the time. The subject matter couldn't have been further away from my world, but that was the point. Still, the incongruity of escaping into the juicy lives of Hollywood starlets battling barbiturate abuse while I was sitting on a muddy rice paddy dike with a M-16 laying across my lap has stuck with me all these years. Reading novels was only a temporary respite, however, and the reality of Vietnam could show its ugly side at any time, as the next cordon and search mission proved.

Our company was the search element for the mission, so we had the Vietnamese interpreters and interrogators along with us. The village we were searching was fairly large and relatively close to the capital, and it had the appearance of being friendly. Lt. Russo was there so I had the radio and tagged along wherever he went. One good thing about carrying the radio was that you were in the loop as to what was going on. I had no idea what the reasons were, but the Vietnamese started picking out people for questioning. There was a lot of loud talk and accusations about one thing or another. Eventually they segregated some of those who were questioned, tied their hands behind their backs, put sand bags over their heads, and had them sit on the ground. Then one at a time they took them to a hut that the interrogators expropriated for the purpose of further questioning.

The hut was at the far end of the village, and only the Vietnamese intelligence guys and a couple of Americans who were accompanying them went down there. The Americans weren't part of our unit. Naturally we were curious about what was going on in the hut. We eventually found out that the Vietnamese interrogators were using field telephones as part of their questioning techniques. The Army field telephone had a hand crank connected to an internal electric generator to power the phone or recharge the battery. There are terminals on the field phone for wiring hook-ups. The Vietnamese hooked up the wires on the phone to different body parts on the Viet Cong suspect and then cranked the phone, giving the prisoner a strong jolt of electricity.

I heard that the Americans in the room didn't take part in the torture but were witness to it. The only conclusion reached was that they condoned it; this was an American operation with the Vietnamese only along to assist. I'd heard stories about this practice before, but I'd never been that close to torture actually taking place. Torture is not part of the US Army's standard interrogation policy, but as in any war, standards are not always met, and many times a blind eye was turned when it came to torture. A couple of soldiers were court-martialed for taking part in a waterboarding incident with a Viet Cong prisoner near Danang in 1968. A reporter happened to be nearby and took a photo of the torture; it ended up on the front page of the Washington Post. That sealed their fate.

One story that made the rounds while I was in Vietnam was the helicopter interrogation technique. It's probably apocryphal but nevertheless the story went like this. Two Viet Cong prisoners were placed in a Huey helicopter. The chopper flew up to a thousand feet or so and the questioning of the prisoners began. The prisoners refused to give up any information. While the one prisoner looked on, the other was tossed out the open door of the helicopter. Having an instant change of heart, the remaining prisoner sang like a canary. I don't discount the possibility of it, but I have never run across a reputable source verifying it, and my guess is that it is something that has gained the status of a jungle version of an urban legend.

There is no doubt how the North Vietnamese treated American flyers shot down over North Vietnam. Many of the US Airmen were taken to the Hoa Lo prison, better known as the "Hanoi Hilton," the moniker sarcastically given the prison by the captured pilots in Hanoi. They were systematically beaten and tortured for years. Pilots incarcerated there spent long periods in solitary confinement in small cells with nothing more than a straw mat to keep them off the cement floor while sleeping and just a bucket in the corner for sanitary purposes. Prisoners suffered broken bones, teeth, and eardrums. They were given the bare minimum of food to keep them alive and medical care was withheld.

John McCain, the Republican nominee for president in 2008, is easily the most well-known of the Vietnam POWs. He was shot down over Hanoi in 1967. He broke several bones while ejecting from his crippled aircraft. Upon capture, he was taken to a hospital where over the following 6 weeks he lost 50 pounds and his hair turned white. He was dumped into the prison in a near-death state where other prisoners nursed him back from the brink. He spent the following two years in solitary confinement. In total, John McCain spent 5 $1/2$ years in prison and returned home with permanent disabilities as a result of his treatment.

Thinking about it now, I'm trying to conger up what my feelings were upon learning that I was in such close proximity to the application of torture. Upon reflection, I can't remember being overly upset. It just seemed like yet another step toward my total disillusionment with the war. It just kept adding up: the dubious tactics, the body count, the kill ratio, the corruption, the black market, officers who saw the war as a career maker, and now torture. You had to have your head in the sand to miss it; it was all around, and it didn't bode well for the future of our involvement in Vietnam.

I finally hit the halfway point in my tour—6 months in, 6 months to go. The first half seemed like forever; I expected no less from the second.

Meanwhile, back in the world:

July 17, 1968— In Iraq, a successful coup d'etat lands Saddam Hussein the job of being the head of security forces in Iraq.

July 20, 1968— The first international Special Olympics games are held in Chicago.

July 1968— The Beatles record "Hey Jude."

July 1968— The Doors release "Waiting for the Sun." August 4, 1968— The Byrds sing "Born to be Wild."

August 20, 1968— Soviet Union invades Czechoslovakia to suppress a budding freedom movement.

August 28, 1968— 10,000 war protesters gather in Grant Park downtown Chicago to voice their opposition to the war. In what would be called a "police riot," over 100 protesters needed medical attention and 175 were arrested.

August 28, 1968— Tammy Wynette releases "Stand by your Man."

September 1968— McDonald's franchisee, Jim Delligatti of Pittsburgh, creates the "Big Mac." It sells for 49 cents.

September 7, 1968— Women's Liberation groups gather in Atlantic City to protest the Miss America Beauty Pageant. The feminists collect "instruments of female torture" such as: cosmetics, false eyelashes, hair curlers, bras, and girdles— and toss them into trash cans for symbolic burnings.

September 8, 1968— first "Miss Black America" is crowned. September 24, 1968— "60 Minutes" premiers on CBS.

September 30, 1968— Roll out of the first Boeing 747 Jumbo Jet

September 30, 1968— The 900th US combat aircraft is shot down over North Vietnam.

July, August and September saw the loss of 3,477 more troops, bringing the total for the war to 29,064.

CHAPTER TWENTY
HALFWAY HOME

October's start was no different than September's end: sweeps, cordons, searches, bridges, and forts were all continued as before. One new change was our AO was extended to the west because another battalion moved out of that area.

Six months into the tour and our original company was barely recognizable from the one that arrived the first of April. Captain Conner was killed in the chopper crash; Captain Williams replaced him. Our platoon leader, Lt. Stockman, was made an advisor for the Vietnamese Army, and Lt. Russo took his place. Our platoon sergeant was gone, replaced by Sgt. Ralstonr. Our platoon was down to about seven original troops; the rest were lost in the infusion to other units or wounded and did not return. We were now a mix of originals, FNGs, and infused troops from other units. The end result was achieving the Army's wish that our whole unit would not have the same rotation date back home. The bad side effect of this policy was that our company was in an endless state of flux. The constant comings and goings of troops was detrimental to unit cohesion, and the influx of new officers (to replace those who fulfilled their six-month combat assignments) only served to exacerbate the problem. Luckily for us, Lt. Russo presented no problem, but some of the other new officers did. It seemed as though they needed to put their stamp of authority on the unit. This did not go over well with the soldiers as it was unnecessary and unproductive considering the troops' state of mind at this point in the war.

There were a few instances where the new officers felt compelled to show who was in charge. The first instance involved a long sweep through the paddies and fruitless searches among the nipa palm lined stream banks. We were met by trucks at a road we reached at the end of the day. We climbed aboard the trucks for the ride back to base. As we were passing through a village, a frustrated troop threw a smoke grenade on the roof of a thatched hut as we drove by. I think a lot of troops found the attitude of the Vietnamese vexing, like the visible hatred we saw in the villagers in the delta or even at best, the indifference seen in so many. That lack of appreciation led to aggrieved feelings by some of the troops. Those sentiments sometimes led to incidents like the grenade being tossed. I'd seen it before: the troops resented the Vietnamese, blaming them for the circumstance they found themselves in and sometimes willing to take it out on them. I'd seen guys hurl C-ration cans from moving trucks at kids running alongside and begging for food. For the most part, this was an infrequent occurrence, but it was reflective of how more than a few troops felt. Unfortunately, most of the troops didn't fully understand the quandary most villagers felt they were in. The Vietnamese government had not shown an ability to protect them. If they showed allegiance to the capital they might expect a visit in the middle of the night by the Viet Cong. Thus was their unwillingness to show any signs of acceptance, let alone gratitude, to any Americans in their midst. It was just a matter of survival for them.

Fortunately, the smoke grenade didn't catch the hooch on fire. Unfortunately, one of the new lieutenants witnessed the event and was determined to make a point out of it. He called the truck convoy to a halt and threatened to make us all walk back to the base like we were still in basic training. To be sure, the troop shouldn't have thrown the smoke grenade, but the lieutenant, being new, was clueless as to why the incident might have happened. The combination of field-tested troops with rookie officers was a recipe for antipathy.

A week later we found ourselves on a long sweep through the rice paddies in our newly expanded area of operations. It was a particularly hot and humid day, we were out in the open with no shade, and the paddy mud seemed unusually hard to slog through. Being strong-legged, I usually handled the paddies at least as well, if not better than most, but I was having an unusually rough time of it that day. I had the radio (which added about 30 pounds to my load), the smoke grenades, and an extra battery to carry. The straps of my pack were digging in, and I kept jerking up my shoulders to relocate the straps and alleviate some of the pressure. I got to the point where all I was concerned about was that next step—then the one after. I didn't know what the problem was, maybe I was dehydrated. I was struggling big time.

Somehow, I made it to our pick-up point alongside a road and promptly lay down in exhaustion to await the trucks. I wasn't the only one ruined that day, and no one was in the mood for doing anything stupid. One of the new lieutenants ordered somebody to do something of dubious worth and was rewarded with some lip. Enraged at this, he threatened to make us all walk back the way we came—through the paddies. The very idea of it was absurd; there was no way that was going to happen, and besides that, he didn't have the authority to make it happen. He made himself look foolish, lost respect from the troops, and set himself up for a difficult time ahead.

Another incident that demonstrated the folly of the Army's 6-month combat rotation for officers happened in AO Laura, of all places. At least ¾ of the company had at least 6 months in-country, some had more. The Army, for some reason, thought it was a good idea to drop a young lieutenant with no combat experience into this situation. Bad Idea!! We were pulling a routine sweep of the paddies in AO Laura when we ran into some trouble. I certainly wasn't expecting any, that's for sure. After all, it was AO Laura and nothing was happening there with the exception of rocket launches into Saigon and some mortar attacks on the cement factory (our battalion firebase) every now and then. This was just going to be a long, hot walk in the sun until the typical afternoon deluge soaked us through and through. Just an ordinary day.

We were walking in a long single file atop a dike that separated a couple of rice paddies. I was around the middle of the group looking ahead at the guys in front of me. Suddenly, I noticed a couple of them react to something that I did not see. Less than half a second later I heard the sound of gunfire coming from a line of nipa palms about four or five hundred yards away off to our left. I, and everybody else immediately dove to the right into the paddy to afford ourselves the cover that the dike provided. It was only about 18 inches high, but it was protection enough from the bullets flying our way. The first guys to move actually heard the bullets whiz by them before they heard the report of the guns.

Fire was immediately returned toward the nipa palms. The new lieutenant was crawling up and down our line of troops telling us to get ready for an on-line assault on the nipa palm stand. *WHAT? Is he crazy? He can't be serious!!* That was the general reaction of the troops when told of the plan. Yeah, I'm sure he was taught this maneuver back in officer school; we were taught it in Infantry Training. I remembered it well because at the time I can recall hoping to God that I never had to take part in one. Whether you survive or not is just blind luck. In effect, what you are saying is: "I'm willing to lose some people to gain a certain objective." But what kind of objective is a stand of nipa palms? Not one you would keep. There was no rational reason for us to get on line and slowly slog our way across four or five hundred yards of muddy rice paddies. There was no way we could avoid taking casualties. The Viet Cong, from concealed and fortified bunkers, would probably fire on us till we were halfway there then hightail it through the palms to the nearest village and blend in with the population. The odds were on their side. I didn't want to do it. It was my longtime nightmare come to life. It was the one fear that nagged at me: the gut shot, the falling in the paddy, the filthy water sloshing into my wound.

Couldn't the lieutenant see how little would be gained at who knew what price? Maybe he felt it was his duty to engage the enemy; the rest of us were well beyond that. If he was looking for glory, he'd be alone in that quest. Whatever his motivation, he was under a full-court press to change it. The guys were trying to tell him it wasn't a good idea, but he seemed intent until a couple of sergeants were finally able to reason with him. We had already done our job: we provoked a reaction, and now we could pour the heavy firepower on its source. Good enough for me, whatever the results.

He called off the assault and we called in an artillery mission to blast the nipa palm instead. The enemy fire ceased after the artillery shells began to fall in the trees. We searched the area after the shelling but found nothing. I was really relieved not to have had to make the assault. I didn't want to die for a body count, a kill ratio, or a stand of palm trees that would have been left behind an hour after it was all over. It was a close call, one that could have cost some lives, maybe my own.

It had been some time since I was fired at directly. Luckily, the Viet Cong were a long way off. A couple of the guys were a little freaked out about hearing those first bullets zip by them through the air. Neither realized what it was until they heard the actual crack from the rifles. The noise lagged behind the bullets' arrival by about half a second because of the distance involved. Somehow getting shot at is even more unsettling if you can hear the bullets fly by.

Once again, I was hugging dirt, lying in the stinky muck of a rice paddy, and not minding in the least. It afforded me protection just as that trench did up in War Zone D. That's where the similarities ended. I understood why we had to leave the protection of the trench up there. We were so close to the enemy that we couldn't call in an air strike or helicopter gunships or artillery for that matter. But this time it was way different. The Viet Cong were hundreds of yards away, not tens of feet. It would have taken forever to cross that open expanse of rice paddy; we would have been sitting ducks. I was concerned that the Viet Cong had decided to ratchet up the war a bit in AO Laura after months of keeping a low profile in the area.

About a week after coming under attack in the rice paddy we were out on a night maneuver to cordon a village about a mile away from the large fuel depot at Nha Be. I'd seen the tanks along the river bank several times when traveling down the shipping channel to the Rung Sat and other points south. Several big companies stored gasoline there: Shell, Caltex, and Esso were represented. We had taken up positions around the village and were settling in for a few hours on watch when we heard some gigantic explosions to our east. In a matter of seconds, we saw flames shooting upwards of 100 feet or more, and from more than one source. The Viet

Cong had either rocketed or mortared the fuel depot. We all joked that the companies must have missed their protection money payment for the month to the Viet Cong. The flames were so bright that we could see our shadows. There was no way to quench that large a fire, so they just let the inferno burn itself out. A dirty grey pillar of smoke cast a pall over the area well into the next morning. It looked like my worries about the Viet Cong stepping up attacks might be coming true. Less than a week after the attack on the fuel depot they rocketed the facility again with the same results. Apparently, the source of the rocket fire was from the east side of the Saigon River—our next mission would be to set up our mortars on the east side of the river on the bank opposite Nha Be.

The "River Rats" of the 1099th Transportation Company showed up one morning with their landing craft to take us down river. We loaded up our mortar tubes and boxes of ammo and headed toward our new position. The trip didn't take long. We were still in the periphery of Saigon, so the promise of a friendly reception was strong. The mike boat nudged up to the bank and dropped the ramp. We unloaded and walked down a short trail to the prettiest little village I had ever seen. The footpath was a hard-packed smooth surface, tan in color, nice and wide and bordered by palm trees, those kind that seem to sweep up from the ground in a graceful curve. The rice shoots were tall in the paddies, and their bright green hue looked almost luminescent as they undulated in the soft breeze. The setting was absolutely idyllic. The broad expanse of the river was on one side, the paddies extended out as far as I could see on the other. The village itself, while composed only of thatched huts, had a look of freshness about it. It was neat and tidy and the local population looked as welcoming as the setting. The place was made for a National Geographic cover story.

We set up our three mortar tubes and began the "laying-in" process. This involved orienting them and placing the aiming posts. We filled some sandbags for mortar pits and built a bunker for ammo storage, and our mortar section was ready to go. But not really. We had fired some illumination and some H & I (harassment and interdiction) rounds, but lack of practice and the influx of new people and the exit of the originals had left us less than proficient. Since I became the radio operator for Lt. Russo, I hadn't taken part in the day to day operations of the mortars and thus hadn't even taken part in the illumination or H & I firing. It didn't really matter how accurate you were with illumination or H & I because the former just lit up the sky, and the rounds landed by parachute. The high explosive rounds used for H & I were fired into "free fire" zones and were by their nature random and haphazard.

An actual fire mission was another story: it required precision and the utmost accuracy to ensure the safety of the troops we were supporting. No one wanted to be responsible for a "friendly fire" incident. Friendly fire is the term used to describe an incident when US troops accidentally fire on other US forces resulting in casualties. This happened many times during the Vietnam war; there are many documented cases, and probably many more that were not. There are many reasons for it happening, a lot of them attributed to the "fog of war," defined as the confusion, chaos, and bedlam that is part and parcel of combat. The fog of war leads to mistakes of position, both of your own and that of the enemy, and also of identity (mistaking your own troops for the enemy). Sometimes the incidents are the result of both.

One of the worst cases during the Vietnam war involved an Air Force bomber dropping a 500 pound bomb on troops of the 173rd airborne brigade who were in heavy contact with the enemy. The errant bomb killed 45 and wounded a like number. During the battle for Hamburger Hill a battalion commander called in for helicopter gunships to attack an enemy position prior to an assault. The gunships mistook the commander's position for the enemy's and blasted it with rockets and machine gun fire. 35 troops were wounded and two died, including the commander who called the mission. Combat is often a fluid situation: troops are moving in response to changes on the battlefield and can become separated from one another and become unsure of each other's locations. This happened to us up in War Zone D when we encountered the enemy base camp. Our platoon and the second ended up almost directly opposite each other with the enemy base camp in between.

Many incidents of friendly fire were caused by artillery and mortar support. When troops are in heavy contact with the enemy they are obviously under a great deal of stress and are usually in a great hurry to call in artillery or mortar fire. The combination of speed and stress can easily lead to mistakes. The same thing goes for the unit providing the support: fellow troops are in trouble and are depending on you to deliver ordnance on target in a short amount of time. Mistakes can be made in a number of ways: the wrong grid co-ordinates can be called in, and errors can be made in deflection, elevation or number of charges—the results can be tragic.

For all those reasons and more I wasn't particularly happy when Lt. Russo told me I was going to be assigned to the mortar platoon's FDC (fire direction center). I was a natural choice since I was always with the lieutenant as the radio operator. As mentioned, we were all out of practice, and the lieutenant was going to take this opportunity to get the platoon back up to speed in case we were ever needed. My first order of business was to learn how to use a plotting board. The plotting board was used to transfer grid co- ordinates from the map. Once your position was located on the grid, you had a reference point to conduct a firing mission. First you needed to plot the target's location on your grid, then you would get the direction from your location to the target, then the distance. From that you referred to firing tables to get the proper elevation of the tube and then how many charges to be attached to the round.

Our first few days at our new position consisted of reacquainting ourselves with the mortars and learning how to work as a team with all the new personnel. In the early hours of the night we plotted H & I fire into the jungle out beyond the paddies. I was starting to get the hang of it but worried what it would be like trying to figure stuff out when speed and accuracy were paramount. Luckily, I never found that out since calling for mortar support was usually secondary to artillery support. We were almost always in range of an artillery battery, and it only made sense to call on guys who worked fire missions all the time.

Using mortars in the delta was problematic: due to the very soft ground around the paddies, the base plates slowly buried themselves into the earth. At one point, we had a mortar tube with us on a nighttime mission. I can't remember what or why, but we were called on to use our mortar. More than likely it was a request for illumination. I would have remembered if it was a support of troops' mission. Anyway, the only ground around remotely capable of supporting the base plate was a rice paddy dike we were close by. We set up the tube, got oriented, and started firing. Each round fired pushed the base plate deeper into the dike until it got to the point that you had to get on your hands and knees to look through the sight. It was a pain digging it out the next morning.

I guess we stayed about a week at the little bucolic village. I enjoyed my stay; we got to know the folks a bit and played around with the kids every day. There were no more attacks on the fuel depot across the river, so someone decided we should re-cross the river and go back to what we were doing before.

We went back to our bridges, which was nice, but we had some new ones to cover as our AO responsibilities had expanded. One new bridge we guarded was the "Y" bridge. As the name implies the letter described its shape. It was the scene of very heavy fighting during the May offensive. We set up on the south side of the bridge close to a dump. The bridge was very important as it fed one of the major roads to the south from the city. The Viet Cong had managed to blow up a span or two in the area, so an increased troop presence was added to the bridge security. Along with the troops were geese—*yes*, geese. Seems like they make a heck of a racket when disturbed, so it was thought that placing them around all the piers was a good idea. The piers were encircled with barbed wire and concertina wire, but between the wire and the pier was home to several geese—watch dogs, if you will— waiting to alert.

Our new bridge location was close to a dump and the rat population was pretty high in the area. Although I had unknowingly eaten rat and now knew that it was not at all uncommon for the Vietnamese to use it as a source of protein, I was still disgusted at the sight of them. These rats were *big*. I won't exaggerate like some guys do and say they were the size of a cat or even a beaver as I once heard. No, not that big, but scary big nonetheless. They probably look bigger in your mind's eye because when you see one of the ugly critters you automatically think of disease, rabies, and even the plague. They didn't give us plague shots for nothing, did they?

One dark and stormy night (seriously), I had crawled into my little hooch made from a poncho to try and keep out of the storm and the soaking rain. In the midst of a thunder storm I was never more than semi-successful at keeping dry. Regardless, I'd drifted off to sleep; but in Vietnam you're never fully asleep, always on the edge of consciousness, or so it seemed. I was in that state when I felt my pant leg move against my leg. The winds were gusting, and in my half sleep I thought that was what caused the sensation. A short time later I felt something on my chest. I opened my eyes to see a rat staring at me. I freaked out and destroyed my little hooch trying to get away from the rat. That same night, McDonald, one of the new guys, was bitten on the end of his nose by a rat. He was sent back to Long Binh for a long series of rabies shots. I bought a hammock from a local Vietnamese the following morning.

Another incident, somewhat comical I guess, happened on the "Y" bridge. Saigon was under curfew and no one was allowed to cross the bridge into Saigon after dark. About three in the morning we heard a cyclo motoring up to the bridge. All of us on guard pointed our weapons at the driver and yelled: "*dung lai, dung lai, stop, stop.*" The driver stopped and began telling us why he had to get into Saigon. None of us knew enough Vietnamese to know what he was talking about, so he went into a pantomime of a woman having a baby and pointed to his wife in the front seat. "Ok, ok," we said. But we had to make sure, so we went over to the wife and tried to explain to her that she needed to let us make sure she was really pregnant. So, there we were on the bridge in the middle of the night, feeling this lady's belly to make sure she was really with child. We finally let them pass, and presumably they went off to the hospital.

This was about the time we started not going out on ambushes if we could avoid doing so. Our AO had expanded to the west, and we were not sure what the booby-trap situation was in these new areas. In AO Laura, the threat had been minimal, but the new area was an unknown to us. That, coupled with the resurgence of Viet Cong actions, engaging us out in the paddies and their rocket attacks on the fuel depot, suggested they were ending their recent inactivity. As noted earlier, the bottom line for the troops at this point in the war was just to get out of it alive. With that in mind, when the first opportunity presented itself to fake an ambush, no one seemed to have any grave reservations about doing so.

It happened one night when we were ordered to go to a village and wait there till nightfall, and then under cover of darkness move into our assigned position. No one was thrilled with moving through an unknown area at night: booby-traps were hard to find in the day, practically impossible at night. We moved into the village as ordered, but after the sun went down one of the troops said: "Why don't we just stay here and call our sit-reps in as though we were on-site." It just took one person to say aloud what was probably in the mind of many others. The die was cast, and we settled in for a night in the village. We called in our sit-reps and no one was the wiser.

Done once, it was easier to do the next time the opportunity presented itself. We weren't alone. One night was spent with 2 other ambush squads in the same village. It was a relatively safe venture as long as you were in a village. If that wasn't possible, you were better off getting into your assigned position because your location would be plotted, and you didn't have to worry about H&I fire.

The practice did lead to a couple tense moments. One night we holed up in a cemetery on the edge of a village. There was a mini mausoleum there that held the mummified remains of a woman. This could be viewed through a plate glass window. *Eerie.* Anyway, in the wee hours of the morning we spied a squad of troops out in the distance coming our way. They were too far off to recognize whether friend or foe. We couldn't call in and ask if they knew of friendlies in the area as we weren't supposed to be where we were. They turned out to be Vietnamese army forces but making contact with them without being fired upon was a bit dicey.

Another time we were in a village and bedded down behind a wall. About 9:00 PM a squad of armored personnel carriers rolled into the village and took up positions about 50 feet from the wall. There was a danger of being fired upon if someone was a little trigger happy when and if we tried to identify ourselves. We decided to just ride out the night hidden behind the wall. We weren't supposed to be there, and if an officer was with the armored cavalry unit he might feel compelled to report us. It was a long night, and it was with great relief we watched the unit pivot their tracks and clank out of the village at first light. I felt no guilt about the subterfuge, just relief in not going out. My only concern was for the young buck sergeants who went along with the program; they would pay the heaviest costs if we were found out. Thankfully we never were.

LBJ, the initials of our president, were routinely seen and heard in the media of the day. It was LBJ this, LBJ that on a daily basis. But in Vietnam, there was another LBJ, and this one was no more popular than the other. The Army built a stockade at their main base at Long Binh, and that prison soon became known informally as Long Binh Jail—and not too long after that as simply LBJ. LBJ had a bad reputation among the troops. Nobody wanted to end up there for a couple of reasons. First, you were in trouble for something or other, and secondly, any time you spent in LBJ was considered "bad time," meaning it didn't count toward your 365-day tour. If you spent two months in LBJ your tour of duty was extended to one year and two months. I never talked to anyone who spent any time there, but we did have a guy in the company who pulled his weapon on an officer, and he ultimately ended up there for the offense. He never returned to the company. By the end of August, 1968, the jail was at near double the capacity it was built for. Tensions in the jail were running high, fueled by the racial antipathy that was simmering on the main bases all over Vietnam.

For the recently drafted black guys, the war seemed onerous. It was a burden they felt was foisted upon them by a country that treated them as second class citizens. These young black men came of age in an era of race riots, inner city burnings, and the assassination of Martin Luther King.

Black leaders of that time, including Martin Luther King, were calling Vietnam a "white man's war" that blacks were being sent to fight. A program started by Secretary of Defense Robert McNamara called Project 100,000 seemed to lend credence to the charges. Squeezed by manpower shortages, the Defense Department lowered the mental and physical standards for military service to allow more people to be eligible for the draft. It was felt by the black community that the lower standards would impact inner city minorities more than white suburbia.

Another way blacks felt shortchanged was in the inequities of the student deferment program. During Vietnam you could avoid the draft by going to school. As long as you were going full-time in either undergraduate or graduate studies, you were exempt from the draft. Poor blacks who didn't have the money to go to school could not avail themselves of that path to escape the draft, but the same could also be said about poor whites as well.

Unlike today when no draft exists, being in the National Guard or the Reserves was considered a safe haven from going to Vietnam. In the wake of growing resentment to the war, the president was afraid of the political consequences that would ensue if he called the Reserves and Guard to active duty. Hence, their rolls were filled, and getting in was difficult. The perception of the day was that you had to "know" somebody or have some political influence to be accepted into those units. Most blacks had neither and felt that the Guard and Reserves, like the student deferments, were avenues to escape the draft that weren't open to them.

For the above reasons, blacks felt that they were taking more than their fair share of the casualties in the war. This perception fed the escalating racial tensions, becoming more and more palpable throughout the main bases in Vietnam. It must be said, though, that by the end of the war casualties among blacks and whites reflected their percentages in the population as a whole. But in August of 1968 perception outweighed truth by a wide margin.

These young black draftees arriving in post-Tet Vietnam brought a host of issues along with them. They felt they were there, in part, because of the inequities of the draft. They felt that they were taking more casualties than their white brethren. They grew up in the midst of civil rights marches, sit ins, and protests. They witnessed that era of relatively peaceful, civil acts of disobedience devolve into more militant stands. Black leaders like Malcolm X, Bobby Seale, Huey Newton, H. Rap Brown and Stokely Carmichael were forming groups and starting movements that moved beyond asking for civil rights to demanding them. The militancy of the new Black Panther Party and the combativeness of the Black Power Movement had to have had some influence on these men. Then came "the long hot summer" of 1967 which saw riots in over 100 American cities. "Burn Baby Burn" became a rallying cry for the rioters. In March of '68 Martin Luther King, the embodiment of the civil rights movement, was slain, triggering another round of race riots across the country.

It is little wonder that a small but significant number of these latest arrivals to the war would be predisposed to rejecting the Army's right to send them into combat to fight for rights they didn't believe they had at home. As a consequence, Long Binh Jail had a prison population made up of not only drug users and thieves but combat refusals as well.

The prison population was predominantly black, and the racial tensions in the jail were no less than anywhere else in Vietnam. Drug use was rampant, and new procedures calling for strip searches pushed some troops over the edge. The black troops starting attacking the white troops the evening of Aug. 29. About 200 troops took part in the riot. Many more did not and managed to escape the prison via a gate the perimeter guards had opened for them. The inmates burned and destroyed tents and buildings, but the riot fizzled out after several days. The final tally showed 63 military policemen injured and 62 inmates injured with one fatality. The inmates earned themselves 129 court-martials.

We heard rumors about a riot at the Long Binh Jail, but at the time I didn't know the extent of it or that it was racially motivated. Surprisingly, with all the media attention on Vietnam the story was not a major news event back in the states. One likely reason for this was that the Democratic National Convention was held during the week leading up to the LBJ riot. The convention drew crowds of protesters to Chicago to vent their frustrations with the war. The day before the riot in Vietnam, Aug. 28th 1968, the city of Chicago had its own riot. About 10,000 protesters gathered in Grant Park for a legal anti-war rally. The mayor of Chicago at that time was Richard Daley. He made sure he had plenty of police and National Guardsmen on hand to take care of any disturbance, and they amassed alongside the park.

I imagine there was plenty of anti-war rhetoric and undoubtedly thousands chanting anti-war slogans like "Hell no, we won't go" and "Hey Hey, LBJ, how many kids did you kill today." At one point, a young lad lowered the American flag from a pole in the park. The police, infuriated by this time, broke through the crowd and began beating the boy, thus starting what was to be eventually called a "police riot." It was a big, big, story played out on national television. The Vietnam riot was overshadowed by the events at the convention. Be that as it may, both riots were emblematic of the fractures in American society back home and in the Army in Vietnam.

If theme songs were assigned to years, Bob Dylan's "The Times They are a-Changin'" would be a shoe-in for 1968. Who could argue? Martin Luther King, the face of the civil rights movement, was assassinated; an aspiring presidential candidate, Robert Kennedy was assassinated; the incumbent President, LBJ, was not going to run again, a casualty of the war now himself.

Although history shows us that the tipping point of the war had been reached in terms of public support, many people were reluctant to suspend their belief that the war was necessary. In many cases, this turned out to be a generational schism: younger folks were clearly anti-war and older folks were unable to make that leap until the war dragged on a couple of more years. While Vietnam was the catalyst for this generational gap, with opponents and supporters of the war providing the friction that sparked the widening divisions in American society, it wasn't the only issue of the time.

It is only fair to point out that the numbers of people actually taking part in protests or living the life of a counter culturalist may be small in terms of the entire population; however, they can come to symbolize an entire generation. This was so in the case of the late sixties. For every war protester who actually took to the streets there were a hundred others who felt the same. For every civil rights marcher there would be a hundred others who believed in what he was doing.

The times they were a-changing in Vietnam as well. By the time the Long Binh jail riot occurred I could see a pronounced shift in attitudes among the troops. As I mentioned before, most of us that came in-country post-Tet were conflicted about the war; the new guys we got were not. The Army was changing before my eyes; it had turned a corner and it was not going back. Discipline, the foundation for any army, was breaking down. There was such a lack of respect between certain segments of the Army that unless you were in a combat unit there was no sense of unity or purpose, even if that purpose was only to keep yourself and your buddies alive.

In addition to racial issues between races there were also frictions within races. The new black guys held some of the older black sergeants with disdain because they toed the line and were Army green first and black second. These older NCOs had chosen the Army for a career because when they enlisted in the late fifties or early sixties it was one of the few places a black man had a real shot at advancement and a good career. This held little sway with the new guys who accused them of being "Uncle Toms."

There were also issues with career minded officers and sergeants who saw Vietnam as an opportunity to advance their careers at the expense of their men. They were of the ilk who believed: "this is the only war we got so let's take advantage of it." I don't want to paint with too broad a brush here. There were plenty of career soldiers who didn't fit that mold, but there were enough to definitely cause some trouble.

One interesting way to follow the progression of the war from a noble undertaking protecting the world from communism to a misguided, misled, misadventure that was in the end a misfortune for all is to look at how the troops looked from year to year. In 1965 when the buildup started, arriving troops looked the part: haircuts were short, mustaches were regulation, if you saw one at all, and uniforms were uniform. Everyone looked alike. If one guy had a helmet on, everyone had a helmet on. If one guy had a bush hat on, everyone had a bush hat on. Boots were bloused, buttons buttoned, faces shaved. That was the story in the early days when the troops really felt like they were fighting for something. As the years went by with no discernable progress despite platitudes by the government that said "we could see the light at the end of the tunnel," the troops in the field could see no improvement, and as the country turned the corner on the war, the troops followed suit.

The new troops who were drafted came with attitude, reflecting the changes that were occurring back in the states. Like most of the guys they would do what they had to, but they didn't have to like it, and they didn't want any of that regimented Mickey Mouse military crap pushed down their throats. By the summer of '68, the new troops and the ones already there who could no longer believe in the cause were ready to push the limits. The troops let their hair grow longer, mustaches were grown bushier, and sideburns began to appear. Black guys were growing afros and wearing "slave bracelets," symbols of black solidarity. Raised fists, the "black power" salutes, were practiced as well as elaborate "dapping" handshakes.

The camouflage helmet covers, and to some extent flak jackets, became billboards for soldiers wanting to let others know how they felt about the war. In the early days, you would not have been able to get away with marking up your helmet or flak jacket with whatever your heart desired. But as the war wore on, many company level officers let their troops express themselves as a way of letting them vent off a little steam, relieving the pressure everyone was feeling so things wouldn't blow up in their faces. It was the same with smoking marijuana or having girls in the bunkers. The platoon leaders knew what was going on, but they turned a blind eye to it as long as the guys did their jobs out in the boonies.

The helmet graffiti ran the gamut from "War is Hell" to "Kill a Commie for Christ," from girlfriend's names, unit designations and maps to philosophy. "Born to Kill," "Born to Die," and "Born Loser" were well represented. One verse seen on a helmet summed up the writer's perception of the entire situation rather well.

> The Unwilling
> Led by the Incompetent
> Doing the Impossible
> For the Ungrateful

Some helmet art referenced the president, such as, "put LBJ on point" or "LBJ's Hired Gun." Skulls and the Grim Reaper were also represented. But the most popular, and the ones I remember seeing the most, were "short- timer" calendars, months or days left in Vietnam, usually scratched out as the time went by, and DEROS dates, that very important date that every soldier in Vietnam knew from the day he got there. DEROS was an acronym for "date estimated return from overseas." The word PEACE was prominently displayed as well as the peace symbol. And last but not least, the very popular letters: F, T, and A. Usually printed boldly in block letters, "FTA" was universally recognized as "FUCK THE ARMY."

Troops were also starting to wear some very unmilitary type items like "love beads" (normally a hippie accoutrement), and "peace medallions" on chains. Some would attach rosary beads to their helmets, which looked oddly out of sync placed next to the pulled grenade pins that some guys liked to display on their helmets. We certainly lacked military decorum back in those days, and military courtesy wasn't practiced openly in the field. Many guys wore no rank (officers included), no saluting was practiced, and there was a minimum of yes sir and no sir.

It was always a shock when you returned to the main base where the Army still practiced being an Army and expected you to do the same. Things were not nearly as loose on the main bases and you could get into trouble if you crossed the line, so you didn't see guys doing what we did in the field. They weren't wearing love beads or walking around out of uniform, but they also wanted to go home and they knew their DEROS dates and they had short-timer calendars as well. I must say their calendars were more artful than the block letter months I printed on my camouflaged helmet cover with a ball point pen then scratched out as they passed by. Usually, when a guy on a base got to be a two-digit midget (less than 99 days to go), he'd get a short-timer calendar to hang in his area. There were different styles but the most popular was usually a naked woman. Usually just a simple line drawing, sectioned off to look like a paint by number project. The soldier would then fill in a block each day: 99, 98, 97, etc., etc…finally getting to 3, 2, then 1. The last block typically was placed where you might expect a hormone fueled young man to put it. The happy day had finally arrived!!

That was pretty much the situation: every unit was was different, and some were worse and some were better in regards to morale, racial tension, and drug use. I think I was one of the ones in a better situation. We had a good group of guys. The infusion of new guys from the other units had caused no problems. Even the brand new guys from the states blended in as well as could be expected for FNGs. The only drug in use was marijuana, and none of the guys used it when we were out on missions.

As it went, we weren't very military. We weren't too concerned with how we looked—or acted for that matter. We were fortunate to still be doing a lot of small unit stuff, off on our own away from the higher-ups who sometimes were clueless as to the state of affairs in the field.

Our platoon had been lucky in regards to the racial issues as well. We got two new black guys in the infusion. One, Thornton Maxwell III, was bi-racial. (He was the one I spent a long night with when he got himself into a semi-comatose state on rice whiskey and scared the hell out of me when I couldn't wake him) The other black guy was named Gary Meinert. He grew up on a farm in Iowa. I would later share a moment with him as well. Both were good guys. The weapons platoon had no real issues, at least overtly, on either side of the racial divide, white or black. Our present group of guys (the few originals of us left, the infusion group, and the FNGs) seemed devoid of even the slight undercurrent of tension that percolated below the surface of a few in the previous group but was never exhibited.

All things considered, as I was nearing the halfway point of my tour I considered myself rather lucky. I knew it could all go bad in a minute, so I appreciated every day we had in AO Laura. We were making more and more trips outside the AO, but we always came back to the bridges and forts that we were so familiar with by then.

CHAPTER TWENTY-ONE
HANSEN'S DISEASE

Practically four months had passed since Lonnie asked me about the brown markings that had appeared on my back. The skin was discolored and a little leathery. Being on my back, though, I would never even know that I had them without someone telling me. They didn't hurt at all, and whatever it was didn't seem to be spreading.

I began my journey to find out what I had by meeting with my platoon medic. He hadn't a clue. Then I tried the most senior medic in the company and walked away with similar results. As the company was always chronically short of troops, and to all appearances I was in no need of immediate care, I was told to wait until we got to a base camp to see the battalion surgeon. That didn't happen any time soon, so weeks went by without knowing what was up. When I finally got my chance to see the battalion surgeon, a real doctor, he proved to be no better versed than the medics. He suggested going to see someone at the brigade level. Nothing had changed regarding my company commander's willingness to let people go back to the brigade main base, but at least I had the battalion's surgeon recommendation that I do so. That helped eventually.

We were serving as base security for our battalion when the company commander finally told me he could spare me for a trip back to Long Binh. I flew back to Brigade Main Base on the evening resupply chopper, all the while thinking how nice it would be to get a shower, sleep on a cot, and have a real breakfast the next morning. It was almost worth having whatever I had for this mini-break from the boonies. Unfortunately, the brigade medical staff had no answers and told me I needed to see a dermatologist at the 93rd evacuation hospital. That wasn't possible that day so I flew back to the boonies none the wiser. But I did have a good night's sleep, I was clean and I ate some real food. Well, at least compared to what I was used to eating. So, the trip was far from a bust.

Weeks passed again before I was afforded the opportunity to fly back for a visit with the skin doctor. I wasn't too concerned about it, to tell the truth; it hadn't troubled me in any way and it hadn't spread. I went into the office, took off my shirt, and he examined me. He asked a bunch of questions and wrote a bunch of notes. He told me he did not know what it was and wanted to take a couple biopsies from my back. I said ok, and he had me lie down on a gurney. At this point I was starting to get a bit concerned. Didn't anybody know what the hell this was?! He told me he was going to give me a couple shots of Novocain at the biopsy sites so the tissue removal would be painless. He was right about the first one but not the second. For whatever reason the Novocain did not take and the biopsy hurt like hell. He got a couple glass jars out and filled them with some type of clear liquid then placed the tissue in the jars. He said he was going to take them to the lab or something and left the room.

I saw the chart he had been writing in lying on a table, so I decided to help myself to a look. Mistake!! I've had a habit of picking up a lot of information of dubious value, and somewhere along the way I'd heard about Hansen's disease. So, when I picked up that chart and read those words, I had a sick feeling come over me. Yeah, it said Hansen's Disease with a question mark after it. Just reading the words in connection with my name was a shock. Unfortunately for me, I knew that Hansen's disease was another name for Leprosy. Sadly, that was the extent of my knowledge. At once, images of leper colonies filled my mind: poor souls with disfigured faces, outcasts from society who lived segregated lives in remote locations. Suddenly I'm seeing myself in one of them, and the picture I'm painting doesn't look very pleasant. Too bad I didn't know more; the following days would have been filled with a little less anxiety. I didn't mention anything about me spying on my chart, and the doctor didn't mention anything about what he wrote on it, either. He said they would get word to me about the results of the biopsy. It would take a while since the tissue samples had to be sent to the Philippines for testing.

When I got back to my unit I didn't tell anyone about what I had seen on the chart. It was darkly amusing when a few of the guys were ragging on me for getting a couple easy days off and asking me if they could rub my back and get some for themselves. I spent a worrisome week or so before I found out the results. Curiously, I have no recollection of how I found out the results, what exactly it was, or how you get it. All I really remember is the relief at finding out I didn't have Leprosy. Unfortunately, it would not be the last of my skin problems.

Diseases were common in the tropical climate of Vietnam: high temps and humidity along with the rainy season were the perfect environment for fungus and bacteria. Skin diseases were at the top of the list but usually only led to temporary disability. Other diseases in Vietnam could be fatal.

Malaria for instance; the US Army alone had over 40,000 cases—78 of those ended in death. Other illnesses accounted for a further 364 deaths.

There were any number of ways you could end up dead in Vietnam without being shot by the enemy. The official US Army statistics on deaths in Vietnam is enlightening. Some of their categories seem curiously named and beg for clarification. Nonetheless, I'll list some of the many ways you could meet your end by non-hostile means.

Drownings	777	Accidental Self- Destruction	680
Illness	364	Intentional Homicides	199
Malaria	78	Accidental Homicide	552
Hepatitis	17	Accidents	834
Heart Attacks	175	Vehicle Crashes	864
Suicides	354	Aircraft Crashes	2182
Burns	97	Misadventure	820

These aren't all the ways, but you get the idea. The US Army alone suffered 7,193 deaths from non-hostile reasons.

CHAPTER TWENTY-TWO
THE PINEAPPLE

We were back at my favorite bridge: the one that crossed a small stream that fed into the canal on the southern edge of Saigon. We were just coming off some cordon and search operations and being sent back to the bridge was always like a vacation for us. Our operation ended late afternoon, and since we weren't too far from Camp Davies, decided to visit their mess hall before going back to the bridge. We really weren't authorized to go and eat there, it wasn't our base. But the lure of real food was too great to let the opportunity pass. We had done this several times before, and nobody had said anything. We traipsed in after an operation, covered in mud and sweat, grenades hanging from our web gear, belts of machine gun ammo crisscrossed over our chests in Mexican bandito fashion, and carrying all our weapons. We'd just grab a tray and get in the serving line. Some even made way for us. I'd like to think that it was because we looked like a bunch of bad asses, but I think we just smelled really bad.

I fell back into the familiar routine of the bridge which included lazy days checking traffic, playing around with the kids, and enjoying the luxury of dry feet. In the evening after curfew I'd string my hammock up on the bridge's truss angles. The girls showed up later on, and we listened to music and ate up some goodies we purchased at Camp Davies. It was a sweet deal that I never tired of. I was excited to have at least a few days on the bridge when Anh, one of the girls, told me we were going to the "Pineapple." Not only was this news that I didn't want to hear, I heard it from someone who really shouldn't know where I was going to go before I did. It reminded me of all those times up in the Rocket Belt when we exited the jungle at a pick-up point along a road, only to find a bunch of Vietnamese waiting to sell us whatever.

We all had heard of the Pineapple. It possessed a reputation no less intimidating than that of the Rung Sat. Choosing between the two was sort of a what's your poison kind of deal. What kind of misery do you prefer? The Pineapple was a name given to an area that began just west of Saigon and extended to the Cambodian border about 25 miles away. Parts of the land were used as plantations in the French colonial era. A vast network of canals laid out in grid pattern laced the area to provide irrigation during the dry season and transportation during the harvest. The canals were dug by the Vietnamese for the French at near slave labor rates. Some of these plantations grew pineapples, and even though all of this land had been abandoned after the war began, pineapples could still be found growing there. They were a treat for the GI's who came across them, and in due course the entire area became known as the Pineapple. For such an innocuous sounding name, it turned out to be a very dangerous place.

I found the Rung Sat special zone to be more physically demanding than the Pineapple. However, we never stayed more than a day in places like the Rung Sat, whereas we would stay a week or longer in the Pineapple. And that was the big difference, the Pineapple wore you down. Day after day drudgery combined with lack of sleep and the constant mental stress of moving across land chock-full of booby-traps left the troops physically and emotionally exhausted. I learned to dread hearing the words, "You're going to the Pineapple."

Lt. Russo told us the following day what I already knew from Anh, "We're going to the Pineapple, and be prepared to stay at least a week." We weren't going to take the mortars with us, so we would be operating just like the 3-line platoons, which meant a steady diet of sweeps and ambushes. Since we were constantly on the move, never in the same place overnight, we had to pack everything we needed for an extended stay. We were loaded down again like we had been up north in the Rocket Belt and War Zone D. We had been spoiled by all the single day missions or at most an overnight on a cordon that didn't require us to be pack mules. That was about to change. Up north we were weighted down, but the ground was firm; in the south, we didn't carry as much but the ground was soft. To the west, where the Pineapple was, we had to contend with both heavy loads and mud.

We left the bridge early the next morning and formed up on a single lane dirt road that was bordered by lush green rice shoots on either side. We split up into groups of 5 or 6 and spaced ourselves out along the road. I was packing the radio and feeling the extra weight already, and we hadn't been doing much more than standing around waiting. Upon hearing the approaching flight of helicopters, we separated again—3 on one side of the road, 3 on the other. It facilitated a fast boarding when the choppers landed.

The flight was flying in trail formation one after the other in a line like the beads in a rosary decade. The ten Hueys in olive drab livery flew a downwind leg before turning back to land into the wind. It was always a pretty sight to see them bank over and begin their descent, the pitch of their rotors catching the air at a different angle producing that classic "whup-whup" sound that has become an audio icon of the Vietnam War. The flight lined up on the axis of the road, all ten, nose to tail, gliding down to our position. The lead ship, upon coming abreast of the first group on the road, pulled its nose up, flared, and settled to the ground in a whirlwind with the following 9 repeating the ballet.

We rushed aboard, bent over against the rotor wash, squinting in an attempt to protect our eyes from being peppered by the blast of dirt kicked up by the rotors, stepping on the skid, rotating to sit on the floor and sliding out of the way for the next guy. The choppers, also called slicks, had no seats and flew with the doors open. Once aboard, the pilot pulled up on the collective, increasing the pitch of the rotors. The blades took a bigger bite of the air, and the chopper got light on the skids. Rising to 4 or 5 feet off the ground, the pilot pushed the cyclic forward, the nose dropped, and the aircraft picked up speed and started climbing into the sky.

Flying in a chopper is a sensory experience. You could feel the vibration through the floor we sat on. The open doors offered an unobstructed view, even more so when sitting on the edge while the chopper banks over and you can almost look straight down—at least it feels like that. The interior is buffeted by the wind and you can feel the air get cooler as you gain altitude. We usually flew at 1500 feet. It doesn't sound like much, but it's usually at least 5 degrees cooler at that altitude; combine that with the wind, and a sweaty body can feel pleasantly cool in no time.

We flew due west, following the canal that marked the city limits of Saigon. It always surprised me to see how abruptly the city ended; there seemed to be no transition. It was city, then rice paddies. We continued west, crossing over the Van Co Dong River which flowed through the heart of the Pineapple. Easy to see was the horseshoe bend created by a meander in the river from which the forward brigade base took its name: Fire Support Base Horseshoe Bend. We started our descent shortly after passing the river. I looked down on all the canals; they looked like the grid iron of a football field.

The Pineapple was a free-fire zone; no permission was needed to blast away. As we got closer to the ground, I noticed the door gunners raise the barrels of their machine guns to the ready position. The helicopters were most vulnerable when flaring to land: their speed is slow till touchdown, and then for the few seconds it takes for the infantry to get off, they are sitting ducks. Sometimes the choppers don't actually land; they'll come to a hover, 2 or 3 feet off the ground and want us to jump out. For as much as the chopper crews want us out of the helicopter in a hurry, it's no more than we want out of it. Shooting a chopper down is a big deal for the VC. Knowing this, we didn't want to be in one any longer than we had to be when they were the most susceptible to ground fire. This time around, though, things went smoothly. Our flight landed in an open marshy area, and we stepped off the choppers into a foot of water.

We had been warned about the booby-trap threat so everyone was on guard and super alert. This was an area where walking the point was going to be very dangerous. The going was slow and methodical. We tried to stay off the dikes which presented the most danger, but that wasn't always practical due to geography or seemingly arbitrary time constraints put on us by senior commanders. The point man was rotated often, so no one man was exposed more than his fair share. Luckily for me I had the radio, and RTOs didn't walk point.

By this time in the war the Viet Cong had moved past the effective but rudimentary booby-traps such as punji pits or stake traps to using explosives that were flowing into the country from North Vietnam. The explosives were easier to set up, and far more deadly. The Viet Cong were clever and didn't pass up opportunities to use our own weapons against us.

One could not help but notice, while flying over the Pineapple, the myriad of bomb and artillery shell craters all over the landscape. The B-52s in particular left a path of destruction that had to be seen to be believed. The big bombers flew in groups of three at the minimum. Some models carried as many as 108 five-hundred-pound bombs, more than 300 for the group. The bombers flew in a "V" formation and dropped their bombs at the same time, laying waste to the landscape. Craters thirty feet wide and fifteen feet deep dotted the earth in sections a mile long and half that wide. The concussion blew trees over and snapped their trunks like they were matchsticks. Not every bomb went off; every now and then a dud would impact but not go off. The VC dug the bombs up and cut into the casings to extract the explosive to make their own homemade weapons.

The Pineapple was peppered with artillery fire as well. Night after night of H&I fire from 105mm and 155mm gun batteries scattershot the area with smaller craters. Some of these rounds were duds as well. The Viet Cong took these duds and rigged them up as booby-traps. The effects of these would be devastating to a line of troops.

A common booby-trap was the hand grenade. Oftentimes fitted with a zero-time delay fuse, the grenade was placed in a tin can. The safety pin was then pulled out. The tin can prevented the "spoon" (safety lever) from flying off and igniting the fuse. A wire (fishing line, thin, clear and hard to see) was attached to the grenade, then the can was placed in a horizontal position alongside the trail, possibly attached to a tree. The wire was then strung across the trail an inch or two off the ground and attached to a tree on the other side. When an unsuspecting or careless troop walked down the trail, his boot would catch the wire, pulling the grenade out of the can. Free of the can the "spoon" flew off, the fuse fired, and the grenade exploded.

After the choppers flew off, we formed up in a long company-size line to move through the wetlands. The fourth platoon was in the trail position and pretty far back from the lead element. We were on the move for a couple of hours. Most of our thoughts were on booby-traps, so it was a bit of a surprise when a forward air controller spotted enemy activity out to our front. I'm not sure exactly what went down—my memory is failing me here—but I do remember that there was an air strike.

Bien Hoa Air Force Base wasn't far from our position and they had F-100 Super Sabres at the ready at all times. The F-100s were single-engine fighter bombers. They were painted in camouflage (matte colors of greens and browns). The ordnance hung from their wings on pylons.

Once the bombers started their circular pattern above the area, the FAC pilot commenced a shallow dive directly at the target. At the right altitude, he fired off a white phosphorous marking rocket. We watched the missile streak for the ground and upon impact leave a large white plume of smoke for the bomber pilots to home in on.

The first Super Sabre banked to the left and initiated a low angle dive toward the plume of smoke. At the correct height, the pilot toggled off two 250-pound bombs, then immediately raised the nose of the aircraft and initiated a sharp climb, wanting to clear the area as fast as possible, not only because someone might be shooting at him but to avoid flying shrapnel from his own bombs.

I followed the path of the falling bombs till right before impact then hunkered down behind the dike. I felt the explosions through the ground before actually hearing them, then a moment later felt the concussion through the air. Sometimes when the atmospheric conditions were right you could actually see the concussive effects move through the air. The jets alternated bombing runs until their ordnance was expended then headed back to base. We moved forward to assess the bombing damage but found nothing of significance to report.

We continued on with our mission, soon coming across some bunkers. We weren't fired upon, but we couldn't pass them up without clearing them and making sure no one was hiding in them. Nobody really wanted to look down inside one, fearing getting their head shot off if by chance someone was hiding inside. Clearing bunkers became a regular chore in the Pineapple. Mostly we just threw grenades down the entrance. I didn't have to clear any that day because I had the radio, but on days I didn't I'd perform this task as well. I never felt fully comfortable dropping grenades into bunkers. In the Pineapple, as in other areas of the delta prone to being covered with water, the bunkers were built a little bit up off the ground. I'd usually check it out for firing ports or other openings besides the entrance. I'd take off my pack so I could move more quickly and freely, and I approached from the rear. When I was alongside the bunker I pulled the pin on the grenade. Then I reached around and tossed the grenade in the entrance, exposing at most my hand and forearm. I'd then jump back to the rear of the bunker, giving me some cover if the grenade was tossed back out. The fuses on our hand grenades were roughly 4 to 4 and 1/2 seconds. That gave somebody a chance to pick it up and throw it back out. However, you could let the grenade "cook' in your hand before throwing it, reducing the time someone would have to throw it back. To let it cook you pulled the pin and let the spoon fly off, triggering the fuse, then you could count to two, if you were brave enough, before tossing it in the opening. None of us were too keen on doing that. I wasn't too fond of even holding it with the pin out, let alone with the spoon flipped off. It didn't really matter anyway as we never found anybody in the bunkers after our grenade tosses. Regardless, for me it was better to be safe than sorry. It was hard to forget that Bill Archer was shot dead peering into a bunker up in War Zone D.

We had used up most of the day by then and looked for a half decent place to put up for the night. My first night in the Pineapple was a memorable one for me because of the bugs. We all knew that there were bound to be lots of bugs, just because of the multitude of streams, canals, and acres of standing water in the marshes and uncultivated rice paddies. Mosquitoes were everywhere. In areas like this the usual routine before nightfall was the application of liberal amounts of bug juice (repellent), buttoning up your fatigue shirt to the neck, rolling down your sleeves, and turning your collar up.

It was a long, hard, tension-filled day and I was ready for some sleep. I had watch later on in the night and wanted some good rest before then. When I awoke for guard duty, I could hardly believe my eyes. I think I was in the middle of some sort of oriental Mayfly madness. You know—those insects that live their whole lives under water as larva or something like that and then one day out of the year they all hatch at once into insects that fly around in some demented frenzy to hurry up and reproduce before they die less than a day later.

While I was asleep the moon had risen and flooded the Pineapple with its silvery light. The gossamer wings of the flittering bugs caught the moon shine and flickered like snow flurries in a car's headlights. There were so many that I was afraid to take a breath for fear of inhaling one. I wrapped my towel around my head to cover my nose, ears, and mouth, leaving just a small opening to see out of. It was an amazing sight; I was both in awe and feeling awful. I was trapped in my towel cocoon to escape the incessant buzzing, as well as to prevent the crazed insects from flying up my nose or down my throat. It was a long turn on guard.

Day three in the Pineapple brought the mortar platoon's first casualty from a booby-trap. His name was John Everest and he was an original member of the mortar platoon. He was one the platoon's forward observers, meaning he was assigned to one of the other three platoons in the company and called in any fire missions back to the mortar squads. We didn't have our mortars in the Pineapple but the FOs stayed with the line platoons anyway.

I heard the blast from the tripped booby-trap out to our front, maybe 75 to 100 yards away. The column stopped, of course. Everything came to a halt while the medics attended to the wounded. The call for a dust-off went out almost immediately. We formed a perimeter in an open marshy area to secure a landing zone for the medevac chopper. There was more than one casualty, but I only knew John among them. My section of the perimeter was next to a small canal that the wounded had to be carried over to get to the LZ. That's when I saw it was John being carried by four troops wading across the canal. He looked up at those of us standing on the bank and smiled. He didn't look to be in any pain; the medics must have given him Morphine.

We spent the next three days roaming the Pineapple, clearing and destroying bunkers, and finding some occasional hidden arms caches. We were generally wet at least a part of every day, our feet sometimes the whole day. There was no way to stay clean, and we added new layers of filth to our bodies as each day passed. I developed a boil on my butt about two inches down from my belt line. It looked like a giant pimple. The skin was raised and red with a yellow center and was very tender to the touch.

The Pineapple wears you down after a few days, which is dangerous because you can lose your focus and make a mistake. I don't know if that is what happened to Jim Martin when he burnt his hand pretty bad with a smoke grenade, but I think it was likely that fatigue played a role. Jim was setting off a smoke grenade—the reason escapes me now—when I heard him yell out in pain. I looked over and saw him plunge his hand into some rice paddy water. I could see he was hurting bad. He pulled his hand out to look at it and saw that his whole palm was one big blister, and a green one at that. Smoke grenades usually have a very minimal fuse delay. After pulling the pin and letting the spoon fly, the fuse ignites the smoke-producing material inside, and the fire burns through the tape that covers a hole at the bottom of the grenade where the smoke pours out. Instead of throwing the grenade right after pulling the pin, Jim held onto it for some reason. Worst of all, he had his hand over the tape when the blast of flame burnt through.

My first trip to the Pineapple ended without me seeing even one pineapple. The choppers flew in to pick us up and fly us back to AO Laura. It felt great to leave.

I hardly recognized B Company when we got together for our flight to the Pineapple. By now, Blackfoot Company was a mere vestige of its former self. All the original officers were gone, thanks to their six-month combat rule. Most of the platoon sergeants had also changed. The infusion accounted for a large group of guys moving elsewhere, and new replacements from the states were filling more and more positions.

We lost people in other ways as well. They were in the minority, to be sure, but every outfit has their share of scammers trying to get out of the field for any number of reasons—mostly medical. Most of them were unsuccessful. It wasn't easy to get out of the field; the company was always undermanned. So, unless it was an obvious emergency, like that heat stroke victim out in the paddies or that guy that went berserk in the middle of the night up in the Rocket Belt, you weren't going anywhere. It took me months to resolve my skin ailment.

There were legitimate ways to escape the boonies, but they came with a price. Some guys hated pounding the bush so bad that they re-enlisted for another MOS (Military Occupational Specialty) to escape the infantry with its physical demands and mortal jeopardy. Garwood, one of our FOs, re-upped for 3 years to get an aviation slot. JP, infused to another company, didn't like his new environs and signed up for 3 more years to get into a Military Intelligence MOS.

Another way of getting out of the field was to extend your Vietnam tour for 6 months to get a better assignment. The Army was always looking for helicopter door gunners (that should have been a warning!) and extending for that job was common. It was easy to see why. I think almost any grunt in Vietnam felt wistful about being a door gunner at one time or another. Part of that yearning was probably brought out by the imagery of that chopper flying away after dropping you off in the Pineapple or the Rung Sat. You are standing there, already sweating, knee deep in mud with 50 pounds on your back, your next real meal a week away, and there's a very real possibility of having a booby-trap blow your leg off in the next few days. You watch the door gunner in his clean clothes climbing skyward into the cool air, knowing that he'll have a hot meal in the mess hall tonight then probably go to the air- conditioned club, have a beer or two, and climb into a real bed. It was a nice vision but I couldn't count how many times I'd seen the big Chinook helicopters flying back towards the air base with a Huey or a LOH that had been shot down, crashed, or mechanically disabled, slung underneath it. Reality check!

Byrdy, my old buddy going as far back as training, extended six months to get into the battalion's 4.2 mortar platoon. His goal of no more walking was achieved in that manner. Don Ocher managed to secure the company clerk job, one highly sought after because you remained on the main base.

There was one caveat to all these avenues of escape: you could not leave the company while on a mission in the field. That was understandable. It wouldn't be too hard to imagine some poor bedraggled troop doing just that after a hard day humping the boonies. Maybe he's burning a leech off his calf or heating up a can of "delicious" ham and lima beans for supper, and he sees the supply chopper coming in. If he knew he could just get on that chopper and go back to base and reup or extend, he might, on the spur of the moment, just decide to do it. I know I thought about it on some particularly bad days. But every time I was back on base and could do it if I wanted to, I had lost the desire. I was closing in on month eight of my tour and I didn't want to add six more to that. There were other reasons too. For as bad as the boonies sucked, I liked the informality of it. There was very little Mickey Mouse crap to put up with. The officers earned respect; they didn't mandate it. I had a lot more freedom, especially when on the bridges or on OPs at the forts. Oftentimes, there were only between two and five us at any of those locations. We were on our own and I really enjoyed that. I liked moving around and seeing new places: from farming villages to the hustle and bustle of the capital city, from hill country jungle to the alluvial plain of the Delta. It was an adventure, albeit a potentially dangerous one. Some guys who worked on the main bases never got further away from them than the little "Sin Cities" that popped up alongside all the big bases to provide "services" for the GIs.

I really enjoyed being able to get to know some of the people who lived in the villages or forts that we stayed at: just regular folks, rice farmers, or fishermen who weren't looking to rip you off, sell you drugs, or pimp their sister. I would never have that experience stationed on a base. I'd have missed catching rides on sampans, an evening meal of rat stew given by some gracious hosts, fishing under a starlit night with a village buddy, and cooking up the catch in the wee hours of the morning. I'd have missed hand grenade fishing— where you threw a hand grenade into a deep stream so the concussion from the blast killed any nearby fish. Then *papasan* took the sampan out and gathered them up as they floated to the surface. I'd have missed just hanging out with and having a beer and a smoke with the Ruff Puffs. I'd have missed the kids, especially; they always brightened my days.

Another thing—and this is hard to explain since I'm not an adrenaline junkie and I really did think the war was wrong and its consequences horrible—it was exciting! Skimming over the tree tops in a chopper or zipping up a stream in an airboat was undeniably a thrill. Especially, say, compared to driving a forklift around all day at a supply depot on a big base, which was the kind of mundane work that so many support troops did day after day. This was just one more case of my conflicting emotions when it came to Vietnam. I hated the war, and yet I had never felt so alive. I hated the physical effort and drudgery of the boonies yet felt a lot of satisfaction in meeting those challenges. My heart told me the war was a great mistake, yet my mind struggled to rationalize my effort to somehow justify the loss of life. I was torn in so many ways, and to be honest, have not been able to resolve all of those issues all these years later. Not the least of which was my increasing ability to distance myself emotionally from the human toll of the war. Whether that was some sort of psychological crutch to deal with the situation or not, I do not know, but either way it bothered me.

For better or worse, I was sticking it out where I was, as most guys did. Only time would tell whether it was the right decision. The next week we would spend in the Pineapple had me wondering.

CHAPTER TWENTY-THREE
TOUGH WEEK IN THE PINEAPPLE

I was back on my favorite little bridge along the canal, resting up and drying out my wrinkled, waterlogged feet. We all fell back into our bridge duty routine without effort. Lonnie and I had some free time so we decided to catch a cyclo and brave the city traffic to visit John Everest in the hospital. John was medevacked to the Third Field Hospital in Saigon after he was hit by shrapnel from the booby-trap out in the Pineapple.

The hospital was housed in what used to be a school from the colonial era. Its architecture was French Colonial: large windows, high ceilings, and shutters. On the grounds were smaller buildings that connected to the main building by covered walkways. In the back of the building was the helipad that unfortunately was all too busy. Lonnie and I saw medics pushing gurneys with wounded troops in from the helipad.

We entered the hospital and asked someone how to find John. We were directed to a large ward; it had a center aisle with beds lined up on either side, maybe twenty all told. Why, I don't know, but all the white stands out in my mind: the white metal frame beds, the white sheets, the nurses in white, and the white bandages. Bandages on everyone, and stark against the white was the red, still oozing from their wounds. I felt uncomfortable and somehow guilty for being able to walk down the aisle whole and without pain amongst this misery.

We found John; he was awake and appeared glad to see us. He was lying in bed, his legs uncovered and without bandages. From his ankles to upper thighs were ugly purple red gashes, the skin split wide enough that you could see the flesh, the result of the metal fragments ripping into his legs. John said the doctors wanted to leave the wounds open for the time being, probably to let them drain as some fluids were seeping from them. He seemed to be in good spirits, pain meds notwithstanding, and told us that he should recover fully, but it would take some time. I think it did John some good to go see him but, looking back on it, I don't see how it could have been good for me. A lot of those guys in that ward probably got hurt in the Pineapple since most of our brigade was working in that area, and I'd be going back there shortly. I pushed any thoughts of John to the far corners of my mind along with any other unpleasant mental pictures I had formed from the ward.

I told Anh we were going back to the Pineapple; she was less than surprised. Going to the Pineapple sucked but leaving the bridge to go there made it seem even worse. We choppered in again, same as the last time.

I had the radio again, thank goodness! We started out the same as we had on our first sweep a couple weeks earlier, only we didn't get very far before the first booby-trap was tripped. The point element of the lead platoon was wounded in the blast and the medics rushed to the front to care for them. The Medevac choppers were called and the rest of us sat down and waited till they got there. This routine was repeated too often in the coming days. It was strange how I dealt with this mentally. I was only 50 yards away from a life or death situation, but I didn't allow my mind to travel those few yards. Better not to dwell on it. It was easier to do now that I barely knew anybody in the other platoons. My platoon had been on its own so much in the last few months that we had no opportunity to get to know any of the new people who came in. Just as well, a lot easier to deal with if there's no chance you'll know who was wounded.

The dust-off chopper comes, the dust-off chopper goes. Time to press on. Less than two hours later it happened again. The same routine, the medevac flew in and flew the wounded out. There was no respite. We started out again with the third point element of the day. The nerves of the guys out front must have been on the ragged edge. We were moving again but slowly and deliberately. The frustration level in the company was high. The Pineapple was living up to its billing. We had five casualties already— and hearing that two other companies out in the Pineapple sustained fourteen casualties to booby-traps in only three days didn't help. Naturally, we weren't keeping up with the plan of the day. Our new battalion commander was flying out over the area in his C&C (command and control) helicopter and radioed down to Captain Williams, wanting to know why in the hell we hadn't reached our check points on time. I can't even begin to tell you how infuriated the guys got upon hearing this. I'll just quote one of the troops to give you an idea: "If that mother fucker flies over us again I'm going to shoot him down." One guy might have said it aloud, but he wasn't the only one thinking it. Having a guy flying around in his helicopter complaining about our slow progress on the ground was pretty hard to take. A battalion commander is usually a lieutenant colonel, meaning he was too old to actually have had any on the ground experience in Vietnam. So, when he puts his push pin on the map he doesn't really know what it takes to get there. Nonetheless, we moved out again and finished the day without further injury. The night was routine: alternating rain showers and masses of mosquitoes.

Our second day was notable for a booby-trap that was spotted by the point element, a 250-pound bomb. It was a dud when dropped by a bomber, probably a bad fuse, but this was rigged to blow if someone hit the tripwire. I can only imagine how bad it might have been: the point element would have literally been no more, and the casualty count would have been very high extending a long way back in the column.

Ordinarily, booby-traps were not defused or rendered harmless; they were blown in place. Usually, say if a grenade was found, some C-4 explosive was set next to it with a blasting cap and a time delay fuse. When the C-4 blew, it blew up the grenade along with it. We usually just fell back on the trail about 50 yards or so till it blew, then continued back on down the trail. This time, though, because of the size of the booby-trap, the company moved at least 500 yards or more away from the bomb site before it was blown.

Day three proved as disastrous as the first. Two more booby-traps were hit, and we suffered four more men wounded. Dust-offs flew in again and again. Everyone was uptight. The odds were worse because we started splitting up. Platoons were doing searches on their own, meaning more people on the point. Sgt. Ralston came to our platoon in the infusion, and he was nearing the end of his tour when we started going to the Pineapple. He didn't have to go on point; his job was really to order someone else to, but he rarely did. When we were on our own as a platoon, Sgt. Ralston usually took the point. It was a gutsy thing to do, even more so because he was so short (time left in tour). He might have thought he was the best man for the job, or maybe he didn't want to feel responsible for someone he ordered on the point getting blown up. I don't know the answer to that but admired his bravery no matter the reason.

Day four saw the arrival to our company of the mine and booby-trap dogs. These dogs and their handlers were trained to detect booby-traps. The dogs could sniff explosives and nose out trip wires. Everyone was happy to see them... *they* would be on the point. Unfortunately, before the day was out, both a dog and his handler were added to the casualty lists. Being a dog handler in Vietnam was dangerous business as they were usually leading the way, be it a booby-trap, scout, or tracker dog. Thousands of dogs served in Vietnam over the war years; 230 of them died in the process and an even greater number of handlers.

The Pineapple was taking a heavy toll on the company and morale was very low. The frustration level was really growing, you couldn't help but ask yourself if we were accomplishing anything at all. Sure, we found some arms caches and we blew up a few bunkers, but the end result didn't seem to be anywhere near worth the investment in blood. The next couple days produced even more casualties. By the end of the week, the wounded count was somewhere in the teens. Everyone's spirits had hit bottom. We were tired both mentally and physically. The weather and terrain sapped our energy, and the constant anxiety of tripping a booby-trap played on our psyches. Even though I didn't have to walk the point because of carrying the radio, it didn't mean I was immune from the danger of them. If someone had tripped that 250-pound bomb, it would have taken out a couple squads, at least.

As far as I knew, no one had died from the booby-traps that week, but the sheer number of the wounded was unsettling. Fortunately, all the wounded that second week in the Pineapple were guys I didn't really know, which made my usual routine of slipping into emotional detachment in the face of the ugly realities of the war far easier. I guess you could say I was aware of what I was doing but was unable to confront myself with that truth just yet.

The upper command figured we needed a rest and assigned us to provide security for the cement factory, our battalion fire support base. That was pretty good news; we could dry out and have at least one hot meal every day. Our platoon staked out a couple bunkers along the southwest wall of the compound for our home for the next few days. It was nice: besides pulling guard at night, we had a lot of free time to write letters, read a book, or just goof off. We got to take a shower and put on some clean fatigues. It still amazes me how those two things alone can do so much to make you feel better. You would be surprised at just how much filth you can carry around in your pores. As you scrub your skin, the dirt just keeps coming to the surface and joins the water to form dirty brown rivulets that course down your body. You keep at it until you've washed away what you thought was a tan, and the water stays clear as it runs off of you. Add some fresh clothes and you feel like a new man.

One of the first things we heard news-wise was that President Johnson made a speech declaring a bombing halt over North Vietnam in the hopes of spurring the peace talks along. I wasn't sure if this was a cause for hope or not, considering the lack of any real progress so far. It took months just to agree on a site. At any rate, it wasn't likely to change anything for my situation any time soon.

Life at the cement factory was good: after a few days of hot food and a few nights of reasonable sleep I started to feel human again. The bunkers allowed us to stay mostly dry so that our cuts and scratches had a chance to start healing. When you are wet all the time, they don't scab over very well. Of course, being young helps you rebound rather quickly from the trials of life in the boonies. My boil burst while at the camp, so I had a chance to tend to it and keep it dry, lessening the chance of it getting infected.

Our "easy time" flew by at the cement factory and before we knew it, it was time to leave. We got orders for a multi-day mission in the south of our AO to begin the following morning.

We got to see a movie on our last night. It was a Vietnam War flick called "The Green Berets," and it starred John Wayne. The movie was projected onto a makeshift screen made of a sheet and some 2x4's. The movie wasn't intended to be funny, but it was so far removed from our experience that we couldn't help but laugh at the standard war movie clichés and be somewhat bemused at the over-the-top pandering patriotism. Nonetheless, it was fun, especially hearing the sarcastic and sometimes ribald comments yelled out by the audience.

A number of APCs showed up at the cement factory to transport us south. The APC stood for Armored Personnel Carrier, officially the M-113 APC. Basically, it was a box on bulldozer tracks and was designed to carry infantry troops inside the box. The M-113 was light, relatively speaking, as it was made of aluminum. It was modified quite a bit after arriving in Vietnam to better meet the needs of the troops. Extra armament was added and armor. The ones we used had a 50-caliber machine gun up front and a M-60 machine gun on either side. One big change in Vietnam was that everyone rode on top, never inside. The M-113 did not stand up well against mines, and if you were inside when one was hit, your chances of survival were slim. The crews sometimes laid sandbags on the floor of the APC to better absorb a blast.

We all climbed aboard for our trip south. After an hour or so, we stopped on a dirt road and jumped off. The armored cavalry left us behind, and we started our mission that consisted of several cordon and searches over the next few days. We were in rice paddy country, which meant, at the very least, our feet would be wet for some time to come. According to the calendar, the rainy season should have been ending, but apparently, it didn't get the word.

Nothing of note happened during the next few days, other than the fact that I was constantly wet. I was on a cordon, a couple nights in a row where I literally ended up sitting in water overnight. I'd been really lucky up to this point with my feet; I never suffered any blisters, or anything else for that matter. But my good fortune ended on this trip. By the end of our mission my feet were a mess, particularly my right foot. I managed to get a case of "immersion foot." I don't really know if it was officially immersion foot, but that's what they called almost everything that happened to your feet if they were wet too long. It was pretty common in Vietnam, particularly in the delta where water-covered rice paddies were everywhere, and the continuous crossings of streams and canals made keeping your feet dry an impossibility.

When the mission was over, our platoon was once again responsible for guarding the small bridge along the canal. Being on the bridge was good for me because I could leave my boots and socks off all day and let my skin dry out and begin to heal. The only problem was it wasn't healing; if anything, it was getting worse. I'd catch rides back to the cement factory to get treated by the medics. They tried a variety of treatments which didn't work. I soaked my feet in some sort of purple solution that stained my feet and made me look rather odd. I tried any number of creams without success. I was starting to get worried. The skin under my toes on my right foot had turned into a soft, fleshy, milky-white mess that no longer even resembled skin. I didn't wear my boots or socks at all, just flip-flops. Looking back, I think the condition caused me more worry than hurt. I don't recall there being much discomfort involved.

Word came down that we would soon be heading back to the Pineapple. Clearly, I was in no shape to get my feet wet again for any length of time, and the medics agreed. I wouldn't be making the trip with the rest of the platoon but would be staying on the bridge while they were away.

CHAPTER TWENTY-FOUR
THE BRIDGE

There wasn't a better place to stay in the whole AO than the little canal bridge, as far as I was concerned. It was as secure as it got. The most likely danger was from a rocket falling short of its intended target, the Capital. I liked its proximity to Saigon and Camp Davies. I enjoyed the hustle and bustle of the traffic during the day. The kids who hung around were always a lot of fun, and they always managed to have cold cokes to sell us. But the nights were the best. Curfew started at sundown: no more traffic other than military, and not even pedestrians were supposed to be out and about. Excepting the girls, of course; they knew the curfew wouldn't apply to them and usually showed up an hour or so after dark.

We got to know the "working girls" pretty well during our periodic visits to the bridge through the summer and fall of that year. I didn't know them that way; I hadn't changed my feelings in that regard but did enjoy their company on another level. I remember three, in particular, rather fondly. Their names were Dally (probably made up), Mui and Anh (real names). Dally and Mui called themselves sisters, but I thought that unlikely, though best buds they surely were.

To be sure, they were all prostitutes, but I could never bring myself to think of them as such, preferring "working girls" instead. There was a war going on, after all, and there were hundreds of thousands of refugees: displaced families uprooted from their villages who flocked to Saigon to escape the war in the countryside. More often than not, they ended up homeless, living on the streets or back alleyways with no more than a cardboard box for shelter. Many were reduced to begging for food. A lot of the "working girls" came from such families, and their earnings went to support them. I never asked any of the girls how they found themselves in the business, preferring to think it was out of necessity—a sacrifice for their families. And it was a sacrifice, one with a high price. The war wouldn't last

202

forever, but the stigma attached to what they were doing would. They were scorned by Vietnamese men, not only for their profession but for consorting with Americans. America doesn't have a patent on prejudice. The Vietnamese were race conscious as well, and even girls who weren't prostitutes but had romantic relationships with Americans were thought of no better.

For these girls, marrying into a respectable family would be problematic at best. Worse still would be a pregnancy, an occupational hazard. One of the saddest legacies of the war were the thousands of mixed-race children left behind after the conflict. The Vietnamese treated them very poorly; many were abandoned to live in the streets or, if lucky, an orphanage. They were looked down upon and were persecuted. The Vietnamese called them the "dust of life": in essence, of little importance or significance.

The girls had to know they would be labeled for life and ostracized if they should happen to have a bi-racial child. It had to have been a burden for them to carry. None of that, of course, came up as a topic of conversation. It's hard to know how badly they were scarred by the experience. They always seemed upbeat whenever they were around; how much of that was an act, I couldn't say. Maybe, like me, they were able to compartmentalize things, put them away somewhere where they couldn't hurt you, maybe to be dealt with later.

Mui and Dally may have been like that, never letting on how adversely their lives could be affected. At first, Dally seemed like the cool professional but over time developed a relationship with one of the guys. They had an exclusive relationship, but it was one he was still paying for. Figuring out where business ended and the personal started left the situation muddled. Mui always put on a happy face, seemingly oblivious to the pitfalls of her profession. She was a lot of fun, and I was always happy to see her.

Anh, the third girl in the trio, was a little different. She was always pleasant but appeared to carry a certain sadness with her. She could be smiling, but her eyes told a different story. Anh's name means brightness in English, but you could see her light had dimmed. She probably was unable to hide from the ramifications of her situation.

For whatever reason, over the course of our multiple stays at the bridge over the summer, we developed a friendship. Sadness aside, she possessed a sweet and sympathetic soul that was touching. It got to the point that I really looked forward to seeing her, and I thought it was reciprocal. I guess we were both pretending she wasn't what she was. Maybe she liked the idea of someone appreciating her for herself, not for what she did.

Although our relationship wasn't physical, it wasn't without contact. We used to lie in my hammock together and listen to the radio. It was kind of make believe for both of us, I know. But heck, she was better looking than most of the guys and smelled better than all of them. Even more than that, it was nice to think there was someone close by who cared, at least a little bit, whether or not I came back from the Pineapple or someplace like the Rung Sat.

The day came when the rest of the guys had to get ready to leave for the Pineapple. I felt equal measures of guilt for not going and relief for not having to. Sgt. Ralston entrusted me with his new expensive camera that he had just bought and told me I could have it if anything happened to him while in the Pineapple. Sgt. Ralston often walked the point whenever our platoon was on its own, so the possibility of something happening to him wasn't exactly remote. His parting words left me with an uneasy feeling, like maybe saying something like that must surely be bad luck. Me and another medical profile or two stayed on the bridge until the platoon returned. Because of our reduced force, we were augmented with some extra MP patrols.

The summer monsoon had finally begun to ebb. Staying dry throughout the day and night felt great, and it couldn't help but aid in my foot's healing process. It felt a little weird that first night without the rest of the guys, knowing they were out in some swamp swatting mosquitoes while I was lying in my hammock with my flip-flops on, listening to some music and waiting for Anh to come up to the bridge. The night air felt cooler without the high humidity of the wet season and when coupled with a gentle breeze was refreshing.

Anh showed up around the same time the MPs did on their jeep mounted patrol. They asked me if I wanted to buzz over to the docks and grab something to eat from an all-night snack bar that provided food for the dockworkers who were there 24 hours a day. I said sure, hopped in the back, and we headed down the road to the big bridge that crossed the canal into the city. We were the only vehicle on the road and passing through block after block of darkened buildings and deserted streets reminded me of those old World War II, newsreels of London during the blitz.

It was handy being with the MPs; they could just about go anywhere they wanted to. The gate guards at the docks just waved us through, and we headed over to the snack bar. I picked up some burgers, fries, and cokes for the other guys back at the bridge and some for Anh as well. The MPs dropped me off back at the bridge before continuing on with their patrol. Anh and I had a little picnic under a clear starlit sky. We sat on top of the bunker, turned on the radio, and listened to some music while she was introduced to an all-American meal. In contrast to many other weeks in Vietnam this one flew by. While the other guys were laboring out in the boonies, I was living the life back at the bridge. It was just about as good as it got for me that whole year, and I remember it fondly.

The platoon returned from the Pineapple intact, and the company as a whole fared much better than the prior disastrous trip. The platoon returned to the bridge for a few days before our next trip. My foot was nearly better so I was probably going along next time out. In the meantime, I'd be continuing my bridge duty.

Hardly anyone bothered us while on the bridge. Lt. Russo stayed at the company base camp more often than not, and when he did show up it was always in the daytime, never at night. Consequently, anyone so inclined felt pretty comfortable smoking some pot in the evening, and no one was concerned about having the girls stay on the bridge with us till late at night. I'm pretty sure that's why no one did come around: they knew what was going on and didn't want to find themselves in the position of having to do something about it—out of sight, out of mind. As long as we did our job in the field, they'd let things go in areas that were relatively secure. One night one of the lieutenants from the company had to stop by to give some new orders for the following day. This was only a day or two after the platoon returned from the Pineapple, and they were still in full stress reduction mode. The guys had girls in the bunkers, and the unmistakable scent of marijuana smoke was wafting through the air as the officer's jeep pulled up to the bridge. All of a sudden it was crisis mode, joints were snuffed out, and the girls were told not to make a sound and not to leave the bunkers. The lieutenant had to know what was going on; the smell was lingering and everyone was trying to studiously ignore it. Instead of coming onto the bridge, the lieutenant waved a couple guys over to his jeep, quickly gave the orders, and left in haste. Clearly, he didn't want any knowledge of the goings on. I think they call that plausible deniability these days. "Hey, I didn't know, I was only there a minute." As the jeep kicked up some dust and sped away, the guys emerged from the bunkers laughing uncontrollably. They were all high but managed to keep it together long enough to avoid giving themselves away. Probably something that neither they nor the lieutenant would have wanted.

I didn't indulge, but I didn't mind others doing so. In fact, I always had a good time being around them. Maybe I shouldn't discount the possibility of second-hand smoke here. Nevertheless, the dopers were more mellow and less prone to stir things up as the juicers sometimes did when they had too much to drink.

Anh had gone to visit her family and, in her stead, Mui started to take her place as my gal pal, which was fine by me but totally different than the friendship I had with Anh. Mui was a lot of fun to be around, and I enjoyed clowning around with her, but as the days went by, our chats became less frivolous and she showed another side to herself. She was spending more and more time with me, but I didn't think anything of it. Then one night we were at the far end of the bridge sitting atop one of the bunkers. Out of the blue she said, "Chuck, I love you too much, beaucoup boom-boom... no money." Well, that threw me for a loop, was totally unexpected, and I was speechless. I didn't know what to say to that, and worse, I'm sure it showed.

Frankly, girls were pretty much of a mystery to me. To begin with, I'm a shy person by nature and when it came to girls, let's just say if there was such a thing as a bashful quotient, my shy Q would have been in the genius range. Being congenitally shy and having gone to an all-boys high school left me bereft of female understanding. Beyond grade school I had only two encounters with girls, neither of which gave me any help in this situation.

My first experience occurred when I was thirteen. I was hanging out on a neighbor's porch with a few other kids, one of them was a friend of a neighbor's daughter who was in town to visit her. Well, Lord knows why, but this girl threw a lip lock on me out of the blue. She was an enthusiastic kisser, and it didn't seem like she was going to let go anytime soon. Now, this was something brand new for me, and I must say the lip on lip thing was a pleasant sensation, but this poor girl's breath tasted like she had road kill for dinner. Inside I was wanting to yell out "Hey, I'm gagging here," but my mom raised me too polite for that. They say you never forget your first kiss.

My second experience happened when I was sixteen. I'd like to say she was my first girlfriend, but in truth she was more like a friend who was a girl. But we did do things together: we hung out, went bowling, went to the amusement park in West View, and went to some other places that weren't so conventional. Valerie seemed to have a fascination with the "other side." I think she actually believed in ghosts and spirits and such. One time she talked me into going on a ghost hunt with her. She had heard of this place where, supposedly, ghosts sometimes appeared in the night. So, off we went to the grounds of Dixmont State Mental Hospital. We pulled off a paved road onto a dirt one and followed it down a hill. The road became more rutted as we went along, and I began to fear getting back out of the place. There was going to be one ghost for sure if I got my dad's car stuck in this place—and it would be me. We finally reached the bottom. There was a small clearing in the woods in the center of which stood an old shack that contained some sort of machinery, maybe a pump, and it was making appropriately creaking sounds for a ghost haunt. Alas, no ghosts or spirits appeared that night.

Another time she had me take her to the morgue. In those days, you could actually walk in off the street and see the sheet-covered bodies lined up on gurneys behind a glass wall. The place kind of freaked me out a little, but Valerie was all into it. "Hey Chuck, if we're lucky we might see some blood spots on the floor." Valerie was a lot of fun but maybe just a little off.

At any rate, these limited experiences with the opposite sex provided little guidance for how to respond to Mui, so it was no surprise when I found out what not to say. So, lesson learned: do not, do not, DO NOT! start off with, "Well Mui, I really, really do like you, but…" I never got past the "but." She stopped me there, not only with her raised hand giving the stop signal but with the look on her face as well. I had obviously hurt her feelings and I felt miserable about that. It was just that I felt a certain fidelity toward Anh. I don't really know what you would call the relationship that Anh and I had, not that it really matters. It was just really nice to have someone to look forward to seeing when I was out in the Pineapple. We enjoyed each other's company, and we were able to set aside the realities of our situations and not think of the Pineapple or the Rung Sat or the rats or the rain, or for her, the dismal future she faced. An hour or two spent listening to music, lying in the hammock, or having a snack together was escape time for me. I really appreciated her company, so I would never have risked hurting her feelings. It probably sounds very naive on my part, considering Anh's occupation, but I didn't regret it.

I didn't really have a good explanation for it and was trying to figure out in my head why in the heck Mui would say something like that. Fairly or unfairly, I began to wonder if Mui was a little envious of Anh having a relationship that didn't involve money changing hands. There was no way of knowing for sure, and I sure wasn't going to ask. Mui was acting a bit overwrought, I thought. I was getting the feeling she was trying to make me feel bad. She accused me of being a "butterfly," flitting from one person to another. In other words, I must be cheating on her. Where did that come from?! Then she said, a wee bit too theatrically, "I think I'm going to jump off the bridge." Now I was pretty sure that this acting exercise was being used as a payback ploy to make me feel worse than I already did. Regardless of the threat to jump off the bridge, I wasn't overly concerned about her safety as it would have been all of a three-foot leap into three feet of water. Despite Mui's histrionics, nobody entered the water that night, and in a day or two all was back to normal. Like I said, women were a mystery to me.

CHAPTER TWENTY-FIVE
RUSH TO THE PINEAPPLE

As usual, the company remained in its continual state of flux: new guys coming in and old guys rotating home. We had to say goodbye to Sergeant Ralston whose DEROS date had arrived. He was headed back to the "world." He was a good guy and we would miss him. He was replaced by Sgt. Robinson, a black career soldier who right away seemed a decent guy for a "lifer." There was generally a lot of tension between the young draftees and the career soldiers in Vietnam; their goals were different. The former just wanted to get out alive, the latter sometimes favored career goals over the soldiers' welfare. We took a liking to this career soldier and tried to give him a heads-up on our situation and more importantly how to keep himself alive while out in the Pineapple. We all knew it was only a matter of time before we would all be back there.

We were all pleasantly surprised when we received orders to move to a base in the southwest corner of our expanded AO. Once again, we formed up at the cement factory to catch our transportation to the new base. The APCs (armored personnel carriers) arrived, and we all climbed on top as usual for our trip down the road. It was a common sight in Vietnam to see flags tied onto the radio antennas of the tracks (another name for APCs). They looked good flapping in the breeze as the tracks zipped down the road. It wasn't uncommon to see confederate flags flown. I'm sure most were displayed by good old boys wanting to show pride in their southern heritage, but I wondered how the black guys felt about it in the midst of all the racial tension that seemed to be increasing as time went by.

We kicked up a lot of dust as the track's treads churned up the dirt road's surface. We were well into November now and the dry season had taken hold. Clouds of the fine powdery particles clung to everything and everybody, and the guys were soon holding up one end of their towels to hold over their faces to filter the dust laden air they were breathing. We passed through several villages along the way. The further away from Saigon we got, the less friendly they seemed.

We arrived at our destination around noon. Thankfully, the base had already been built. It bordered one side of the road and consisted of large well-fortified bunkers laid out in a stand of palm trees. The area was pancake flat, and we were surrounded by rice paddies. The fields, no longer covered with water, had baked under the sun until the hated muck turned hard as concrete. Our location alongside the road held the promise of hot food being delivered on occasion, the palm trees provided shade for our encampment, and it wasn't raining any more. All in all, it looked like a pretty good deal.

I was selected for ambush duty our first night there. We were in unfamiliar territory and no one wanted to go walking about after dark, which is what they wanted us to do. The group of us headed out of the compound at dusk and started down the road. It didn't take long for us to reach a consensus on what to do, we had done it before under similar circumstances. Instead of turning off the road and crossing the paddies to our designated spot, we continued down the road to the next village and holed up there overnight. By this point in my tour, I was in survival mode. I'd seen nothing to make me feel what we were doing was worthwhile enough for me to lose a leg to a booby-trap in the middle of the night, just to set up another ambush that so far for us had led to zero results. We met two other squads in the village with the same idea. We all did what we had to do, but if the opportunity arose where we didn't have to, we took it. We ambled back into base the next morning at an appropriate time, and no one was the wiser—or if they were, they said nothing.

Captain Williams told us the Red Cross Donut Dollies were going to visit the compound around noon that day. The "round eyes," as the guys called them, arrived as promised. I can't remember if they brought donuts or not, but they brought some sort of word games to play and generally just hung out and talked.

Just as they were getting ready to leave, Captain Williams came running out of the communication's bunker yelling that another company was in contact with the Viet Cong out in the Pineapple, and we were going to be choppered in to help out. He told us to take everything we had because he didn't know when we would be coming back. *God Damn It!* My stomach was starting to tie up already. Flying in under fire was the last thing I wanted to do. I started packing up my ruck, grabbed the radio, an extra battery and some smoke grenades, and made sure my rifle was clean and I had all my magazines full of ammo. Everything was rush rush, and we were soon grouped in lift sections strung out along the road waiting for the choppers to come and get us.

I heard the low-pitched beat of the chopper's rotor blades before I saw them: ten dots in a row out over the horizon and heading our way. They began their long, slow, descending turn to align with the road. Continuing down, they all began to flare about ten feet off the ground and settled down into their own self-made dust storms. Squinting to keep out the dirt, with heads lowered against the whirlwind, we climbed aboard. We rose up into the clear air and banked west toward the Pineapple.

Choppers are noisy, they vibrate, and the wind is buffeting through the open doors. But at times like this you don't notice any of it. You are alone in your thoughts, shutting everything else out. This was the worst kind of fear, the kind you had to wait on, the "let's just get this over with cause I can't stand waiting for it to happen any longer" fear. But wait we would. We arrived over the LZ, only to be told that the area was going to be prepped with artillery fire, and our flight should move to the north and circle until the barrage was over.

From our new vantage point, we could see the red-orange flashes and ugly grey-black smoke plumes rising up from along the tree lines. Yeah, blast them with all you got— all the better for us. Then I saw something new to me, a helicopter flying low over the ground trailing a long cloud of white smoke. It had some nozzles shooting oil into the hot exhaust of its turbine engine, creating a fog bank that our flight could land behind, obscuring us, at least for a little while.

Our lift lined up to land parallel to the smoke cloud, and the door gunners opened up with their M-60s on approach. The pilots dropped to a hover several feet off the ground so we could jump out, then they immediately lowered the nose and began to lift out to clear the area as quick as possible.

This was about the time that the fear took a back seat to focus. As the chopper descended and neared the ground, I slid my legs over the edge of the craft's floor and slipped down till my feet hit the skids. I wanted off the chopper just as much as the crew wanted us off. The pilot started to flare into a hover, the door gunner beside me was blasting away. I didn't see any indication of incoming fire but I jumped anyway, a tad too soon, and hit the ground a little fast. I was a little off-balance and landed awkwardly, collapsing hard and splitting my lip open on my knee.

I lay down on the ground and looked for cover. The noise of the choppers soon faded as they gained altitude and exited the area. It was dead quiet, except for my heart pounding, no incoming fire at all— but who knew. We all waited there for something to happen, having a moment. I realized we landed in the remnants of a pineapple plantation. After three trips to the Pineapple, I finally saw a pineapple.

Apparently, the Viet Cong had melted into the trees once again, which was ok by me. It was their MO to fade away when confronted by a larger force. We began a sweep of the area and found nothing of significance. We wouldn't be going back to our base, though; we'd be staying in the Pineapple. Naturally, I was disappointed to be back in the Pineapple, but at least we were now in the dry season. We wouldn't be getting rained on all the time, and the mosquito population should be down.

We continued our sweep till we hit the river, the Van Co Dong, which coursed its way through the middle of the Pineapple. Many of the canals that provided irrigation and transportation for the plantations were connected to it. We fixed our NDP (night defensive perimeter) along the eastern bank of the river.

We had a talk with Sgt. Robinson again about the dangers of the Pineapple, and how not to go wandering off searching for stuff if you don't have to. I made a habit of not walking anywhere I wasn't required to, and even then, I always tried to take the same path someone else already had. The place just had too many ways to blow yourself up. I don't think Sgt. Robinson fully understood just how deadly the place could be; he failed to heed our advice several times during that first day. He was a career soldier after all, and I guess he felt it was his duty.

Our first night wasn't bad, I had a little show put on by the B-52s. I was on guard around midnight when I felt the ground begin to shake beneath me; it was an odd feeling. I looked all around and noticed the tell-tale rhythmic red flashes of a B-52 raid traversing the horizon from north to south. It was always an awesome sight to behold at night. In the morning, we saddled up for our first full day. We were going to head east from the river and cover some open fields that still had some standing water in them, probably from irrigation ditches connected to the canals.

We headed out in a long line, following the path that the point element led. I was right behind, fourth man behind the lead. Mindful of mines and booby-traps, I kept my distance from the man in front of me. I was looking toward a tree line a few hundred yards distant when a mortar round hit in the paddy, maybe a hundred and fifty yards in front of us. My first thought was our advance was being supported, but nobody had mentioned that possibility. A couple seconds later, a second round hit, only it was 50 yards closer, and the two explosions formed a line pointed directly at us. It was time to move now; if the pattern continued the next one could put me in its burst radius. I did a 180 and started running directly away but realized immediately that the mortars would overtake me so I pivoted and ran perpendicular to the line of progression. I heard another round go off. I was still ok, but I suddenly remembered that I was running through a booby-trap area with abandon. Damn! I said hell with it and dived into the muck and tried to immerse myself in it for any cover I could get. Then it was over, stopped as quick as it started. I waited a few seconds, then I heard the cry for medics. The three people in the line in front of me were all hit.

Two had relatively minor wounds but one had his jaw nearly torn from his face. A medevac was called in and flew them to an army hospital near Saigon. Then we continued on with our mission.

I can easily picture the open fields, the far tree line, the troops in line in front of me, the first mortar round impacting and sending up a geyser of wet mud and dirty black-grey smoke thirty or forty feet in the air. I can see the second one hit and remember turning heel to take off running, knowing the next one could land on my head. But try as I might, I can't recall the emotions of the moment. Surely, I would have had some, but like the other incidences I'd lived through I hid them away, almost instantly it seemed. Maybe for me that was the only way to keep going. Medevac completed, the company moved on as if it just had a flat tire that needed to be taken care of. I hardly knew those guys; they were fairly new and had not shared any bridge duty with us. I didn't even know the name of the guy with the mangled jaw, and now I never would. It was truly one of the obscenities of the war, dropping new guys into a combat zone, not knowing anyone. Imagine it yourself: two days in the boonies, getting hit and lying on the ground, scared and hurting, without even a friendly face to look out after you and offer some comfort. They must have felt a terrible aloneness.

We finished the day without further incident. We set up for the night in an area of tall grass. I matted some of the grass down and set up some overhead cover with my poncho, like a few other guys responsible for that part of the perimeter did. We were well into darkness, and the resupply chopper had yet to arrive, so I went ahead and blew up my air mattress, slid it under my poncho, and crawled in. You were always tired in Vietnam it seemed, so falling quickly asleep was never a problem, although it was rarely a deep sleep.

At any rate, I was cutting some z's when the supply chopper showed up. I heard it in my half sleep and figured I would wait to get what I needed in the morning. I was lying comfortably on my air mattress and didn't want to get up. I usually didn't have one but I was liking it. The choppers were usually guided in, and especially this time because it was night. Well the guy doing the guiding must have forgotten about us guys in the tall grass as he was guiding the chopper in. I heard it getting louder and louder but I really wasn't concerned. The chopper was a Chinook, a big twin-rotor behemoth, and unbeknown to us, the troop was guiding him in on top of us. The downwash from the rotors was getting stronger and my poncho was really starting to flutter. I was fully awake now and getting ready to scramble out from under my poncho when it got caught by the whirlwind and blew away. There, right above me—the Chinook; it seemed to be falling on me. I scooted off to the side and saw out of the corner of my eye my air mattress being launched into the sky by the swirling blast of rotors. I found my poncho the next day but never did recover the air mattress.

The day started like any other in the Pineapple: dreading the walk through the booby-trapped fields, dikes, and even canals. The Viet Cong were known to have set up booby-traps under water. They chose likely crossing sites and set the tripwires underwater, making them almost impossible to detect due to the murkiness of the streams and canals. We tried to avoid dikes as much as possible since they were the most likely locations for the hidden killers. But the dikes were the fastest way to go, and we had to resort to their use when time was an issue.

We made it through the morning without incident, staying mostly to the fields—a tougher go, but far safer. We stopped at the intersection of two dikes for lunch. We checked them out for about 30 feet on each leg of the cross that the intersection made; we wanted a dry spot of land to sit down and eat.

I was eating my usual lunch, a can of fruit, when I heard the explosion. I looked up and saw Sgt. Robinson falling off the dike. Apparently, he had seen something he wanted to investigate further down the dike. He ignored all our warnings about not walking anywhere he didn't have to. Probably out of a sense of duty, he went to check it out and tripped a booby-trap. His legs took the brunt of the blast. Thornton took off, racing across the field, disregarding the danger of any other booby-traps to get to him. He was bleeding profusely and Thornton applied tourniquets to both of his legs.

We called for a dust-off, the medics gave the Sgt. some Morphine and bandaged up his many wounds as best they could, then we waited for the medevac chopper to arrive.

I felt bad for the sergeant. He was a decent guy, and what happened to him didn't really need to happen. Getting hurt was one thing, getting hurt when you could have avoided it would be a lot harder to handle. A few weeks later we got a letter from him; he was in an Army hospital in Japan. He told us his legs were really messed up, and he wasn't out of the woods yet as far as the possibility of losing one. But he said the doctors were optimistic.

Sgt. Robinson joined many others on the long list of Pineapple victims. It was hard to see what we were accomplishing. The poor sergeant blew himself up for nothing; we neither found nor learned anything of value from his sacrifice. After receiving his letter to the platoon, I wondered if our warning was haunting him. "Don't walk anywhere you don't have to," we all told him. I think he was compelled, both by his nature and his sense of duty, to go beyond the bare minimum required. Sgt. Ralston was the same way, walking the point when he didn't have to. He felt he could do it better than anyone else; therefore, he didn't want to order anyone else to do it.

The war seemed to bring out both the best and the worst in people, both the noblest of actions and the most shameful. But I must say that I was witness to far more of the best and noblest. Which was all the more remarkable, considering the sense of futility and lack of purpose experienced by the troops. The Pineapple exacerbated these feelings. Maybe we were accomplishing something, but it never seemed evident to us what that might have been.

The booby-traps were impersonal, they lay in wait to seal some unlucky soul's fate. You couldn't fight them or vent your rage on them. They demoralized you. They drained you psychologically and sapped your will to keep on going. And yet, the troops did keep on going. The pressure on the point men was intense: not only were they under the strain of tripping one themselves, but of missing one that a few men down the line might trip. I was so fortunate to have the radio; it spared me the unrelenting strain of leading the way. Nonetheless, the Pineapple could send me to some dark places filled with gloomy thoughts and morose musings on my situation. I had been tremendously lucky so far, but rather than that being a relief, it actually reinforced my foreboding that something bad was going to happen. How much good fortune can you have before it runs out? I'd landed on the favored side of circumstance and fate more than my fair share should have warranted. My company was in the Rocket Belt during the May Offensive, missing the heavy fighting around Saigon that other companies in our battalion saw. While there was fighting all around our Rocket Belt AO, some even within sight, we escaped contact. When we thought we were surrounded, in the deep jungle north of the Dong Nai River, listening to the Viet Cong signaling with their bamboo sticks through the night, sure that an attack was certain, our only casualty, as it turned out, was lack of sleep.

Even when things did go bad, I emerged unscathed. I'd escaped the fusillade of fire when I was on the point entering the base camp up in War Zone D. I managed to low crawl under withering fire to the safety of the trench. I had a grenade bounce down the trail in front of me and explode without effect. When I was ordered to draw fire, bullets came within a few inches of the top of my head. When we moved south to the land of streams and canals, I scared myself badly when I slipped into a hole crossing a stream and found myself underwater with sixty pounds of gear on. Down in the Rung Sat I came within inches of being squashed into the river bottom by a landing craft, only to be nearly done in by a smaller craft minutes later, in the same fashion. I'd escaped having to make a nightmarish assault across open paddies when we took fire from a distant tree line, only by the good fortune of having two sergeants talk a wacko lieutenant out of attempting something so foolhardy.

I'd made it through 3 trips to the Pineapple without a scratch, but my latest close call really made me ponder. When you are fourth in line and the first three get hit, you can't help but wonder... *what if?* What if I was third in line that day instead of fourth? You can drive yourself crazy. What if that landing craft didn't jink at the last second and miss me by inches? What if that rope cleat on the patrol boat was one inch higher, just out of my reach? What if that hand grenade bounced toward me instead of away?

I guess it's just human nature to look for meaning in our lives, to wonder if the chain of events that constitute a life are directed somehow, as if there was a master plan in play and the role we act out isn't entirely in our hands. Those thoughts often surface when fate seems to overly favor you. You can look at it in different ways, I guess. Some might take it as a sign they are living right and that their good fortune is their reward. I liked to think that of myself, but knowing a whole lot better people than me had been killed or wounded put that hope to rest. It was hard for me to accept, at first: that blind luck played such a pivotal role in whether you survived your year or not. I'm not dismissing skill and competence, just recognizing that a lot of your destiny is out of your hands. Realizing that was hard; I had had so much good luck that I was sure it couldn't last. I must say, though, most of the time I wasn't haunted by those thoughts. It took a few days in a place like the Pineapple or the Rung Sat for them to surface and increase my feelings of vulnerability. Thankfully, those dark thoughts were transitory and usually contingent on circumstance. So, I was lucky even in that. Others weren't. It wasn't uncommon for soldiers to have a "preoccupation with thoughts about past occurrences which may result in feelings of anxiety," so say the psychologists. They have a name for it: "anxious ruminations." It's not a condition exclusive to soldiers, but it is one that troops are certainly susceptible to. But I'd think it is more of an occupational hazard for them than a psychiatric disorder.

The start of day four in the Pineapple was no different than any other we spent out there. Just being there seemed to generate a malaise that infected the whole company. No one really wanted to start the day. We were well shy of motivation: stalling, unwilling to step out onto the dikes, forge into the fields, or cross the canals. Every step delayed might mean one less taken, bettering your odds for the day. You could only put it off for so long before the daily lottery began.

Another company was in our area and together we were making a broad sweep through the fields. They must have made contact with the Viet Cong. They called for helicopter gunships to rake over the area to their front with their mini-guns and rockets. We weren't far from their position, and we held ours until the air-strike was over.

Two Huey Cobras soon arrived. They were sleek gunships exclusive to the job, not troop carriers modified for that work. They carried an assortment of air to ground rockets, multiple barrel mini-guns capable of spewing out thousands of rounds a minute and rapid-fire grenade launchers. The Cobras set up a circular pattern: while one was banking away from a firing run on the target, the other would be entering the pattern to begin his, keeping the enemies' heads down for as much of each pass as possible. On rocket runs they fired the rockets in pairs, paused a moment, then let another salvo loose, usually three sets per pass, then followed up with long bursts with the mini- gun. The guns made a fearsome sound—an angry growl—from the torrent of lead spitting out of the barrels. You almost felt sorry for those on the other end... almost. We waited till the gunships had expended all their ordnance on the target before continuing on with our mission. The other company moved up to investigate the impact area while we headed out to search a stand of nipa palms close to a canal.

The area next to the canal was thick with vegetation: a great place to hide arms in bunkers that were not visible from the air. It didn't take long after entering the thicket to run across our first bunker, and soon thereafter another. It soon became apparent that we had found a major stash. Captain Williams was excited by the prospect and wanted a very thorough search. That prompted a lot of activity; the troops were moving about the area between the bunkers and in turn flattening down the vegetation. All this walking about had lulled me into a false sense of security, and I let my guard down and walked without concern along the newly formed paths of tamped down foliage.

I was working with a guy named Gary Meinert. He was a black farmer from Iowa, a minority within a minority. Anyway, Gary said, "*I'm going to grab a smoke*," and wandered off a few steps to find a place to sit down. I finished up and headed off to another bunker, following the newly trod track in the tall grass. I got close to Gary and he looked up from staring at the ground, as I came nearly abreast of him, and he yelled out, "*STOP! Don't move!*"

I didn't. From Gary's position close to the ground, he saw an opening in the tall grass that you would never notice if you were upright and walking. I carefully stooped down and looked into the opening and saw a grenade tied with wire to a stake that was planted into the ground. A tripwire was tied to the pin. We followed its path into the grass. Apparently, other people had walked over it, trampling the grass atop the line in places. There must have been some slack in the line, and it must have been close to the ground because a vertical movement was too short to pull the pin from the grenade. Luckily, Gary spotted it. I could have easily snagged the line with the toe of my boot and within a step pulled the pin out of the grenade, and that would have been that, probably for both of us. Once again, luck was on my side. Why was fate so kind to me? I had no clue, but now I had another item to add to my growing list of experiences to ponder about, and when feeling low and vulnerable, to "anxiously ruminate" over.

I woke up on day 5 scratching at itches all over my legs. I checked my legs out at first light and found little round red circles all over from ankles to waist. I had picked up a case of ringworm, a fungal infection, just one more of the legion of skin diseases that plagued the troops in the field in Vietnam. The constant hot and humid conditions encountered in the boonies made us very susceptible to fungal and bacterial infections. In fact, skin diseases accounted for 70% of hospital visits in Vietnam. The rest were almost equally divided between battle casualties and non-hostile injuries.

It was a long day for me; I started feeling poorly and worsened as the day progressed. Thankfully, the day was uneventful in a military sense. The night wasn't so kind; I ended up throwing up a few times. I felt better for doing so, and whatever I had didn't linger. I have no idea if the ringworm had anything to do with it or not, but I had to live with the itching for a number of days.

We left the Pineapple on day 6, none too soon for me.

CHAPTER TWENTY-SIX
GOODBYE LAURA

Luckily, our platoon was assigned to the small bridge alongside the canal again. It was great to be away from the Pineapple. As usual, I slipped back into the bridge routine effortlessly. I never brought the Pineapple with me whenever I returned from an operation there. It was bad enough to be there; I wasn't going to let it be a black cloud over my head while I was away. Easier said than done, at times, but for the most part I was successful at it. Besides being delighted to be back at the bridge, I had another reason to feel good. It was now December and I could scratch the eighth month off my calendar—four more to go!

The bridge didn't just mean no Pineapple. It meant clean clothes and getting clean. It meant an occasional hot meal and my nights spent comfortably in my hammock. It meant the company of Anh and the other girls. It was a world removed from the Pineapple and I appreciated every minute of it, as I knew lots of other guys were not nearly as fortunate.

We did have some single day missions, but they were all in AO Laura, which had proven to be benign 90% of the time and were conducted in the company of the ARVNs. These joint exercises with the Vietnamese Army were a new tactic initiated by the high command, but their purpose escapes me now. I didn't mind at all, though, as any search and destroy mission with the ARVNs would more than likely end up as search and avoid mission. Just another long walk in the sun.

We had been on the bridge about a week. I had just finished up another one of those joint missions with the Vietnamese when I got the news. Anh met me when I got back to the small span. "Chuck, you go Pineapple, no come back," she said. At first, I thought she was telling me she had a premonition that something bad was going to happen to me, but that wasn't it. No, the word was that our whole battalion was leaving AO Laura for a new AO in the Pineapple. *Damn!* I was hoping that this was the one time that Anh didn't know what I was doing before I did. I wished she didn't have such a good track record.

Unfortunately, she was proven right the next morning. Lt. Russo showed up at the bridge with the news. We were pulling out of the AO the next day. We met up at the cement factory, packed up all our stuff, including the mortars and ammo, and loaded it on the trucks that would be coming for us.

It was a sad day for me, I knew we would never again get as good a gig as this one had been. I'd be seeing a lot of the regulars from the past few months. There was the contingent of kids that stopped by and brightened my day. The young girl who sold us biscuits: she passed our way every morning, always wearing a perpetual scowl that she seemed to be daring us to try and remove. We rarely did. The old lady with the blackened teeth and opaque eyes who was always smiling and always ready to sell something that was probably stolen from the docks.

The night was no better, the girls came up to say goodbye. Anh gave me a picture of herself, as did Dally and even Mui. The mood was melancholy and I felt a genuine sadness in leaving.

We gathered at the cement factory in the morning to pack the trucks with our stuff. We would convoy through the city to the west of Saigon to set up our new base camp adjacent to the Pineapple. The long column of Deuce and half's left the cement factory and headed up the highway toward Saigon. I was feeling nostalgic for AO Laura already, and we weren't even out of it yet. I had perched myself on top of a load of boxed mortar shells that were stacked about 4 feet high on the bed of the truck. I had a commanding 360 degree view all around me. We were on the same road where we hitched rides on the tanker trucks, riding the running boards and hanging onto the mirrors. The Pineapple had no bridges to guard. It had no Ruff Puff forts to man OPs. We wouldn't be on our own with two or three of us living in those forts with soldiers and their families, getting to know them, having a good time with them. No more fishing off sampans in the middle of the night, no more rat stew. We passed the entrance to Camp Davies. I'd miss that too; no more sneaking into the mess hall for a real meal every now and then.

Then the trucks reached the big bridge that spanned the main canal. We climbed up the approach ramp and onto the deck. I could look down and see the little steel truss bridge that provided us with regular respites from the Pineapple, the Rung Sat and Riverine Operations. It was about 150 yards down the waterway. I kept my eyes on it all the way across. I actually felt a little twinge in my chest as it passed from view. I didn't know who I would miss more, Anh or Laura.

CHAPTER TWENTY-SEVEN
SOLDIER OF THE MONTH

The convoy coursed its way through the always crazy Saigon traffic till we reached the western outskirts of the city. The road we traveled transitioned to dirt, and the long line of trucks in our convoy kicked up quite a dust cloud in their wake. The trucks pulled off the dusty road after a couple miles into a large clearing. We weren't quite in the Pineapple but we were close. This was where we were going to build our new base. I saw plenty of sandbag filling in my future.

The first few days were spent building. Then we began patrolling our new area and getting the lay of the land. We probably continued the pattern that had been set the past couple of months: a week in the Pineapple then a week back here or another place like it. My future was looking kind of dismal at that point. I had 3½ months to go and at least half of that would be spent trying to avoid booby-traps while trekking the fallow fields of the Pineapple.

One morning while we were still at the camp, Lt. Russo called me over to tell me I'd be flying back to the Brigade Main Base in Long Binh on the afternoon supply chopper. He told me I would be competing for Brigade Soldier of the Month. That was a surprise to me. I'd basically been in the dark about the whole thing, going weeks back to when the process started. Heck, I didn't even know there was a process or what it would lead to.

Nearly a month earlier, Lt Russo told me I was going to be the 4th platoon's representative for B Company's "Soldier of the Month." Three other representatives from the other platoons and I would vie for the "honor." This was all new to us; we never had a "soldier of the month" before and didn't know what it meant for the person who got it. Knowing how the Army works, Captain Williams probably just got a directive to pick one, not knowing why. Lt. Russo told me that we would be interviewed by the company first sergeant, then he would select one of us to be the soldier of the month for company B.

I didn't feel particularly comfortable being selected to stand for the mortar platoon. I thought the lieutenant should have picked someone a little more aggressive, a little more "into it" than I was. Of course, that narrowed his list of candidates considerably since most guys in the platoon were on the same page I was—as in, "let's just get out of this place alive." Still, I was uneasy about it; I didn't want people to think I was chosen out of favoritism. I spent a lot of time with the lieutenant: I was his RTO, (radio operator), and I was in the FDC (fire direction center) along with him. He was responsible for putting me in charge of the beer and coke money for the platoon, as well as being the company postal clerk. Besides that, I was an "old-timer" at this point, being an original member of the platoon and having served 8 months in-country. As it turned out, I don't think anybody really cared who was chosen. Such was the antipathy toward the Army at the time that no one thought that anything good would come from it anyway.

I have absolutely no recollection of the interview with the first sergeant. I doubt whether I even combed my hair. The interview was held out in the field so we were all in our filthy fatigues anyway.

A few days later Lt. Russo told me I was selected as SOM. Great, now what? Apparently, nothing. There was a rumor floating around that you would get a three day in-country R & R, but nary a word was said to me about that. And that's where things stood; I was Company B SOM—big deal! Things went on as usual and I stopped thinking about it.

Ten or so days later the lieutenant told me to go down to the cement factory for an interview with the battalion sergeant major. He was going to be evaluating all the company SOMs in the battalion and choose one to be the Battalion Soldier of the Month. Once again, I can't conjure up any memories of that interview at all, meaning that I probably did nothing to prepare for it and considered the potential honor next to meaningless to boot.

As before, a few days passed before I heard the results that I was selected. I was now the Battalion SOM. What this meant, I had no idea. It seemed that neither Captain Williams nor Lt. Russo knew, either.

In the meantime, we packed up and left AO Laura, moved adjacent to the Pineapple and began operations in the new area. That's when I got the word about going to Long Binh to vie for the Brigade SOM.

I didn't know what that would entail, but I was finally going to get some benefit out of the whole business. I was going back to the main base, at least for that night. I was excited about that. I'd get a hot meal in the mess hall and get to sit in a chair to eat it. I'd get to take a shower, and I'd get to sleep on a cot the whole night through—no guard duty!

I grabbed my stuff and hopped aboard the departing supply chopper. It lifted off out of the cloud of dust that the rotors had kicked up and banked toward the city. It was the first time I saw all of Saigon from the air. I looked down and was able to recognize a few places I had seen from the ground. We followed the track of Highway 1 north to Long Binh. Long Binh's size could be better appreciated from the air. It was a sprawling complex that was home to 50,000 logistics and support troops, the largest base in Vietnam. The 199th's headquarters were at the northern terminus of the base. The chopper descended and landed at the Fireball helipad, the home of the aviation unit assigned to the Redcatcher Brigade.

I walked back up the same dusty road that our platoon had walked down over 8 months ago to catch our first chopper ride to the boonies. I remembered how loaded down we all were, making the rookie mistake of carrying too much. A lot had happened since that first day. I hadn't turned into a warrior during that time, by any stretch, but I was able to do what I had to, and I felt a certain amount of pride in that.

I reported to the XO (executive officer), the second in command of the company who normally remained back at the main base along with the first sergeant. The XO told me to find an empty cot in one of the tents and he would see me in the morning.

It didn't take long to figure out that this time, somebody else cared about who won. I was issued brand new fatigues with the proper patches and name tag sewn on. I was given a new hat and new boots as well. The first sergeant gave me some tech manuals to look at since I probably would be questioned about weapons. In addition, he told me I might also be asked about current events.

For the first time, I heard what all this might actually mean for me. Turns out that the winner would be the enlisted aide for the brigade commanding general for one month. In my case, it would be January—if I was selected. I can't say I was overly excited about that prospect. In my mind, I had a picture of me making sure his laundry was done, maybe polishing his shoes and running errands for him. On the other hand, it meant a month out of the Pineapple. For that alone, it would be worth the effort to try my best.

I went down to the Vietnamese barber on the base to get my hair cut and my mustache trimmed. By this time in the war, the usual standards of military deportment and appearance had slipped dramatically, particularly in the field. As a reporter for a major news weekly stated, "The US Military faced deep and widespread insubordination." Hair was longer, mustaches bushier and sideburns extended. Shirts were left open, pants were rolled up, and not a care given to what your boots looked like. Adornments were common in the form of love beads, peace medallions and graffiti-covered helmet liners and flak jackets. Uniformity was a lost cause. Guys wore their bush hats in every way imaginable: brim curled up in front, down in back, one side up like an Australian bush hat or both sides up like a cowboy hat.

Anyway, I got my hair cut short, but nowhere near what a military cut looks like today. I asked for my mustache to be trimmed but the guy made it uneven. By the time he got both sides even, I had a pencil-thin mustache like Vincent Price, so I told the guy to just shave it off.

I knew if the guys back in the field saw me now, all properly attired, boots with a shine, sporting a haircut and sans mustache I'd be razzed mercilessly for being a "lifer." But sometimes you got to do what you got to do. Not going back to the Pineapple was strong motivation.

I had it pretty nice back at Long Binh. I had no duties other than to get ready for the Board, and what I did for that was entirely left up to me. I started studying up on all the weapons that we used in the field. I refreshed my memory on the maximum effective ranges of rifles and machine guns and the burst radius of grenades and artillery rounds. I went over radio communications and hand signals. Just generally brushed up on anything I thought might be important to the Board. I even went over the General Orders, something I had not seen or heard about since boot camp. I went to the post PX and bought copies of Time and Newsweek to brush up on what was happening in the world and read the Stars and Stripes newspaper as well.

I found out a little more about how the Board worked. There was a panel of 5 sergeants major, one each from all the battalions making up the brigade. Each candidate would meet with them as a group. The sergeants took turns asking the questions. They considered not only if the questions were answered correctly but your appearance and the manner in which you conducted yourself.

I felt lucky, if not deserving, to be in the position I was in. It's easy to get spoiled back at the base. I did feel some guilt thinking about the guys out in the boonies, but it would have been foolish not to take advantage of the situation. Life isn't fair. For instance, it was nearing Christmas and Bob Hope was coming to Long Binh as part of his annual holiday tour of the bases in Vietnam. I was going to get a chance to see him, but the guys actually doing the fighting out in the boonies were not afforded that opportunity.

Long Binh had an outdoor amphitheater that could hold several thousand troops, and none of the 2x10 boards that constituted the seating arrangements had any empty spots. The place was standing room only. Bob Hope came out onto the stage to start the show and did a little stand-up routine and one-liners. I thought the performance was a little stilted, then I noticed that toward the middle of the amphitheater there was a stand with two guys turning cue cards over as Bob Hope talked. The cards were huge so that he could see them from the stage. I thought his material was a little dated, but I, like everyone else there, was primed to have a good time, and so we went with the flow and got into the spirit of things.

Bob never came by himself, of course. Knowing his audience was made up of a lot of young men, he brought a bevy of beautiful babes along with him. Not the least of which was Penelope Plummer, the reigning Miss World. Also on stage, were the "Golddiggers," an all-girl song and dance troupe that proved to be the crowd favorite. Music was provided by Les Brown and his Band of Renown. A singing group called the "Honey Limited" entertained. A husband and wife team of Roger Smith and Ann Margaret said a few words, he of the TV detective series "77 Sunset Strip" and she a movie starlet. Rosie Greer appeared. He was an all-pro defensive lineman for the Los Angeles Rams who purportedly did needlepoint in his spare time.

At the end of the show, Linda Bennett sang "Silent Night," and everyone joined in. For the first time since I got to Vietnam I truly felt homesick. I'd been down and blue before and at times had wanted to be anywhere but where I was, but this was different. I had never missed a Christmas before this, and I guess that hit home. It got me to thinking of Christmas Eve at home and how my brother Mike used to write the words we were singing, "Silent Night" or "Peace on Earth," on the mirror above the fireplace using glass wax. He was a good artist and he'd write the words in a calligraphy style. He'd usually draw a star of Bethlehem above a small village with a church nestled in a valley. We always put our tree up the day before Christmas. We'd put the nativity set under the tree, but my mom wanted us to wait till later to put the baby Jesus in the manger. I started thinking of all those little traditions, the eggnog and peanut butter cookies, the anticipation when you were little, how long it took to get to Christmas. All those kinds of things ran through my mind. Heck, in the grand scheme of things it wasn't all that long ago that I couldn't wait to see what Santa brought me. Not long ago and forever ago, that's what it felt like.

The day of the board arrived, and I was as ready as I could be. The panel of sergeants was using a room in the NCO club for the interviews. I was called in and told to take a seat that was placed in front of a long table they were all sitting behind. They began by asking me how long I was in-country and what my job was in my unit.

After the formalities, they got down to asking me some questions. At first, they were all military questions: the kind of material I had studied for and even some things I hadn't studied but just happened to know anyway. Then they asked me some questions about current events. Luckily for me, it seemed like they read the same issues of Time and Newsweek that I did.

Things were going along pretty well, I thought. I wasn't sure what they were looking for exactly, but I felt I hadn't made any gaffes yet. If any of my answers were wrong, they hadn't corrected me.

It felt like things were winding down when one of the sergeants major asked me the correct procedure to follow if my unit had been exposed to a nerve gas attack and everyone had donned their gas masks successfully but now needed to check if the air was clear. The problem was there was no gas detecting equipment available to use. Well, if I ever knew the answer to that I'd long forgotten it. I was really struggling to come up with something, but nothing at all came to mind. Finally, thinking I'd blown my chance, I admitted that I had absolutely no clue.

The sergeant major then began to explain how it is done. "If you have no gas detecting equipment and you need to check if the air is safe, you get the lowest ranking man in the unit and ask him to look you in the eyes. Then, while observing his eyes, you crack the seal on his gas mask and look for any dilation in his pupils." Wow, I was incredulous. It just seemed so unfair to make the lowest ranking man a guinea pig. Not thinking, in the midst of my amazement at this news, I blurted out: "Good luck finding him."

This evoked a lot of laughter from the sergeants, after which I was thanked for coming and then dismissed. All my good feelings about the day evaporated. I thought for sure I had blown it, particularly because they ended the interview at that point. I figured I'd be headed out to the Pineapple on the next supply chopper. I tried to salve my disappointment by reminding myself that I got out of the field for a few days, I got some new clothes and boots, and I got to eat real food and sleep all night. Playing those kind of mind games rarely works. I was actually starting to think that it might have been better if I had lost at the company level, then I'd never have to regret what I lost out on back here in Long Binh.

I went down to the club that afternoon, figuring it was going to be the last time I would see it before I rotated home. "Hey Jude" was playing when I walked into the club. It wasn't very crowded at that time of day, and I immediately saw Thornton Maxwell III sitting at one of the tables. I walked over to see him. He had just come in from the field, his tour was almost over, and he'd be heading back to the "world" in a couple of days. I kidded him a bit about the night he was in a near coma from rice wine or whiskey or whatever that potent potable was that he had drank. We wondered how Sgt. Robinson might be doing, both hoping that he hadn't lost a leg. I was a little surprised that he didn't seem more excited about going home, but I kept that to myself. He was a really good guy and I wished him well. I think of him every time I hear "Hey Jude."

The next morning I got up, figuring that this would be my last day here on the base, but I sure wasn't going to ask anybody about it. I'd wait as long as I could till I was ordered back to the boonies. A little later in the day I ran into the first sergeant, and I was totally shocked to hear him say: "Specialist Hensler, you've been selected. You are to report to Brigade Forward at the fishnet factory." He told me to catch a truck or jeep going to FSB Horseshoe Bend, the official name of the base that everyone just called the fishnet factory. He told me that I would be trained by the outgoing SOM for a few days before taking over the duties of Soldier of the Month on January 1st, 1969.

I got a ride in a jeep headed to the fishnet factory the following morning. We headed south on Highway 1, passing by almost the whole length of the Long Binh complex. It was huge. We passed the Vietnamese National Military Cemetery then crossed over the Newport Bridge into Saigon. The driver took us through a residential area that looked quite prosperous. It was probably an area that the French lived in during the colonial era, with large houses on broad tree-lined boulevards. We drove through Cholon, the Chinese section of the city, then hit Highway 4, the main road to the Delta. The fishnet factory was about a mile down that road.

Like the cement factory, the fishnet factory was rented by the US Army who then took sole possession for whatever use they wanted. The building itself was enclosed with a tall wrought iron fence about 6 feet tall. Inside the fence were some grounds that led up to the building's front entrance. The structure had some offices in front and then a large factory floor behind it. All the machines for making fishnets stayed in place. This would be home for at least the next 5 weeks.

I reported to the lieutenant whom the first sergeant had told me about. He told me where to grab a bunk and stash my stuff and that the current SOM would be filling me in on my duties when he had a chance. I scoped out my new digs. I'd be out of the weather, the place was big enough to warrant having a mess hall, and I'd be eating 3 squares a day. Across the road was a battery of 155mm self-propelled howitzers and an infantry unit tasked with providing security for the base. There were a lot of folks stationed here at the Brigade Forward Headquarters and a whole lot more brass than I was used to seeing—Lt. Colonels and Majors were coming and going all the time. I was not used to exercising proper military etiquette in the field; it just wasn't done. But here, I'd have to watch my P's and Q's.

My first day ended without meeting up with the current SOM, so I was still in the dark as to what my duties were. Outside, though, it was a little brighter, and I went out to look up into the heavens and check out one of the current events we talked about during my interview with the board a few days earlier. For the first time ever, man was escaping the gravitational pull of the earth to venture out into space. Apollo 8 was nearly to the moon. It was really exciting, especially for those of us that grew up with the space program. It was real life adventure wrapped up in the politics of the Cold War. For someone like me who liked history, current events, and aviation, it just didn't get any better than that

Christmas arrived and went without leaving me with a distinct memory of the day. Likely because I spent it with nobody I really knew. I was in a new location for all of two days and had no time to really get to know anyone yet. Many memories are manufactured out of shared events; the lack of someone to partake in the holiday spirit is probably the reason for my dearth of memories of the day.

The day after Christmas I met up with the SOM for December. He laid out the duties for me and I was pleasantly surprised to find out that my fears of being a servant of some kind were unfounded. He told me that there might be some odd jobs here and there to take care of, but the primary task of the Soldier of the Month was to be the radio operator in the general's command and control helicopter. He told me that I would be flying every day.

The general's chopper was the latest model UH1-H Huey helicopter. It flew in every morning at first light from Long Binh and rested on the helipad in front of the fishnet factory. The chopper and crew were at the general's beck and call all day. His office was probably less than 100 feet from the helipad, so it took no time at all to get aboard. That was also, part of my job: to always be ready to go at any given moment.

I had flown in Hueys before, of course, but none of them had seats. The general's chopper had a bench seat attached to the rear cabin wall; that's where I sat. Directly in front of the bench seat was a single seat positioned so the general could look directly out the always open door. Behind the bench seat was the door gunner's position. The normal routine had only the general and myself aboard, along with the crew of four—two pilots and two door gunners.

Slightly offset from the general's seat was the rack that held at least three radios. There was also a crypto unit that scrambled radio transmissions so that only a person with a descrambler unit could understand what was being said. I was told that it was my responsibility to destroy that unit if we were ever shot down.

Since part of the job was keeping in touch with other units within the brigade as well as artillery support, air support and medevacs, I needed to have in my possession all of those frequencies and call signs down to the company level. I was given a booklet with the frequencies for the month of January. (All the frequencies were changed once a month for security reasons.) The booklet was called the SOI (signal operating instructions). Obviously, you never wanted that booklet to fall into the wrong hands, and it was impressed upon me how important that was. I ended up buying a thin chain and threaded it through the booklet so I could wear it around my neck. It would stay there the whole month.

The last three months back in the "world:"

Oct. 17— The Olympics, held in Mexico City, are boycotted by 32 African nations because of the participation of apartheid South Africa. Additional controversy occurs when Americans Tommie Smith and John Carlos, who each medal in the 200-meter dash, stand on the medal stand and hold black- gloved, clenched fists high above their heads in a "Black Power" salute during the playing of the Star Spangled Banner.

Oct— Cambodia admits it permitted the Viet Cong and North Vietnamese Army sanctuary in their country.

Oct. 31— President Johnson announces a complete bombing halt over North Vietnam.

Oct— Anti-war protests organized and led by Vietnam Veterans are held in San Francisco.

Oct— Peace talks begin in Paris between the US and North Vietnam.

Nov. 5— President Nixon, elected President, ran on the promise that he had a "secret plan to end the war."

Nov 5— "National Turn in Your Draft Card Day" is observed by many thousands of students at colleges and universities all across America.

Dec. 9— The world's first word processor using the first "mouse" is demonstrated at Stanford University.

Dec 24— Apollo 8 astronauts orbit the moon.

Pop culture:

"Night of the Living Dead" premiers in the city of Pittsburgh.

The Beatles release the "White Album."

"I Heard it Through the Grapevine" is released by Marvin Gaye.

O. J. Simpson is awarded the Heisman Trophy for being the best college football player in the country.

October through December would see the deaths of 2,590 servicemen in Vietnam, bringing the total for the war to 31,174.

CHAPTER TWENTY-EIGHT
JANUARY'S START

It was New Year's Day and my first day on my new job. I was a little nervous, to be sure. I'd never even spoken to a general before. One of the lieutenants on his staff introduced me to General Heyward that morning. He gave me a binder to carry and said, "Let's get to work." He wore a 45 automatic on his hip. I grabbed my M-16 and a bandolier of magazines.

The rotors on the Huey were already starting to wind up as we walked out to the helipad. The chopper, being the general's personal aircraft, was always kept clean and sported special graphics on the nose and doors. We climbed aboard and sat down, him in his special seat and me situated in front of the radio rack. I donned my earphones and microphone as we began to lift off. The pilot dipped the nose, we rose up and over the wrought iron fence and started our ascent into the early morning light. We headed west toward the Pineapple.

The general told me to contact the headquarters of the 4th Battalion and let them know we were coming in for a visit. We flew out to their base camp and landed. The general grabbed his binder and went in for a meeting with that battalion's commander. The crew shut down the chopper and we waited for the general to be done. When the meeting was over, the crew fired up the turbine and we headed off to the next confab. We spent most of the day flying from base to base. I was told to keep a log of the hours spent in the air and what type of flights they were.

We returned to the fishnet factory in the late afternoon. The chopper normally stayed at the base till almost dark, then returned to the air base for overnight maintenance; it could easily be recalled if needed. The general had a small trailer parked inside the factory that was his sleeping quarters. I had a cot that was inside my own personal bunker made of culvert halves and sandbags. It was close by the trailer.

The first day was a breeze. The only time I was really with the general was when we were flying. He hadn't asked me to do anything other than to carry his binder and work the radios. I was thinking, *Man, this is the best ever.* I had fresh clothes every day, hot food, and a clean place to sleep. The following three days did nothing to change my mind about the job. It couldn't have been any better. They say all good things come to an end.

General Heyward was called back to the states on an emergency leave. The brigade executive officer, the second in command, Colonel Jones, became the acting commander in the General's absence. Right away I could sense a difference in style and demeanor from the General. He seemed hard-core, a no-nonsense kind of guy. His radio call sign should have given me a clue, "Angry Axeman." Besides that, he gave me a list of things to do and let me know that I wasn't saying "yes sir" enough.

The colonel proved to be different in the air as well. We left the fishnet factory in the morning as usual, but we didn't head to a firebase for a consult with a battalion commander. Instead, he directed the pilots to fly low over the nipa palm lined canals that crisscrossed the Pineapple. He was scanning the area, looking for anything that might be suspicious.

At some point, he saw something that he felt should be further investigated. We called a company commander whose unit was operating in the area of interest. Colonel Jones told the captain on the ground that he would land his chopper at his position and wanted the commander to give him four men to go and check out the area of concern. They popped a smoke on the ground at their position, and the pilot guided in on it for a landing. Four guys walked up to the helicopter and climbed aboard. The pilot lifted off and banked toward the site in question.

I had two guys squeezed in on either side of me on the bench seat. I looked over at them and saw they were none too happy about getting plucked up by some Colonel who ought to be minding his own business and not fucking around with the guys on the ground. I knew how they felt: we hated it when some battalion commander flew over our position and demand to know why we were moving so slow or redirected our direction of travel to suit his needs. Two of the guys looked like FNGs: their fatigues hadn't faded, and their boots hadn't had all the dye leeched out of them yet. You could see fear in their faces. The other two guys looked like old hands, and they looked mostly pissed.

I was feeling a little ashamed of myself. The guys who hopped aboard had probably just crossed a canal or something as they were all wet and muddy. When they sat down next to me, I tried to avoid contact with them. I didn't want to get that slime on me. I felt bad because just a couple weeks ago I could have been in the same position as they were, and here I was now, trying to avoid touching them. They couldn't have cared less, of course, and probably took some joy in mucking up the nice clean clothes of the guys flying around in the helicopter and causing them grief. We dropped them off and then circled above as they searched the area. Nothing was found and we returned them to their unit. It seemed like things were going to be a little different with Colonel Jones running the show.

January 6th started a little later in the day than the previous few day's activities. It was probably about noon before we took off and headed toward the Pineapple. We picked up a radio transmission from a LOH (light observation helicopter, pronounced loach) stating that they had spotted an unarmed Viet Cong soldier running across a dry rice paddy. The LOH pilot was able to cut off his retreat to the trees by maneuvering the chopper in front of the soldier who would then run off in a new direction. Hearing this, Colonel Smith directed our pilot to head to that area.

We arrived on scene in about 5 minutes. The action was taking place in an open field bordered on each side by canals. It was about 1 mile away from the horseshoe bend of the Van Co Dong River. I spotted the LOH flying very close to the ground, and a moment later I saw the Viet Cong soldier running away from the chopper. The LOH is an incredibly agile helicopter. It's a lot smaller than a Huey and normally carries a crew of two, although it could fit four. The VC troop was carrying no weapon; however, it was a free-fire zone, and the helicopter crew could have engaged him if they had wanted to. From our vantage point, it looked like the LOH crew was trying to capture him.

The Viet Cong soldier ran toward one edge of the field, then the loach would try to knock him down by flying close to him and whacking him with the skid. The enemy troop then jumped back up and run in another direction. He was obviously in a panic as the scenario was repeated over and over again. I thought the enemy troop would stop and give up, knowing that one burst from the chopper's mini-gun would tear him in half. But no, he kept at it, running again and again after the nimble little chopper knocked him down again and again. I don't know why the chopper pilot didn't just zap the guy. It was obvious he wasn't going to surrender, and you never knew what might happen.

I think in the pilot's zeal to get a prisoner he lost track of just how close the enemy troop was getting to the nipa palms alongside the canal. We were circling above (about 500 feet) the whole time, counter-clockwise so the Colonel could see the whole deal play out from his side-mounted chair on the left side of the helicopter.

The VC was flattened again by the steel skid of the chopper. He jumped up and sprinted toward the nipa palms. This time he was too quick and too close. He disappeared into the thick foliage before the loach crew could swing around for another pass. There was no way to see him now: the palms were 15 or 20 feet high and densely packed. The LOH pilot, probably frustrated at this new turn of events, popped up over the nipa palms to the canal side of the heavy vegetation. Our pilot dropped down several hundred feet for a better look. The loach was directly over the canal, six feet above the water at most. I could see the ripples in the water from the downward blast of rotor wash. The LOH pilot faced the little chopper directly at the wall of green and started a slow traverse along the canal, looking for any sign of the VC.

I was watching intently and was alarmed to see the small craft tilt sharply over. I knew it didn't have enough forward speed to be able to maintain an angle of bank that steep. My fear was confirmed when I saw his rotor blade strike the surface of the canal and send up a large spray of water. The blade broke backwards on impact and was ripped from the center hub. The trailing blade fared no better and the resulting force caused the chopper to fall, spinning into the murky canal and sinking in a second. The little loaches flew without doors: this caused the LOH to sink like a rock, but also provided the crew with an avenue of escape. This was one of those times when it was hard to believe my eyes. Did I really just see that? It was there, and then it was gone.

The enemy soldier must have had some buddies in the palms. The LOH was nearly standing still in a hover when it was hit by enemy fire. The two man crew didn't have a chance from that range. The canal couldn't have been thirty feet wide at that point—maybe less.

Our pilot immediately banked over into a steep descent to catch a better view of the crash site. I spotted the two crew members in the water, swimming toward the opposite bank from where the enemy fire was coming from. Plumes of water were shooting up all around the swimmers, the result of enemy bullets striking the water. The door gunner on my side of the chopper started firing into the nipa palms, pouring slugs from his machine gun into the green wall that lined the bank. Maybe it was enough. The two crewmen were able to scramble up the far bank and blend into the foliage. They were on their own in there and probably lightly armed at best- —if they managed to hold onto their pistols through the crash and their swim to the canal bank. It was only a matter of time before the VC could cross the canal and kill or capture them. Colonel Jones ordered our pilot to continue making gun runs up and down the canal to keep the enemy from crossing over and getting to the downed crew.

We radioed for help right away. An Eagle Flight, an infantry troop with helicopters on standby back at Long Binh, responded to our call. Developed for situations just like this, they could have troops here pretty fast. But we were the only hope the downed crew had now. Our pilot lined up parallel to the canal and made several gun runs, alternating directions to give each gunner a crack at them and to not deplete all the ammunition on one side of the chopper. Of course, the Viet Cong were firing back, and the light aluminum skin of a helicopter body provides only the illusion of protection— not to mention the wide open doors.

On one of the gun runs the door gunner on my side of the helicopter was hit in the leg by ground fire, and the chopper took some hits as well. The gunner said he was ok and to continue on, and so we did. While we were making our call for help, a gunship crew stationed at Di An heard the urgent request and rushed to get their Cobra helicopter into the air and on their way to help us out. In the meantime, we continued to make gun runs during which Colonel Jones was hit twice, once in the leg and once in the shoulder. He did not let this deter him and he ordered the pilot not to let up.

Finally, the Cobra gunship arrived. It was a sleek machine that carried rockets and fired mini-guns and had a rapid-fire grenade launcher. Our pilot oriented the Cobra pilot to the locations of both the enemy and our own downed aircrew. We flew alongside of the Cobra as he initiated a gun run. He soon outpaced us, and our pilot banked away from the line of attack. As we were in our turn, I heard the opposite side door gunner yell out, "He's inverting!" I didn't see what happened since I was on the far side when we began our bank away. Our pilot, who did see it, set up a very rapid descent, finally leveling out about 100 feet above the surface of the ground. I could see the Cobra clearly now; it lay broken and on its side. The tail boom was ripped away from the chopper's body, the aluminum was torn and jagged like a shredded beer can, the crumpled rotors were ripped from the mast, and lying a few yards away was the wrecked fuselage.

All eyes on the cockpit of the downed bird as we flew overtop the crash site. The crew sat in tandem under a large plexiglass canopy, but no one noticed any movement. They were dead still. It looked like the Cobra crew was beyond help, but the downed LOH crew were still in jeopardy, so Colonel Jones said to continue with our own gun runs. Our chopper took more hits on the succeeding pass, and the master warning light on the instrument panel began to glow. The door gunner reported that we were trailing black smoke from the back of the helicopter. Colonel Jones wanted to do another run, but the pilot said we were in grave danger of losing the aircraft.

The Eagle flight from Long Binh was only a few minutes out, so we departed the area, hoping to find some friendly forces before we went down. The pilot got on the radio and transmitted a distress call: "MAYDAY! MAYDAY! MAYDAY! Fireball one going down, five clicks south of Firebase Kathy, acting brigade commander aboard and wounded."

Luckily, we spotted a small outpost along one of the larger canals in the area, and our pilot headed straight for it. I was crossing my fingers as we neared the landing area, what with the engine smoking and the alarms, the possibility of an engine failure was real. Fortunately, everything held together long enough for us to touchdown in one piece. I jumped down and tried to help Colonel Jones out of the chopper. He winced in pain as I supported him while he was stepping down. Medics ran out to the chopper to assist the Colonel and took him inside a tent so he could be checked out.

I walked back to the chopper to retrieve my M-16 and magazines. While I was there, I looked the helicopter over, checking for bullet holes. The evidence was there; it confirmed how, once again, I had lucked out. Not only had Colonel Jones been shot twice, not two feet in front of me, and the door gunner had been shot not two feet behind me, but there were holes in the floor close to my seat. Seeing them, I instinctively looked down at my feet. There, sticking out of my boot, was either a bullet fragment or part of the helicopter floor. The holes in the floor were just inches from where I normally placed my feet while sitting in front of the radio rack. And, speaking of the rack, there was a bullet hole in that, just inches away from where my knee would have been. I'd seen enough. I don't know how many holes were in the helicopter altogether, but they didn't try to fly it out. A big Chinook helicopter was dispatched to sling the disabled chopper underneath it and haul it back to a repair depot.

The door gunner's wound was minor. But the colonel needed hospital attention, and a medevac was called for him. I did not see the colonel again. Another chopper arrived to get the crew and take them back to their base at Long Binh. I went along, too, and they dropped me off at the fishnet factory.

I ran over the day's events as I lay on my cot in my little bunker late that night. I heard that the Eagle Flight assaulted the enemy in the nipa palms and were able to rescue the downed LOH crew, but I didn't know at what cost, if any. I kept replaying the images and emotions of the day: the rotor blades being ripped off the hub as they struck the water, the LOH violently spinning into, then sinking below the opaque waters of the canal, the miraculous appearance of the two crewmen, swimming for their lives amongst bursts of automatic weapons fire kicking up geysers of water all around them. How they made it to the far bank, I'll never know; but I'm certain our door gunners had to have been of some help. I was so excited to see the Cobra come on-station. The deadly gunship was blasting the Viet Cong with rockets and mini-guns. With two guys wounded and damage to our helicopter, their arrival was a Godsend. I went from elation to despair upon hearing the two words anxiously voiced by the door gunner: "He's inverting!" Helicopters don't fly upside down. It could only be bad, and bad it was, as evidenced by the broken and crumpled gunship lying on its side in an open field. There would be no miracles for those two. Nobody survives an impact from that high up. I thought about the Colonel not giving up on the downed crew, though twice wounded himself. He relented only when overruled by the aircraft commander whose main responsibility was to save the helicopter and all the souls on board.

The image that bothered me the most was of that Viet Cong soldier running in a panic and being knocked down repeatedly by the skid on the LOH. I wasn't sure if what the LOH pilot did was only done to capture the enemy troop. I kept replaying the scene over and over, and I got the uneasy feeling that the loach crew was having fun with this guy, tormenting him for kicks. It was the way they let him get up and run away again and again after knocking him down. All these crews carried personal weapons. If they really wanted him as a prisoner and didn't want to risk killing him with the mini-gun or machine gun, they could easily have shot him in the leg with a pistol or an M-16. I can't be sure, of course, and I truly hope I'm wrong. But this was a free-fire zone, and every Vietnamese knew you were fair game if spotted in the Pineapple. There were no friendlies in the Pineapple. The crew had every right to blast him, weaponless or not.

And I kept thinking back to a thought that crossed my mind as I was watching the scene play out before my eyes: "They should stop fucking with this guy and waste him." I even thought myself cold-hearted for thinking that. As it turned out, it would have been for the best. The LOH crew, more than likely, wouldn't have been shot down. The Viet Cong in the nipa palms would have been unlikely to fire unless they thought they were discovered, and at that point they were not. There would have been no need for the Cobra crew; now they were dead. Colonel Smith and the door gunner would not have been wounded. I never did hear how the Eagle Flight fared, other than them saving the LOH crew. Lastly, two helicopters were destroyed and one badly damaged. I wish I hadn't had those thoughts. Maybe the LOH pilot just didn't have the heart to shoot an unarmed man. But it would have been better if he had.

It's just one more reason why war messes up so many people's heads. Can you imagine how that LOH pilot must feel if he was, in fact, just messing with the Viet Cong, and that's how he got himself shot down and how two people lost their lives trying to save him? Even if he was just so good-hearted that he couldn't shoot an unarmed man, what do you think would happen the next time around? A sure way to turn a warm heart cold.

CHAPTER TWENTY-NINE
THE NEXT DAY

Life goes on, as they say, particularly for a combat brigade in a war zone. People die or get wounded every day; it's the nature of things. Despite my midnight musings on the previous day's events, this was a new day, and I quickly set aside any further pondering for down the road.

With the general in the states and the colonel hospitalized, the brigade turned to my old battalion commander, Lt. Colonel Behm, to lead the unit. He was not at full song just yet. He was still recovering from his wounds incurred in early August on our riverine operation into the Rung Sat Special Zone. When we were introduced, he extended his left hand to shake, inverting it so as to be able to shake my right hand. It works, but is awkward if you are caught unaware. Obviously, he couldn't use his right hand; he always held it down by his side. He didn't mention it and I didn't ask. Maybe he was waiting for another operation, but I just didn't know.

But the war goes on. A new helicopter awaited on the helipad that morning in front of the fishnet factory, along with a different crew. Col. Behm and I walked out to the pad to start our new day out over the Pineapple. We made a few stops, like the general, but he did not seem inclined to go looking for trouble as Colonel Jones was want, which was fine by me.

We had just taken off from a battalion base camp at the western edge of the Pineapple and gotten up to cruising altitude when I noticed a bit of disconcerting body language from the pilots. I was looking out ahead when I saw the two pilots who sit side by side suddenly turn and look at each other. I interpreted the body language as a "what the hell" moment. But I was unaware of any danger, either outside or inside the helicopter. I was to learn later that the pilots felt through their controls a loss of the hydraulic system. This was not a major problem in straight and level flight, but any change of altitude or direction carried some risks. The Huey helicopter we were flying in had a single hydraulic system that was used to boost the force the pilots exerted to move the flight controls. The aerodynamic forces on the rotors are at such a level that it would be difficult for a pilot to control the helicopter without this assistance.

If you want to know what this would feel like, go out into your car, turn the key to unlock the steering wheel, but don't start the car. Now try turning the steering wheel; you will be able to do it, but it will be hard. Now imagine you are driving down a very curvy mountain road and you lose your power steering and power brakes. You might keep up for a little bit, but soon you will be fatigued. On one of those curves, you won't be able to get the wheel turned back fast enough for the next bend, and off you will go.

This was what was confronting our pilots. Some folks say flying a helicopter is really a continuously controlled crash, meaning that flying a helicopter is never a hands off affair. You can trim a plane to practically fly itself straight and level, but that isn't true with choppers; you are constantly correcting for attitude, speed, and direction. Faced with this situation, the copilot had his hands on the controls along with the pilot to give him an assist. The major danger was in moving the controls too far and then not being able to get them back in time to make a correction. This condition eliminated the possibility of a normal helicopter landing. There was no way to hover without the hydraulic system working. We would have to land like an airplane on a runway. We had no wheels, though, just skids, and that's what we would be doing—skidding along the runway.

There was a gravel airstrip close to Duc Hoa on the northern edge of the Pineapple and it was the closest runway to us. We were headed east, but Duc Hoa had a north south runway, so the pilots had to orient the aircraft to a northerly compass heading. It was just a left turn, but it seemed to take forever to make it. Both pilots, holding the controls ever so carefully, slowly put the chopper in a very slight bank and held it there till the right heading was reached.

With Duc Hoa in sight, the pilots had to gradually lose altitude till we reached the end of the runway then fly the chopper onto the gravel. This chopper had seats like the general's had and seat belts as well. I usually didn't wear them, but I buckled up for the landing and cinched it tight. The pilots told us to get out of the chopper as soon as it came to rest. I don't know how fast we were going when the skids started dragging along the surface, but they made an unsettling sound for far too long till we finally came to a skewed stop. Everybody was fine. I was beginning to think that this Soldier of the Month gig was not nearly as good a deal as I had first thought.

Thankfully, things settled down for a little bit and we got into a regular routine. Colonel Behm was not very demanding of my time and I started "living the life" again. I think I started to gain a little weight, too, but my appetite still didn't seem to be what it should be. I had access to a lot of food now—3 squares a day—but I rarely took advantage of it. They even showed some movies at the fishnet factory and I got to see "The Graduate" with Dustin Hoffman.

I was nearing the halfway point of my stint as SOM and was starting to wonder what would happen to me after my month was over. At the end of January, I would have two months left in-country. Frankly, I didn't want to spend them in the boonies; I was spoiled. Even though I felt undeserving and even experienced a little guilt about leaving the guys, I did not want to go back. But it was out of my hands.

We started the next day by flying out to a base occupied by the 4th Battalion. Colonel Behm wanted to have a consult with their battalion commander. We landed at the camp in the usual cloud of dust that marked helicopter operations in the dry season. The crew shut the engine down, and after the dust cleared I noticed a poncho-covered body lying on the ground on the other side of the perimeter.

I stepped out of the helicopter to look around for someone I might know while Colonel Behm went into the Command Post for a meeting. A lot of my original platoon got infused into the 4th Battalion back in June, and I was hoping to find one of them here. I did. His name was Jim Wallace and he was a pretty good buddy of mine going back to Fort Lewis. He told me that not 15 minutes earlier the GI under the poncho was killed by a booby-trap on the far side of the stream that bordered the base camp. The booby-trap was set up not far from a village also on the far side of the stream.

A squad came back into the base from an overnight ambush and saw the body lying there. Apparently, one of those guys was a very good buddy with the dead soldier. He sat down beside the body and began to weep. It was a sad tableau: the young man, alive just minutes ago, now lying in the dirt covered by a mud-spattered poncho that wasn't quite big enough to cover him. His boots were sticking out from underneath. They were the boots of a veteran: practically grey, and leather cracked.

It was around 11:00 AM and I had this sudden thought: "Here I am, looking at this tragedy for some family halfway around the world, and they don't know yet that their lives have been irrevocably changed." It was nighttime back in America. A girlfriend might be writing a love letter that will never be read. His mother, possibly getting ready for bed, may have just thanked God for keeping her son safe for another day.

The man sitting on the ground next to the body was sobbing uncontrollably now; his head, bent over and resting in his hands, was heaving up and down. I looked on at this picture and was disgusted with myself for being able to observe it so clinically. How could I understand the sadness but not feel it? What the fuck was wrong with me?! I felt envious of the man crying on the ground. It was true that I didn't know the person lying there, but he was a fellow troop and it wasn't right that I could be so detached from the situation. I suddenly realized I hadn't even given a thought to those two dead helicopter crewmen since the day it happened. Ever since I had heard my friend's name, Dan Morris, announced while I was looking at the field crosses during the memorial ceremony back in April, I'd been keeping my emotions in check, although not by design. Now, it felt like an important part of me was missing.

The following day was a Sunday. Sunday meant a visit to Capital Military Assistance Command (CMAC). It was formed in June of 1968 for the sole purpose of protecting the capital. June was when we were yanked out of War Zone D and convoyed to Saigon to blunt an anticipated attack on the city. The 199th Light Infantry was an integral part of the command that also included other units.

Once a week the commanders of these units met at the CMAC headquarters in downtown Saigon for a meeting. The building they were housed in had a helipad on the roof, and we landed on it to let the commander out then take off again to open up the pad for other choppers to land.

We had to kill time until the meeting was over so the pilots used this time to go joyriding in their helicopter. Flying generals around was usually mundane (unless you had someone like Colonel Jones), so when the pilots had a chance to do some fun flying they took it. They headed out to the countryside to do some low-level flying that gave you a much better appreciation of speed. The most fun was when they found a canal that had tall growths of nipa palm on each bank. They flew down the canal just a few feet off the water. With the wall of green on both sides you felt like you were flying in a tunnel. I really liked Sundays.

A few days later General Heyward returned from the States and I said goodbye to Colonel Behm. The following days were fairly routine. We flew to Cu Chi once so General Heyward could meet with the commander of the 25th Division. One other time we flew down to the Mekong River and landed on a boat in the middle of it to meet with someone from the 9th Division. Landing on the boat was pretty cool but a little scary; the helipad was very small.

Intelligence reports during the last couple of weeks in January were indicating a new build-up of enemy troops entering the Pineapple. Those reports were proven to be true on Jan. 26th when elements of the 199th encountered a large enemy force in the western Pineapple not far from the

Cambodian border. It was late afternoon when we got on scene. The general wanted to check out what was going on, but at that time things were chaotic on the ground. A true sense of what they were up against was yet to be established. We headed back to the fishnet factory as darkness fell.

We were back at it at first light and headed west toward the Cambodian border. Things had heated up overnight and additional units were being flown in, including elements from my old battalion. There was bedlam in the skies over the battlefield. The airspace over the battlefield looked like a swarm of bees searching for a new hive. Helicopters were everywhere. There were 3 C&C choppers, including ours. There were medevac helicopters and hunter killer teams made up of LOH's and Cobras. There were Huey's ferrying in new troops to bolster the numbers of those already on the ground. There was a FAC (forward air controller) for the Air Force and F-100s ready to bomb any identifiable target that the FAC could point out. Besides that, an artillery battery was lobbing shells into the area, and we had to make sure our flight path did not intersect their trajectories. I still have my logbook entries for my daily flight times, and for Jan. 27th 1969 it says over 10 hours. We stayed on scene all day except for a few hot refuels.

The fighting was pretty intense below us and everyone was on a razor's edge. I could hear it in all their voices. The general was trying to keep in touch with everyone and keep his fingers on the pulse of the battle. You could sense his great concern for everyone on the ground, which made what happened later that day very difficult for him to handle, I'm sure.

Firefights are mass confusion at times, and it is hard to keep track of everyone involved. It's easy to get separated and isolated from the rest of your group. If you are a leader, it's the last thing you want to be confronted with when an air strike or helicopter gunships have been called in to support you, particularly if the mission will be close in. That was the situation as we flew over the battlefield that day. The F-100's were on station with their bomb loads ready to strike. Problem was, a company commander on the ground could not account for all his men, and the general was reluctant to give clearance for the air strike until all the men could be spoken for. The F-100 fighter-bombers had jet engines that burned a prodigious amount of fuel, particularly when flying on station at low altitude the way they were now. They can't stay on site very long.

This battle was a major to-do, and it attracted a lot of attention. Apparently a major general from the II Field Force, responsible for combat operation in III Corps, was monitoring General Heyward's unit frequency—thus his conversation with the company commander on the ground who could not account for all his people. The II Field Force Commander was on-site in his own helicopter and contacted us on a different frequency. I took the call and put General Heyward in touch with him. I could still monitor the conversation. The major general told General

Heyward to start acting like a professional. In other words, make the tough call and send in the air strike.

I don't know how it must have felt to give the ok, knowing someone might be in great jeopardy, but he did, however reluctantly, act professionally. Whether it was the right decision or not isn't always easy to answer; it's what is referred to as "the fog of war." Six men from the brigade died; five bodies were sent home to their loved ones. One was never found. He was originally listed as an MIA. No evidence of him being a prisoner of war was ever discovered. After that air strike, PFC Crawford was probably no more than a red mist, at most. If a 500 pound bomb drops nearby, there won't be anything left to find.

We headed back to Brigade Forward after the long day. My ears hurt from wearing the headphones all those hours, I couldn't wait to get them off.

The next morning, we returned to the area but it was just about all over. The Viet Cong had slipped back across the border into Cambodia, but they had left 50 of their compatriots lying dead in the tall grass. We had 5 companies involved in the battle, including 2 from my old battalion. In addition to the 6 dead, there were 20 wounded and 9 helicopters took hits.

It was the last significant event of my stint as the general's enlisted aide. I only had a few days left and I had to train the incoming aide to his duties.

On balance, it was a great month: a lot of new experiences, a little too much excitement on a day or two, but overall pretty routine. Had good nights of sleep, hot food, and clean clothes. No complaints.

THIRTY
CIVIC AFFAIRS

I finished up on the 31st and returned to Long Binh on Feb. 1st to an uncertain future. Upon my return I somehow ran into Colonel Behm. He remembered me from his stint as acting brigade commander and asked me what I was doing. I told him I just completed my turn as SOM and now was uncertain what would come next as nobody had said anything yet. Unexpectedly, he asked me what I wanted to do. I really didn't know if he had any pull or not since I was technically still a part of the 5/12 and he was in Headquarters. They were always short of people in the field and they probably wanted me back. But I figured what the hell, I've got nothing to lose. So I told him I'd like to work in Civic Affairs. I'm wondering what he's going to think about that. After all, this is the guy who back at Fort Lewis wanted to award anybody who brought him the ears of a VC or NVA colonel or above a money bounty. And Civic Affairs isn't exactly the calling of a warrior. Well, he just laughed, and I wasn't sure what that meant. But then he said, "Ok, we can do that." Maybe 10 months in Vietnam and being seriously wounded had softened him a bit. I still was holding my breath; I wasn't counting on anything until I was actually assigned to the Civic Affairs unit. But Colonel Behm was true to his word, and I would start my new job in a few days.

The Civic Affairs unit was a small group tasked with coordinating efforts by the US Army to strengthen the bonds of friendship between itself and the civilian population. The Army used its engineering units to build roads, repair damaged housing, and dig wells for villagers. They also sent out medical teams to outlying villages to treat the civilian population. They called these Medcap (medical civic action programs).

I had seen Medcap programs in many villages that we cordoned and searched in the upper delta. That's how I knew about them, and I liked what I saw—something good actually coming out of the war. So that was part of my motivation for wanting to work with them. I'd still get off the base, but I wouldn't be humping the boonies. To be honest, I'd have done practically anything to avoid spending my last two months in the Pineapple.

There were only 4 or 5 people in my section and I can't remember a single person's name. I was working on my own a lot, so I really didn't have much chance to form any friendships. I worked both from the main base at Long Binh and the forward base at the fishnet factory. One of my duties was to locate building supplies for village projects. I got a truck and a driver from the motor pool and headed off to different compounds to scrounge for lumber.

I learned right away that Civil Affairs was treated like a stepchild in the Army, and there wasn't much prestige in being a part of it. Much of that most likely stemmed from the problematic feelings most GIs had with the Vietnamese in general. Fairly or unfairly, most US troops did not feel that the Vietnamese Army was up to the task and felt we were doing more of the missions that they should be doing. The GIs could see that corruption was rampant; the wide-open black market was proof of that. In the hinterlands, there were few signs of support for the combat troops by the locals. This fostered resentment by troops looking for some appreciation for their sacrifices. For many troops, most of their interactions with the Vietnamese were limited to prostitutes or shysters trying to rip them off. Then there were those stories that everyone heard about the Vietnamese who worked on the big American bases. How the Vietnamese day laborers surreptitiously paced off distances to certain targets of value inside the base to better the accuracy of the mortar shells they lobbed onto the compound at night. Or the Vietnamese barber who cut GIs hair on the post during the day, and then that night was found dead in the barbed wire perimeter after an assault on the base.

Those feelings were not without merit but were not the whole story. Unfortunately, most troops did not have the opportunity to get to know the Vietnamese on an individual basis. I was lucky to have had the chance to live with them and get to know them and form some friendships which gave me a little better perspective on things. Anyway, I soon found out that I could get a lot more stuff if I said I needed some building supplies to fix up an enlisted men's club rather than a Vietnamese village out in the boonies.

It was a good job. I got to move around a lot. We went to the Saigon docks or Newport docks or Tan Son Nhut Airbase to beg for stuff. For the most part, I was working out of Long Binh during those first weeks of February. During that time, my old unit was still out patrolling in the Pineapple and suffered some more injuries due to booby-traps. There was still talk of an offensive that centered around the Lunar New Year celebrations as possible redo of last year's great clash, but the Tet Holiday passed without incident.

I finally got something for winning the SOM; the brigade sent me to Vung Tau for a three day R&R. Vung Tau was located about 65 miles southeast of Saigon on the South China Sea. The Army leased some hotels there for the troops who came to the old French Colonial resort town. I got a ride out of Bien Hoa Air Force Base on a twin-engine cargo plane en route to Vung Tau. Luckily or unluckily, I left the day the new offensive started across the country. Luckily, because Long Binh and, specifically, Camp Frenzel-Jones (where I was staying) were rocketed and mortared the same night that I left. Unluckily, because Vung Tau, ordinarily a very secure area, was thought to be under threat of an attack and was put under curfew every night.

But the daytime hours were mine to do as I wished and I swam in the South China Sea every day and ate some really good food (like steaks every night) at the R&R center. I also roamed around the small town a bit. There were bars, like in Saigon, named after American locations. But I wasn't much of a drinker; I never had more than a beer or two.

I guess the concerns about an attack had some merit because a communication unit got rocketed one night. They were stationed high on a hill at the end of the beach. I looked up at the hill one night and saw a large fire up there. But it turned out that the most danger I was in came from the ocean. I was swimming one afternoon and got caught in a riptide. It started pushing me out to sea. I panicked at first and tried to swim against the current back to shore, but all I was doing was tiring myself out. Suddenly, I was out of it and in calmer water. I must have been swimming somewhat diagonally and eventually swam out of the current. I really felt at the mercy of the ocean. I know about riptides now, but I didn't then. Thankfully, by chance, I escaped it.

I headed back to Long Binh, again by cargo plane. The offensive was still going strong but mostly in terms of rocket attacks. I learned that over 80 rockets and mortar rounds had hit the base at Long Binh the night after I left for Vung Tau. Saigon was being hit again as well, just like they were last June when we moved south.

The captain in charge of my unit sent me to the fishnet factory to go on some Medcaps. Luck followed me there; Long Binh suffered some ground attacks right after I left. The fishnet factory was right on the edge of the city, and the city was being rocketed nightly, but none of the rockets hit close to us. Nonetheless, I was taking no chances and slept in my bunker every night. The B-52s were really pounding the infiltration routes and staging areas to the west of Saigon. Every night the ground shook, the windows rattled, the skies to the west lit up from the blasts of the bombs going off, and the sounds of rolling thunder crept through the night air. It was a comforting sound.

The post-Tet offensive of 1969 concentrated more on military targets than the previous years when many cities were attacked, resulting in high numbers of civilian casualties. The Viet Cong and North Vietnamese Army struck American and South Vietnamese military bases up and down the length of the country. Long Binh and Camp Frenzel-Jones, the 199th's home base, were hit with both rocket attacks and ground assaults. Fortuitously, I had missed both—by a day each time. I went to Vung Tau the day the offensive started (missing the rocket attacks that night) and left for the fishnet factory a day before the ground assault occurred.

Curiously, the post-Tet offensive of 1969 is not nearly as well-documented and reported on as the Tet Offensive of 1968, even though American casualties approached the benchmark losses of that previous battle. US losses were approximately 300 a week with an official total of over 1100 for the offensive. Part of the reason for that was that Saigon was never really threatened the way it had been in 1968. Still, rockets hit the city nightly, some of which thrust their way over the fishnet factory on their way to targets in the city.

March began with me distributing rice that was uncovered out in the Pineapple by the 4th Battalion. It was a really big find, 4800 pounds, and included a large arms cache as well. I got the number 4800 pounds from one of my letters home in which I was describing my duties in the Civil Affairs Unit. I bought myself a unit history of the 199th Light Infantry Brigade a few years ago, and it was pretty neat to see a log entry for March 2nd 1969 describing the operation that found the rice—4800 pounds of it.

Speaking of March 2nd, it signaled the completion of my 11th month in-country. I had 30 days to go; I was really short now. Short enough to sit on a curb and not have my feet touch the street. So short that I could walk under the door instead of opening it. There were tons of "I'm so short" phrases.

A month to go was a milestone for sure; the end was in sight. It didn't hold quite the emotional and psychological edge for me as it did for the guys in the boonies. I was doing something I liked and was operating at the low end of the risk scale. For those in the field, particularly those in heavy combat, 30 days meant both hope and despair. Hope that it now seemed possible that they might actually live through the war, and despair in that they might end up suffering through 11 months of hell only to be killed or wounded in their last days in-country.

For the combat infantrymen that 12th month was torture. They were always on edge, trying to be too careful, too cautious, or too tentative for their own good. You couldn't blame them. They wouldn't know for sure when they would be called back to the base. Every unit was different, but most tried to get people out of the field as soon as practical. Most infantry units were chronically short of people and some poor guys ended up out in the field with as little as 3 days to go. Can you imagine the tension they must have felt? When are they going to bring me in? 10 days to go, 9, 8, 7…?? The last days must have felt like agony. 10 days to go and you want me to go out on ambush??? As short as I am and you want me to walk point??? Yes, for some 30 days was both a blessing and a curse.

THIRTY-ONE
LAST DAYS

I got down to about 3 days to go and couldn't believe it was really happening. There were many times during the previous year when I thought that this day would never come, particularly during those early months in the jungle. But here it was, I was finally going home. Trouble was, I wasn't nearly as excited about it as I thought I would be. My current job was great. I wasn't stuck on a base all day: I could travel around and see new places, interact with the locals, and come back every night to a hot meal and a clean cot to sleep on all night. Besides all that, I felt like I was doing something worthwhile. The captain of the unit asked if I would consider extending my tour, promising some incentives like another R&R and a promotion. I considered it, but not too seriously. If I could have been absolutely certain that I would retain my position and the area I was working in, I might have done it, but the risk of everything going bad was too great. I had an infantry MOS (military occupational specialty) that was always in demand out in the field. The infantry companies were chronically short of people due to combat deaths, wounds, and sickness. I could easily have been sent back to the field at any time. On top of that, there was no guarantee that we would stay based around Saigon; the unit could be sent north just as fast as we moved south last June. And then there were the rocket attacks; though they were sporadic and not great in number, you never knew when you might be in the wrong place at the wrong time.

Part of the out-processing routine was an obligatory visit to the re-enlistment sergeant for a re-up talk. Mine was short— No thanks! In a way, I didn't mind the Army, but it was the army in the field that I didn't mind. I wasn't that fond of the garrison army with all the rules, regulations, and demanded respect for those who didn't deserve any.

The Army I served in was under a lot of stress, some of its own making, some not. But regardless of the causes, the fabric of the Army that was already frayed when I arrived in April of 68 was now coming apart at the seams as I was leaving in April of 69. By the end of the war, it was in tatters.

It was just a really crazy time to have served. People could get away with a lot more, not just because there was a war going on but because of the times. The anti-war and the civil rights movements were forces in Vietnam as well as at home. The troops brought these issues along with them to the war zone, and their displeasure with the Army manifested itself in drug and disciplinary problems on the large bases and eventually resulted in combat refusals out in the field. While we may have faked ambushes, troops in later years sometimes just refused to go on certain missions. For the Army as an institution, Vietnam had to be a low point in its history. For individual soldiers sent to Vietnam, it was without question the most significant event of their young lives, one they carried with them long after the "Freedom Bird" took them back to the "World."

The "World" was my next stop. I had said my goodbyes to those at the Civil Affairs unit and caught a ride down to the 90th Replacement Battalion, which is your last stop before leaving for the airport. I got there on the evening of April the 1st and was scheduled to leave the next morning. It was a reunion of sorts because I ran into a bunch of guys who had been transferred to other units during the infusion but were scheduled to leave the country on the same day as me. It was fun comparing notes on the different paths our tours in Vietnam had taken us.

There were plenty of barracks to sleep in for our overnight stay, but many of us elected to stay in a bunker overnight. I didn't want to risk having a rocket or mortar round land on me my last 24 hours in-country! I spent part of the night on top of the bunker, sitting on the sandbags and BSing with some of the guys I knew. The night was dry and clear. Just like my first night in-country, I watched the gunships raking over the hills in the distance and tracked the smoky paths of falling flares. The big guns were pumping out the H&I fire, and the troops were manning their machine guns in the guard towers. Not much had changed.

Morning eventually dawned on my last day—#365. It looked like I was going to make it. Buses picked us up and transported us to Bien Hoa Air Base where I had landed a year earlier. I was filled with a curious mixture of excitement, anticipation, and melancholy. I guess it should have been no surprise that departing Vietnam left me conflicted; I was conflicted coming and conflicted while I was there.

The big DC-8 sat out on the tarmac waiting for us to board. It was a Seaboard World Airlines jet, and it would take about 260 of us back home. But before we could board we passed an amnesty box. The amnesty box was a big wooden square container, probably 5 feet in every dimension, with a wide slot about 3/4 of the way up on the front. There was a large sign stating that if anyone had in their possession anything of an illegal nature, it could be placed into the box with no questions asked. It also stated that once we passed the box if we were found to have anything illegal we would be prosecuted. Illegal items were listed to make it easier for an individual to make up his mind whether to ditch something or not. The list was comprised mostly of drugs and weapons. I read the sign over again, I wasn't sure if my bayonet was considered contraband or not. Colonel Jones had given me the bayonet as a commemorative token of our helicopter mission over the Pineapple to help the downed crewmen of the LOH. There was no way I was going to throw it in the box. I decided to risk it and walked by.

Climbing the steps to board the airplane had a surreal feel to it. It didn't seem right to be leaving, even though I didn't want to stay. There was no pay-off from my year of service. I guess it's just human nature to need an achievement, a goal, an end, or a resolution for an effort put forth. If you work all week you want to be paid at the end of it. If you study all night for a test you want to be graded on it. If you are playing a game you finish it to see who wins. I know full well how crazy this must sound. How can I feel the war is wrong and at the same time feel reluctant to leave it? I don't have a good answer; it is what it is. It was like leaving that hilltop Viet Cong base camp after the firefight: I wanted out of there, but it felt wrong to just up and leave that land—hard fought for and stained with American blood.

For all of us one-tour vets, Vietnam was like a baseball game where you walk into the stadium off the street, play an inning, and then go back home. In the timeline of the Vietnam war, I probably played the 5th or 6th inning. Leaving the game before it was over, without a resolution, left me feeling empty, unsatisfied, and with too many unresolved issues. I guess I wanted to see what the nearly 12,000 guys who perished during my year tour died for. But there was no answer and never really would be.

All aboard, the pilot taxied to the end of the runway, turned into the wind, let the big jet's engines spool up, released the brakes, and sped down the runway. The instant the tires lost contact with the concrete, a cheer rang out from one end of the plane to the other. The voices didn't all carry the same level of exhilaration, though: some resonated with genuine elation, some were muted, some just obligatory. I guess mine fell into the latter classifications, and I envied those who fell in the former.

We climbed steeply and banked east toward the ocean. I looked down and saw the languid waters of the Dong Nai River meandering through the dark green jungles of War Zone D. I wondered if anyone was down there now and looking up through a gap in the forest canopy, catching a glimpse of our "Freedom Bird" and longing to be on it. I clearly remember spying the bright orange livery of that Braniff airliner through the tall branches during a lull in that firefight last June and wondering if I would ever make it out on one.

Obviously, I did. But sadly, the thrill of finally being on the "Freedom Bird" did not live up to my expectations. I felt strangely guilty about leaving. I was safe but didn't feel like I deserved to be. I know it sounds screwy, but I felt like I didn't do enough, even though not believing in what I was doing. It was hard for me to get my head around that. Nonetheless, I was going home.

Our first stop was Japan, and all I remember about that was how cold it was. The next stop was Travis Air Force Base in California. Flight time over the North Pacific Ocean was about 11 hours.

We landed at Travis around 11:00 AM and were bussed to the Oakland Army Base across the bay from San Francisco. It was a major transit center for troops returning from overseas deployments during the Vietnam War. There was a large sign at the base with the words "Welcome Home" that we walked under on our way into the out-processing area.

I had some time left before my two-year obligation to the Army was over, but the Army wisely decided that returning Vietnam Vets with less than 5 months to go would be discharged upon their return to the states. The process of being discharged out of the Army was done assembly-line style: visits to personnel, finance, medical, and uniform issue. I was issued a set of dress greens with all the right patches sewn on, ribbons in place, and my combat infantry badge pinned on above them. Officially, I could wear it for less than 24 hours; I'd be out of the service in less than a day. Dinner time came and we were treated to a steak dinner. Afterward, with only a few more details to be attended to, I'd stay overnight and start my way home in the morning.

I didn't sleep well that first night back, probably a combination of jet lag, excitement, and anticipation. I can clearly recall lying on the top of a bunk bed in the transit barracks, wide awake, my mind racing with all that happened over the past year, and sort of being in shock that it was all over— just like that. The night before, I watched the war from atop a bunker, and now I could look across the bay and see the glow of lights in the nighttime sky over San Francisco while listening to the Mamas & The Papas singing "California Dreaming" on the radio. It all seemed a bit surreal.

In the morning, I had my last meal in the Army and then got my discharge papers. I went together with a few other guys to catch a taxi ride to the San Francisco International Airport. I bought a ticket for a Trans World Airlines flight to Pittsburgh. It still didn't seem real to me: the idea that I was actually going home. But 4 or 5 hours later we were pulling up to the gate at Greater Pitt. Mom and Dad were waiting for me.

I guess this would be the logical place to end this story, since it is about my time in the service and Vietnam. But it didn't take long for me to find out that just because your body made the trip home, it didn't necessarily mean your mind came along with it. I might have been home, but Vietnam was still with me every day. I found it impossible not to think of it, and I still carried with me those unresolved issues that troubled me.

During my last 3 months in-country,

January 12, 1969— The New York Jets defeat the favored Baltimore Colts in Super Bowl III, giving the upstart American Football League equal status with the National Football League.

January 20, 1969— Richard Nixon is sworn in as the 37th President of the United States.

January 25, 1969— Paris Peace Talks resume.

January 30, 1969— The Beatles perform for the last time in public.

February 22, 1969— Major communist offensive begins in Vietnam. Army bases all over South Vietnam are targeted. Over 1100 Americans were killed in action during the 3-week offensive.

February 27, 1969— President Nixon arrives in Rome and is greeted by thousands of students protesting the Vietnam War.

March 1, 1969— Mickey Mantle announces his retirement from baseball.

March 10, 1969— James Earl Ray pleads guilty to the murder of Martin Luther King Jr. He is sentenced to 99 years.

March 18, 1969— The United States begins carpet bombing Viet Cong and North Vietnamese Army sanctuaries in eastern Cambodia

March 20, 1969— John Lennon marries Yoko Ono.

March 25, 1969— Midnight Cowboy with John Voight and Dustin Hoffman is the first X-rated movie to win the best picture Academy Award.

During my last 3 months in-country, 3,836 GIs lost their lives, bringing the total for the war at this point to over 35,000 dead.

THIRTY-TWO
HOME

I had hardly slept since leaving Vietnam. I hadn't slept on the flight over the Pacific, nor had I slept much during the night while in the out-processing center at the Oakland Army Base. I was too keyed up and out of sync due to jet lag. A lot had transpired in the last 48 hours. I had traveled over 10,000 miles through 12 time zones. I was discharged from the Army, no longer a soldier but a newly-minted veteran. I went from jungle fatigues to dress greens to a T-shirt and blue jeans in 2 days. It was all a blur and too much to absorb in such a short amount of time. From war zone to home in 48 hours was just too quick.

You would think going to a war zone would be the more difficult of the two, but there were key differences between coming and going, at least in my case. Going over, I was with guys I had known for months: we had trained together, we were traveling together, and we would be in the war together, at least for a while. Coming home I did alone.

I wanted to be more excited about getting back to "The World," and I did my best to portray that to my Mom and Dad, but inside I was all out of sorts. I was home but felt lost. I guess I wasn't capable of letting go. I felt like a football player who's plucked from the field and forced to sit in the stands. It was too abrupt, and the shock to my nervous system came to manifest itself in long periods of restlessness. I might have been out of the war, but the war wasn't out of me.

I recall looking at the bare trees on the ride home from the airport and contrasting their look to where I had just come from. I was antsy and wanted a cigarette but felt funny about lighting up; my mom and dad had never seen me smoke.

We pulled into the driveway; it felt surreal. It didn't seem possible, yet here I was. I walked into the house and immediately went to my room. I opened the door and was shocked to see a TV and a couch and a recliner but no bed. My bedroom had been turned into the family room. Years later my mom told me how bad she felt when she saw the look on my face. I'd be moving upstairs to the small bedroom. After being outside for practically the whole year, my new abode seemed claustrophobic. I'd had little to no sleep the last couple of days, and it finally caught up to me. I zonked out on my bed and slept the rest of the morning and all that afternoon.

Mom prepared a big spaghetti dinner for me, thinking I must have been half-starved. I didn't know it then, but she thought I looked like I just got released from a concentration camp. I had lost over 25 pounds during the year I was away, living mostly on cigarettes, cocoa, cookies and canned fruit. I tried my best to chow down, but I just wasn't used to eating food in any quantity. It seemed like I was eating and eating, but the big plate of pasta looked pretty much the same as when I started. I told everyone that I thought it was growing. It was sort of a family joke for a while, my struggles with the spaghetti on welcome home day.

When I was in Vietnam I used to dream about doing nothing and promised myself to do just that when I got home. During those early days in the jungle, especially when we were humping all day with heavy packs, staying up half the night on an ambush, or manning an observation post, the thought of relaxing with nothing to do seemed like a fantasy. Now that I was home I could do just that, but found it impossible. I was unsettled, anxious, and antsy. I couldn't sleep at night and didn't know what to do with myself during the day. Doing nothing was driving me crazy.

Less than two weeks after coming home I went back to work. Fidgety days and restless nights staying up watching old movies until the test pattern came on was getting old. I got my old job back at the Alcosan plant on the grounds crew. It felt good to be doing something, especially something physical; it helped relax me.

I'm sure I didn't recognize it at the time, but I was probably going through some type of withdrawal. Being in a war zone is a heightened experience. There was a certain tension in the air at all times in Vietnam no matter where you were stationed—in the field, on a base, or in the city. No place was entirely safe; a rocket or mortar round could find you anywhere. The mechanics of war were all around: the truck convoys of troops and supplies, the low-pitched throb of the chopper blades overhead, the drumbeat of the artillery lobbing shells day and night, the distant thunder of the B-52 strikes, the roar of F-100's in full afterburner taking off from Bien Hoa AFB, the bright flares that floated down from circling gunships that cast an eerie amber glow across the night sky and left lazy smoke trails coursing across the horizon, and the drone of the old radial engine gunships that fired the growling mini guns, laying down thousands of rounds a minute that ripped through the night air like laser beams. It was the backdrop of the war. There were few moments when you weren't acutely aware of where you were, even when stationed on a base. If you were in the field, you could go into sensory overload.

To leave that environment where life is lived in an elevated state of awareness and go back home to what feels like sensory deprivation is a big leap, particularly when it's done in two days. Vietnam was a 24 hour a day gig; it was all encompassing. It was your life. Stopping that life in an instant isn't possible. It feels like when you brake your car to a sudden stop; it's still, but you feel like you are still moving. I was still moving, I couldn't get Vietnam out of my head. I'd scan the papers every day and watch the news every night hoping to see or hear something about my old unit. It was as if my body had made the trip home but my mind was still there. Suddenly, everything had changed. What I had been hoping for, wishing for, and counting down for had arrived. But I wasn't feeling it. There was no elation; I felt flat, let down, with no wind in my sails. I felt like there was something wrong with me. I should have felt wonderful: I was safe, I had a bed to sleep in, a roof over my head, and good food to eat. Yet I didn't feel wonderful. I guess I had got a hint of what was to come when I didn't feel that elation I expected when my "Freedom Bird" left the ground and headed back to "The World."

I kept these feelings to myself. I thought no one could possibly understand them; I didn't understand them myself. How could I possibly tell anybody that I missed Vietnam? Besides, it was all too apparent to me that no one wanted to talk about the war anyway. The country was more divided than ever about the conflict, but the tipping point had been reached and the percentage of those against it had been steadily rising. The topic of the war was a sore subject for many, and conversations about it could easily become heated. I can't recall, even in my own family, anyone asking me how I felt about the war. It was like, "Thank God he is home safe, now we don't have to think about it anymore." My coming home was like turning the page on the war—time to put it behind us and move on. I couldn't move on; I was stuck, still mired in Vietnam, for better or worse.

I had no one to talk to about it. I missed the camaraderie of the guys with whom I had shared the Vietnam experience. There is something about sharing an experience that makes something good even better and the bad more tolerable. I couldn't really call coming home bad, but it certainly wasn't what I thought it would be. It wasn't anybody's fault; it just was what it was, and I didn't fully understand it. I think it would have helped if I had someone who had gone through the same thing to share my thoughts with. I felt a bit isolated, a bit different—changed. It was hard to step back into my old world as if nothing had happened, but it seemed like everyone else was going about their lives as if nothing had happened. It made the homecoming a bit unreal.

I think part of me felt let down. I wanted my family to be proud of me (regardless of the merits of the war) for serving honorably, for just making it through. I was no hero, I didn't see a lot of combat but I did what was asked of me and survived a tough day or two. I was proud of myself for that but didn't feel that same vibe from my family. I don't think it was intentional by any means, and I probably didn't fully realize how tough it must have been for them. I think they were just so relieved to be over the stress of it that they probably thought that I felt the same way. Over and done with!

Besides, by the Spring of '69 being a Vietnam Vet didn't carry much prestige. The honor and respect given returning vets from other wars was absent this time around. The early part of the war had earned a lot of positive press, but in this post-Tet era the tables had turned. Negative press on the war had become the norm. The nightly news was much more likely to carry reports on racial strife, drug use, and insubordination among the troops than on how many villages had been pacified.

It was the public's perception that we were losing the war. We actually weren't in a tactical sense, but strategically the writing was on the wall—it was over. The generals had promised too much for too long, and now nobody was believing it. As the attitudes about the war had changed among Americans, so too had their perception of the troops. Unfairly in some quarters, and even more sadly among some older veterans, the returning troops were looked upon as losers. There were stories floating around about certain VFWs or American Legion Halls not being particularly welcoming to the newest of their brothers in arms.

I could remember when I was younger—maybe 12 or 13—seeing some of the older guys in the area come home on leave and continue to wear their uniforms while at home. I'd see them at church or driving around, at the store, wherever. I saw guys walking around the firemen's carnival with their girlfriends, and I thought they looked really cool. Point was, they thought they looked really cool; but more importantly, I think they felt proud to be wearing the uniform. There wasn't much of that going on in 1969. If you were proud of your service in Vietnam, you more than likely kept it to yourself. Many vets wouldn't even tell people that they were in Vietnam. It was just easier that way.

I spent the spring and summer cutting grass, trimming hedges, and spraying trees. I was outside all the time, which was good: being at home felt claustrophobic. I planned on going to school in the fall, mostly because I didn't know what else to do. Besides that, it offered some cover for somebody who hadn't a clue what he wanted to do with his life. In the meantime, I'd continue the yard work, all the while thinking about Vietnam. I couldn't get it out of my mind.

We still got Life magazine every week at home, and my habit of reading it cover to cover hadn't changed. Toward the end of June, the weekly picture magazine arrived as usual, but its content that week was very unusual. It sparked a lot of controversy, some praising and some damning. The cover showed the face of a young man, the boy next door if you will. Atop the cover page: "THE FACES OF THE AMERICAN DEAD IN VIETNAM, one week's toll." Inside, a 10-page spread showed the photographs of 242 young men who had died during the week of May 28-June 2nd. The total reflected the average losses for a typical week during that time of the war.

Most of the pictures showed them in their uniforms, mostly army and marines. Some looked to be senior portraits from high school. Hearing the number 242 is entirely different than seeing the faces of 242 young people who were no longer with us. The issue made an impact, and the responses to it reflected the divisions in the country. Some said it was "long overdue," others said it supported "the anti-war demonstrators who were traitors to this country."

The magazine affected me as well: it brought back into focus some of the unresolved issues I brought back with me from the war. First and foremost, among them, was my inability to feel the losses from the war. Ever since my friend Dan Morris was shot dead by a sniper in the jungle, I had closed the door on my emotions. I wanted to open it but it wouldn't budge. I studied some of the faces on those pages, willing myself to somehow feel the sorrow that their loss should evoke, but it didn't happen. The door was locked, I couldn't find the key, and I continued to feel some shame in that.

Reportedly, some of the dead in the picture spread were from the Battle of Hamburger Hill. The battle occurred during the month of May, 1969. I believe it was the quintessential example of how poorly the war was run. The battle was fought in the A Shau Valley far to the north from the area I was in. The valley provided a corridor into Laos and the Ho Chi Minh Trail from which men and supplies infiltrated into South Vietnam. The valley had long been a stronghold of the North Vietnamese Army. At the head of the valley lay Ap Bia Mountain, the Vietnamese name for the massif. It rose to an elevation of over 3000 feet and was covered in dense double and triple canopy jungle. The NVA had entrenched themselves on the mountain slopes for years, and their fortifications were strong.

The US Army wanted to deny access to the valley, to shut off the infiltration route of the enemy. They wanted to rid the mountaintop of the NVA troops that rose up over the valley. Officially, for the Army the objective was Hill 937, the designation reflecting the mountains height in meters. Before the operation was complete it gained a new one. The 101st Airmobile division was tasked with the job along with some South

Vietnamese Army units.

A frontal assault up the mountain covered the span of several days. Frontal assaults aren't the preferred strategy in most cases because you are throwing yourself into the teeth of the enemy's fortifications. Worse yet, for the troops of the 101st, was the fact they were going uphill to boot. The enemy was dug in deep and had cleared fields of fire along likely attack routes. The fighting was close in: too close for artillery or direct air support. The GIs advanced as far as they could under withering fire then dropped back and called for artillery and air support. Once the shelling ended, they advanced again. The hilltop was taken on the tenth day of the operation; most of the NVA had withdrawn back into Laos. The cost was troubling: 72 dead and 372 wounded. Not many days afterward, the hill was abandoned by the Army, and not long after that the NVA returned. The troops began calling Hill 937 "Hamburger Hill" because of the amount of troops it had ground up. The genesis of the name may have also been an allusion to "Pork Chop Hill," a famous Korean War battle noted for large casualty numbers.

Stories started to surface in the press about Hamburger Hill. The casualty numbers and the fact that we abandoned it after shedding so much blood to take it hit a raw nerve with the public, the majority of which were against the war. The Life magazine article on the Vietnam war dead came out a couple of weeks after the battle, and many people wrongly assumed that all those faces were the Hamburger Hill dead. Rightly or wrongly, it further inflamed emotions. Congressional hearings were held to investigate the Battle of Hamburger Hill. It was a watershed event and ultimately caused a change of tactics for US troops. Senator Ted Kennedy on the floor of the Senate declared the battle: "Senseless... Irresponsible... Madness." In addition, press coverage was devoted to reporting one of the more notable friendly-fire incidents of the war where an errant air strike killed 2 and wounded 25 Americans on the side of the mountain. Sadly, what wasn't reported on amongst all the stories on flawed tactics, unacceptable casualties, and questionable leadership was the guts and fortitude it took for those GIs to get to the top of the mountain.

The stage was set now. President Nixon had earlier announced his Vietnamization policy, namely turning the war over to the Vietnamese. I think most people in the government realized the war was unwinnable under the current circumstances and were looking for a way out. Nixon wanted "Peace with Honor." Vietnamization was an instrument to achieve that goal. We would hang in there, gradually reducing our forces over time and holding the enemy at bay until we could get out. Then, if things fell apart, the South Vietnamese only had themselves to blame, and it wouldn't look like we lost the war. Unfortunately, this strategy cost America many more of its young men—over 15,000.

Half a world away from Vietnam an event occurred that summer of 1969 that would long be remembered. The Woodstock Music Festival took place in upstate New York. It was probably the high watermark of the counterculture movement that began in the early to mid-sixties and mushroomed in large part due to the Vietnam anti-war movements. Although largely overlooked now, the festival did not lack anti-Vietnam War sentiment. The festival's original name was, "AN AQUARIAN EXPOSITION: three days of Peace and Music." This was acknowledging "The Age of Aquarius" as the high point of the hippie movement. The counterculture movement and anti-war movement were intertwined.

Coverage of the festival centered on the hippies, music, drugs, nudity, and free love, but the anti-war sentiment was there, probably best exemplified by Country Joe and the Fish singing the "I FEEL LIKE I'M FIXING TO DIE RAG," a protest song of the anti-war movement.

I finished the summer out working at Alcosan until the start of the fall semester at Slippery Rock University began. I chose Slippery Rock for no better reason than it was close and had reasonable tuition. I had no clear idea why I was going; it was more like I didn't know what else to do. I signed up for some prerequisites that I needed no matter what direction I might eventually take: an English course, biology, philosophy, geography, and something else I can't remember now. Ready or not here I come.

Unfortunately, I wasn't ready, and it was apparent from the very start. I was still incredibly restless, and I struggled to concentrate on my classes. I was barely getting by and was sorry I had bothered to sign up for the semester. I was conflicted as to why I had such trouble. I felt at the time that it might have something to do with my Vietnam experience, but on the other hand I was never a very good student. With no concrete goal in mind, the courses were more like obstacles than paths to wherever I was going.

On Oct. 15, 1969, demonstrations were held all over the country including college and university campuses, and Slippery Rock held one too. The protest was called a "Moratorium to end the war in Vietnam." Students gathered along Campus Drive across from North Hall. They held up signs with anti-war slogans and were even flying the flag of the National Liberation Front. It gave me a strange feeling watching that half-blue, half-red banner with the yellow star in the middle of it rippling in the breeze. I had no issue with the demonstration: I had long ago come to the conclusion that the war was wrong but flying the colors of the Viet Cong also seemed wrong. Although I certainly didn't disagree with the protesters, joining them would have made me feel disloyal to the troops in Vietnam. I know it sounds like a contradiction but it was the way I felt.

One month later, in November, over 500,000 people marched in Washington DC to protest the war. President Richard Nixon said of the march: "Now, I understand that there has been, and continues to be, opposition to the war on campuses and also in the nation. As far as this kind of activity is concerned, we expect it. However, under no circumstances will I be affected whatever by it." Apparently, the fact that 58% of Americans now felt the war was a mistake and that 69% of students considered themselves Doves could not dissuade the President from the path he had chosen to take in Vietnam. "Peace with Honor" was the goal. How much honor does 15,000 lives buy???

November would also be the month that news broke about the My Lai Massacre. The massacre actually took place in March of 1968, but the news would not reach the public for over 18 months. The basics of the story were this: On March 16, 1968, members of Charlie company, a unit of the Americal Division, entered a village called My Lai and killed over 350 old men, women and children. The disclosure of the incident resulted in world-wide condemnation of the United States and increased anti-war sentiment at home.

The story was shocking to America. It garnered plenty of media attention and focused attention on the young men who were sent over to fight the war. People didn't want to believe that American boys were capable of such things.

The revelations and continuing intense media coverage did nothing to help the already tarnished image of the Vietnam Vets who had returned home. Protesters of the war had long referred to Vietnam Vets as "baby killers." Graphic pictures of the My Lai Massacre were published in magazines and newspapers that showed not only women and children but infants as well. The pictures gave the allegations credence.

Wars present people with situations rife with moral ambiguity and ethical dilemma. The rules of civilian life seem to be set aside as if they aren't really relevant in a war zone. Thankfully, I was never put in a position that put my own ethical standards to the test, but I had seen or heard things that I recognized as questionable behavior and accepted it too readily as just what happens when a war is going on.

I remember Colonel Behm announcing his bounty plan for the first person that brought him the ears from a VC or NVA colonel or above. It certainly isn't official US Army policy to provide cash rewards, and Colonel Behm's announcement was practically tacit approval to the troops to cut off the ears of the dead.

We once had a Night Defensive Position in a place we called the snake pit. While digging in for the night, some skeletons of dead Viet Cong soldiers were found. Some of the guys made use of the skulls as ersatz soccer balls. Back in "The World" that would have been considered abuse of a corpse and subject to criminal prosecution. In Vietnam, it meant no more than a macabre game.

Is torture ever ethical to use? I can remember finding out what the Vietnamese interrogators were doing to the detainees in a hooch of a village we searched. Americans were with them but just observing, not administering the torture. I was surprised but not as shocked as I thought I should have been. It wasn't uncommon to see the South Vietnamese soldiers slapping around suspects when we searched villages.

Was it ethical for us to avoid going out on ambushes when we could get away with it? I knew one thing, I would feel bad about it only if we had gotten caught. What is the right answer when faced with calling in an air strike while knowing that some men on the ground will be in grave danger if you do? General Heyward was faced with that decision. He was under pressure from the higher ups; he relented, and rightly or wrongly, called it in, and a price was probably paid for it. How do you choose a man to take the point in a heavily booby-trapped area? Should everyone take their turn? Or do you put someone who you think would be better at it but by virtue of your choice endanger him more than the others?

Is there ever a moral justification for prostitution? Can your ethics be suspended in a case where you need to feed a family? Can a case ever be made for terrorism? Depending on whose side you're on, one person's terrorist is another person's freedom fighter. Is it ethical for the Army to tell parents that their son died in combat when it was really the result of "friendly fire?"

If nothing else, war presents a sea of grey when it comes to ethics and morals. Few things seem black and white. One thing I noticed was that morality seemed to be inversely proportional to your distance from home—the further away, the less moral constraint.

I thought about these questions after I got back from Vietnam. When I started school at Slippery Rock, I saw that I could fulfill a social science requirement by taking a philosophy course in ethics and signed up for it. I thought in light of the times and all that was going on in the world that a course in ethics would really be interesting. The war was still at full bore with all the ethical questions that surrounded it: from massacres to draft dodgers to war profiteering. It never occurred to me that we would never broach any of those questions that were relevant to our times. Instead, I found myself having to read Pride and Prejudice by Jane Austin. I couldn't believe it. I had just come from a place where real ethical conundrums existed. I struggled to find answers to my questions by studying the tortured romance of Elizabeth Bennet and Mr. Darcy. In hindsight, I'm sure there was value in what we were studying, but at that time, in my state of mind, contemplating the moral attitudes of early 19th century English landed gentry while there was so much going on in the real world that deserved attention was just beyond me. My grade reflected my apathy.

Frankly, I didn't feel all that comfortable that fall semester at Slippery Rock. I kept wondering: "What the hell am I doing here?" I was struggling with my studies. I felt older than my fellow classmates, although I wasn't by much. I just couldn't get into it. I was floundering.

There was a Vets group on campus, and I went to one of their meetings, hoping that I would find someone to talk to. The group was small and generally older than me, and none had served in Vietnam in a combat capacity. It wasn't what I was looking for. I couldn't talk to anyone at home about it, and there was no one at school to talk about it. But to be honest, I didn't know if I even could talk about it. For as much as I thought about the war, I really didn't know how to go about talking about it. I had so many different emotions and conflicted feelings that I probably would have sounded like I was "round the bend." So, the few times I was asked, I found myself very reticent to engage in a conversation, fearing I wouldn't be able to explain myself to someone who hadn't been there.

I became resigned to the idea of keeping the war to myself. Anyway, being a Vietnam Vet on a college campus in the Fall of 69 was not something you brought attention to yourself about. I decided not to return for the spring semester and withdrew from Slippery Rock that December. I was hoping to go back when I got my head together.

THIRTY-THREE
FINDING MY WAY

Still restless, and now out of school and blessed with no marketable job skills, I ended up driving a cab through the early part of the year. In the spring, I went back to work on the grounds crew at Alcosan and cut grass and hedges through most of the summer. I took August off and drove to Los Angeles to visit my brother Mike. I started back to Slippery Rock for the fall semester. As yet without any direction, I somehow completed the year, albeit without scholastic distinction. I returned to Alcosan for the summer months.

It was a really nice summer. I had a no-brainer job during the week that I actually liked and met a girl who lived in an apartment next to the one of a friend of mine. I ended up spending a lot of evenings on the front porch of Carol's apartment. We played a lot of cards and just sort of hung out a lot, very casual, though, which was good for me as I was still very shy when it came to girls.

So, with that fact in mind, when I finally asked your mother out for the first time, I was in no way sure of what she would say. I asked in the most casual manner I could muster so it wouldn't be too awkward if she said no. She didn't. We went to the movies; "Ryan's Daughter" was playing at the Denis theater in Mt. Lebanon. I held her hand as we walked down to the theater from the parking lot and she didn't seem to mind.

What was a nice summer got even better, and I was sad to see it coming to an end. I was registered for the fall semester at Slippery Rock, but I returned without much enthusiasm. I was taking some geography courses. I always liked that subject, but it wasn't of much use unless you wanted to teach it. And teaching, for someone as shy as I was, was really out of the question. I had dreaded, then hated, speech class. Standing in front of a class all day speaking clearly wasn't for me.

I came home every weekend to see Carol and over time began to envision the possibility of a life with her. There was one catch, of course; I had no way to support a family someday, at the rate I was going. I did a lot of soul-searching and decided to enroll at the Pittsburgh Institute of Aeronautics to become a licensed airframe and power plant mechanic. It was a bit of a leap of faith for me. I wasn't one of those kids who liked to take things apart, or made go-karts out of lawn mower parts, or started working on cars when I was 14. No, the most mechanical work I ever did was probably taking broken parts off my bike, never to be returned. I remember taking those aptitude tests they give you in high school to see what I might be suited for; it always came back saying I should be a social worker. But, heck, I liked planes, and I needed a trade to make some money, so off I went.

I started school in Feb. of 1972. I liked the atmosphere right away. Ninety percent of my class were veterans and most were aircraft mechanics in the Air Force or the Navy. I had no trouble with the academic part of the course, but I was definitely behind the curve with the practical half. I realized I had no innate ability when it came to mechanics. I'd have to learn everything; it didn't come naturally. But I was motivated, I wanted to be able to make a life for myself and Carol, if she was willing. I graduated 11th out of 44.

I got a call from school one day asking me if I wanted to interview for a mechanic job in Florida with Mackey International Airlines. I said yes, and a phone interview was arranged. I was surprised when the guy I talked to hired me right over the phone. I was also a little concerned: what kind of place hired somebody with no experience and not even ask for references, all on the basis of a 10-minute phone call?

Nevertheless, I felt I had to take it: my career needed a jump start and maybe this would be it. I knew nothing about Mackey International Airlines; I'd never even heard of them. I'd agreed to go down to Fort Lauderdale not knowing what I would be doing or what kind of aircraft they had. I left for Florida in a 1965 Rambler American that I bought from my Dad for $150 bucks. I took my tools, clothes, and my most valuable possession: a 13 inch black and white TV complete with rabbit ears.

I worked at the airline for about six months and enjoyed it, but was concerned about persistent rumors about the health of the airline. When a mechanic's job opened up at the Post Office I took it, albeit reluctantly.

The Post Office was hiring a lot of Vets back then, but my 5 extra points for being a disabled one made a big difference for when I was hired. The Bulk Mail Center hired 70 new mechanics, and I ended up being the eleventh hired, ensuring me a daylight bid and at least part of the weekend off. Others further down the list would have to wait many, many years to get on daylight, let alone get the weekend off.

I came back to Pittsburgh feeling I had made the right decision but still feeling a little down about leaving the airline business. At the end of the day, though, it was the right choice. In 1978 Congress deregulated the airline industry and it has been in a state of flux ever since. If you were working for the airlines the only certainty was uncertainty.

Newly engaged, and finding a secure job, I felt like I was ready to move on with my life.

THIRTY-FOUR
POST WAR DAYS

Your mom and I were married on April 26, 1975, four days before the war ended in Vietnam. The whole sad finish of the war played out every night on the evening news. It was hard to watch, but I couldn't turn away from it. Watching the tanks roll down streets that I had walked and seeing the flags of North Vietnam and the National Liberation Front (Viet Cong) flying over the city that my unit was tasked with protecting was very disturbing, even though I and anybody else who served there from '69 onward knew it was inevitable. My restlessness had gradually diminished over the years. I can't honestly say whether the war had anything to do with me feeling so unsettled for so long or not. But even though my uneasiness had ebbed, my interest had not. I scanned the paper every day and listed to the news every night for every bit of information about the war. I was tied to it in a way I didn't really understand. Still am, I guess, or I wouldn't be writing this. It's funny, those first couple years I was home I was so fastened to the war that some songs that remind me of Vietnam weren't even released until after I left the country. My body may have been home, but my mind was still far, far away.

The war was now officially over, but for many Vietnam Vets it would not be over for a long time to come, if ever. PTSD isn't anything new; it's been around for as long as there have been wars. It just went by different names, and, unfortunately, the symptoms would have to be relearned and accepted after each conflict. A difference for Vietnam Vets was that they were all painted in an unfavorable light. The War was a long one and with one-year tour of duties and the drawdown of troops in the later years, most Vets were home long before the end of the War. They had to watch the whole sad affair play out to a bitter and acrimonious end, and the Vets themselves became the focal point for a lot of that acrimony.

The Vietnam Vets were not welcomed home to a nation appreciative of their service to their country, let alone as heroes. The divisiveness that enveloped America over the long years of the conflict distorted the image of the Vets for years to come. Yes, Vietnam was different: our enemy wasn't well defined, and we weren't fighting an obvious, tangible threat to America. We were fighting more of a theoretical foe. We weren't engaging evil incarnate as manifested by the Nazis, and we weren't combating a country that attacked us and sunk our battleships. Our enemy was indistinguishable from our allies. How can one be a gook, a dink, or a slope and not the other? The situation was ripe for confusion and conflict; the very nature of guerilla warfare lends itself to innocents caught in the crossfire. Things happened that weighed heavily on the troops. Now those Vets would have to deal with what they had done without the moral high ground that could assuage those actions that counter man's natural instinct not to kill.

I was very lucky during my tour of duty in Vietnam, I didn't see a whole lot of action, and what I did see didn't involve anything on my part that I would fret about later on. Killing someone is hard to get over, even when it is justified. At the end of the day, I was fortunate in that regard. The enemy came a lot closer to getting me than the other way around. Anytime I fired my weapon it was always at an unseen enemy and always with others doing the same; it was a shared endeavor. Any guilt felt at the result is a collective one; one that is easily assuaged by dint of the fact that a hundred other guys are firing away, and artillery, gunships, or even an airstrike could have been involved. Any personal responsibility is alleviated by the sheer numbers involved. It's like traveling down the freeway, before cell phones, and seeing a car broken down on the berm of the road. You have a thought that maybe you ought to stop and see if they need help, but you don't. The fact that you knew 500 cars had already passed him by and 500 more will after you drive by eases your conscience to the point that two miles down the road you have forgotten all about it. Not so easy if the scenario is a lightly-traveled back country road, at night, in bad weather. Passing by someone in need of assistance in those conditions is not so easy, and if you do, you are not apt to forget about it two miles down the road. No, it will linger with you for some time to come. So, too, for that soldier who has taken someone in their sights and pulls the trigger and watches him go down. No matter how justified he was (it is a war after all), it will be something he will have to live with. He doesn't have the luxury of sharing the guilt.

I never thought I had any symptoms of PTSD. When the condition was first talked about in the media, it usually refereed to the most serious of symptoms. The usual scenario was some poor Vietnam Vet suffering a psychotic breakdown from flashbacks or nightmares. The range of and seriousness of the symptoms of PTSD are wide. It is probably naïve to think that you could be a combat veteran and not experience some sort of psychological issue, no matter how subtle it may be. I realized even when I was still in Vietnam that my reactions to certain situations was out of the norm. At least I thought they were out of the norm at the time. One symptom is emotional numbness. It is the suppression of emotions to avoid feelings of sadness and grief. Unfortunately, escaping the emotional shock of trauma may protect you from feeling anguish, loss, and suffering but often comes with a price. It may also prevent you from feeling love, joy and happiness.

I could not have put a name to that feeling while I was in Vietnam, but I knew I was living it. But for me, and I have no idea if it is unusual or not, I only experienced one side of it. I was able to detach myself from the horrors around me without losing the ability to appreciate the wonders. It wasn't like I was pretending the bad things weren't happening; I was always fully aware and cognizant of the realities, I just didn't *feel* them. It would be one thing that would disturb me after coming home. I would feel guilty about it for a long time. To be sure, my detachment was a coping mechanism, but I still felt down on myself for needing it, even though it was never a conscious decision to use it.

I've read some psychology that seems to intimate that my detachment, that to me felt a bit heartless, actually protected me to the point that I could survive the war mentally intact and with my personality largely the same. It made me feel a bit better. My dad always said that the war didn't change me, that I was the same Chuckie. I guess in some ways he was right, but not so much in others. How could he know? I never talked about the things that troubled me—to anybody.

Mostly it was guilt, on several different levels. But first and foremost was that detachment. I thought there was something wrong with me, and it dispirited me. I had a bit of survivor's guilt as well, not that I was in a lot of heavy combat. But I did have a number of very close calls, and you just can't help but wonder about what if and why for. I guess it's just human nature. I also felt guilty about missing Vietnam. In a way it was an adventure, it was exciting, and I had some really good times; but it sounds wrong to admit that. Somehow, along with the detachment, I was able to compartmentalize my experiences. I could separate the good from the bad. I psychologically ignored the worst of the war and relished the best. I enjoyed myself when I could, I lived in the moment.

The mid-seventies and early eighties proved to be a struggle for a country trying to get over the hangover caused by the war. President Jimmy Carter called it a "malaise," a sense of being out of sorts, not quite well.

America had lost a war for the first time in its history. At least that was the perception, even though we were no longer involved at the end. Many vets disagreed with that assessment, no doubt struggling with the idea that their sacrifices were made for naught.

The economy was sick, we had spent too much money on the war, causing deficits and causing both rising inflation and unemployment. Economists called it stagflation. Whatever they called it, it played havoc on the stock market, and the Dow Jones Industrials lost 45% of their value by the end of 1976. Interest rates continued to rise and by 1980 if you planned on buying a home you had to be prepared to pay a 16% interest rate for a mortgage.

Politically the country was a mess. The "Watergate" scandal eventually brought the downfall of President Nixon, the only president to ever resign from office. President Ford, who succeeded the disgraced Nixon, was the target of two assassination attempts within three weeks in September of 1975. The first, by Lynette "Squeaky" Fromme," a member of the Charles Manson family cult, went wrong because she had not chambered a round in her 45 automatic. The second attempt by the politically-radical Sarah Jane Moore failed because the sights on her newly purchased 38-caliber revolver were not set up correctly, and her first shot missed the President by six inches. Her second shot's aim was disrupted when a bystander, a former marine, lunged for her gun.

An oil crisis in both 73 and 79 saw long lines at the gas pumps throughout the country and further damaged an already weak economy. In the late seventies, there was a precipitous decline in the steel industry's fortunes, further fueling worries that America's role as the industrial giant of the world was coming to an end. The Iranian hostage crisis and the disastrous attempt to free them made us look weak in the eyes of the world, and our prestige was at a low point.

Even though the war was over, Vietnam would just not go away. Jimmy Carter caused controversy anew when he pardoned a couple hundred-thousand draft evaders who had either fled to Canada or failed to register for the draft. Vietnam apparently didn't have enough of war and invaded Cambodia and also had a conflict with China in the late seventies.

The communist victors in Vietnam were harsh on the people who fought for or worked for the South. Approximately 65,000 Vietnamese were executed after the war and a further million sent to "reeducation camps" in which more than a 100,000 died. These measures contributed to the exodus of hundreds of thousands of Vietnamese from their country. Most left by boat, usually small coastal vessels not suitable for the high seas, and many drowned. The idea was to get the little crowded fishing boats out into the international shipping lanes a couple hundred miles off the coast and hope to get picked up by passing freighters or naval vessels. The escapees were known as the "Boat People," and many nations opened their arms to them. The US alone accepted 825,000 refugees.

The specter of Agent Orange began to haunt the thoughts of Vietnam Vets who were exposed to the defoliant that contained the toxin dioxin. I was one of them. Reports had begun to circulate about the high number of babies born with birth defects in Vietnam attributable to exposure to Agent Orange. There was also increasing evidence (mostly apocryphal) of an increase in birth defects among American babies whose fathers had served in Vietnam. Naturally, this caused me a lot of anxiety during your mom's pregnancies, particularly the first. I'll never forget the look on Carol's face the first time I saw her after the delivery. I walked into the hospital room and she told me the pediatrician said the baby might have cretinism (mental retardation). Carol said, "There is nothing wrong with my baby" and told me to tell the doctor that she didn't want to see her again. I wasn't so sanguine, I was prepared, as much as one could be, for bad news in light of all the agent orange rumors. I was afraid that she might be thinking with only her emotions, so I was looking for any signs that the doctor was wrong. I was relieved when Jenny turned out to be precocious; Carol could not have been more right.

The bicentennial of the United States was celebrated in 1976. Our country should have been ready for some grand festivities, but the country was still in a bit of a funk. Although there were many things happening, I think the birthday was a bit muted. America didn't have its mojo back yet.

Ronald Reagan won the Presidency in 1980 partly on the promise that he was going to make us feel good about ourselves again. Iran released 52 American hostages (after 444 days of captivity) on Reagan's first day in office. The freed prisoners returned to the states and were hailed as heroes.

Two months into his presidential term, President Reagan was shot in an assassination attempt by John Hinckley Jr. The would-be assassin was mentally ill; he somehow thought that killing the President would impress the actress Jodie Foster whom he was enamored with.

In 1983, the Marine Corps was sent to Lebanon on a peace-keeping mission. A suicide bomber driving a truck laden with explosives crashed into the entryway of the marine barracks and detonated. Two hundred and forty- one American servicemen died.

The mid-seventies to the early eighties were pretty sad as far as the nation went. Even Elvis died. But personally, they were the happiest years of my life.

I can't honestly say that I couldn't wait to have kids. For me, it was just what you did: you got married, you had kids. It's estimated that there are 350,000 births the world over every day, a pretty common event; but when it happens to you... it's magic!

In the movie Jerry McGuire, Tom Cruise famously tells Renee Zellweger, "you complete me." Well, that's how I felt when you girls arrived. I wasn't aware that I needed completing, but I guess I did. There was a void that needed filled, and you made me whole.

There are all kinds of love in the world: the love of a spouse, parents, siblings, friends, and yes, country; but there is nothing quite like the love of a child. It is a singular sensation. It is love in its purist form: absolute and unconditional. One of the true joys in life is the gift of giving unconditional love. It's a liberating feeling. In so many relationships in life we hold back a little— afraid to give 100%. But when you first see your baby, all the restraints, those inhibitions, those lessons learned in order to protect ourselves crumble under the weight of an instant and unbreakable bond. The emotion of it is a bit overwhelming at first, and one that, frankly, I wasn't prepared for. Babies and young children put complete trust in their parents. The gift of unconditional love is the reward for honoring that trust as best you can.

All seemed good in the world: good marriage, good kids, good job, and a house that was a home. Vietnam had become a much smaller part of my life by now; it wasn't the preoccupation it once was. It was still there, always present, but on the back burner. I still had some unresolved issues, but my life was full enough that they had fallen dormant. They were about to be reawakened.

THIRTY-FIVE
THE WALL I

As the seventies came to a close, most of the veterans of the war had gotten their lives together and moved on. The war was still a sore subject, however, and most people just wanted to forget about it. For those who fought in it, having moved on or not, there was no forgetting about it. For them, a memorial seemed only fitting, but unlikely to be built unless they did it themselves. Jan Scruggs, a Vietnam Vet who served in the same unit that I did, the 199th Light Infantry Brigade, founded the Vietnam Veterans Memorial Fund in 1979.

The work of raising funds began, much of which came from the veterans themselves. A competition was organized to choose a design for the memorial. Some guidelines were set: it was to be reflective and contemplative without having political or military content, and its emphasis was on those who had died. Over 1400 designs were submitted. A distinguished panel of architects was formed to judge the entries.

Maya Lin, an architectural student from Yale University, had her design selected. The memorial consisted of two black, polished stone walls, each nearly 250 feet long, meeting at a vertex of 125 degrees, forming a slight inverted V shape. The vertex where the two walls met was 10 feet tall; from that point, each wall tapered down to less than a foot at the far ends. The unseen side of the walls were backfilled with dirt to make it appear as if each wall was sloping down into the earth. Each wall had 72 panels; on these panels the names of all the Vietnam War dead would be etched— over 58,000.

This being a Vietnam Memorial, it was no surprise that the selection caused controversy. One critic called it a "black scar in the earth," another described it as "a black gash of shame." Many had wanted a more traditional monument, more heroic in nature. I was ambivalent myself, at first. James Watt, then the Secretary of the Interior, even threatened to withhold the building permit for the construction of the memorial. Nonetheless, controversy aside, it was built and would be dedicated on November 13th 1982. I wanted to be there for it and traveled down with a Veterans' group to attend the ceremonies.

Thousands of veterans showed up for the dedication, many wearing old fatigue jackets and bush hats they had kept from the war. It seemed like the uniform of the day. Time Magazine said: "The convocation had an edge, a sense of catharsis, mainly because it was large and public in the end, with a splendidly ragtag march down Constitution Avenue and the dedication of the Veterans Memorial, the spectacle seemed like the national homecoming the country had never offered."

As Time Magazine reported, it was a ragtag march down Constitution Avenue from beyond the Washington Monument where we formed up by state. There were no ranks of perfectly aligned troops marching in cadence; it was more of a stroll, chatting among ourselves along the way and basking in the warm applause of those that lined the parade route. It was kind of fitting for us: marching in our own way, dressed in our own way, and feeling pride in our own way.

The speeches given that day had a somber tone, as they should have. The weather cooperated, providing a cool grey day with low-hanging dark clouds that reinforced the solemn mood, one appropriate for the dedication of a memorial that had 58,000 (mostly young men's) names on it. Time Magazine: "Its long walls, inscribed with the names of 58,000 killed or missing in America's last war, are simple, elegant, and dignified, everything the Vietnam War was not."

Earlier in the week of the dedication, a service was held at the National Cathedral in Washington. Two hundred and thirty volunteers read the names of all 58,000 dead on the wall. It took three days. Thirteen years earlier, this same month, half a million protesters gathered on the mall around the Washington Monument to demonstrate against the war. As part of that protest, 40,000 names were read, all the Vietnam War dead up to that point in the war, 1969.

Many hoped this coming together would help to change the perceptions of Vietnam Veterans. Stan Horton, the director of the Vietnam Veterans Leadership Program, said: "Only a small fraction of the war's veterans, after all, came home with serious emotional problems, even though for a decade the Vietnam Veteran has been portrayed in the films and on TV as a doped- up maniac itching to mow down strangers. More and more the public is seeing vets not as baby killers but, at worst, as dupes— and at best, as people that did their patriotic duty."

Most Vietnam Vets just hungered for some respect and to be allowed to show some pride for what they did. One observer stated: "If the war they went to fight made it almost impossible for Vietnam Vets to be treated as heroes, they are at least no longer made to look like pariahs."

After the dedication, the wall was opened to all. Directories were available to look up names on the wall, providing the panel and line location to find the name. I went to Panel 61 on the west wall to search for the names of those killed in the firefight on June 2nd 1968 up in War Zone D. I found them starting on line 10. There, etched in the stone, was the name William Archer. He was only 18 years of age when he died halfway around the world from his home in California. I stared at the name, hoping to feel something, but it wouldn't come. I looked around me at other vets, touching the names and obviously emotionally touched by the experience. I felt, once again, the longing to connect, but for some reason I could not. I felt not only frustrated with myself but ashamed. What was wrong with me?

I didn't linger at the wall, reasoning I shouldn't be taking up space that might be better filled by someone more capable of connecting with it. The experience nagged at me, rekindling dormant feelings of frustration that my emotional detachment from the war had caused me.

I was glad I made the trip, though, no doubt about that. The memorial was obviously doing its job of inviting reflection and stirring contemplation for vets and visitors alike.

THIRTY-SIX
THE WALL II

In appreciation of some vets' concerns, the Memorial Fund decided to erect a statue on the memorial site. The bronze statue consisted of three young soldiers dressed and equipped in the style of the Vietnam era. They represent a Caucasian, an African American and a Hispanic. The statue was placed about a hundred feet south of the wall so the faces of the soldiers appear to be looking at the names on the memorial.

It was going to be dedicated on Veterans Day 1984, and I planned on attending. There was a larger group that went down to Washington this time and more of a party atmosphere as evidenced by the keg brought on the bus. We'd be staying the weekend. Many Division and Brigade associations were holding gatherings and reunions at different hotels around the city. It became our mission to visit every unit reunion that had a member represented in our group. Saturday was a party day, the vets had taken over the city. The scent of marijuana was everywhere. It seemed the Washington metropolitan police force had issued a free pass for the weekend. It was a really enjoyable day. Even my unit, the 199th, had a reunion and a reception suite. This surprised me as ours was one of the smaller units in Vietnam.

Sunday was dedication day and I attended. I went down to the wall to pay my respects again. Since the wall was dedicated in 1982 it had become somewhat of a shrine. Those that came to see a name on the wall (family, friends, or service buddies) began to leave a memento of their visit: usually something that reminded them of that person or even something that the person on the wall once owned. Many offerings had no obvious connection to the war, their meanings secret to those who left them and the name on the wall. Many were quite obvious: helmets, bush hats, medals, dog tags, ribbons, and boots. There was also money, cans of beer, and whiskey bottles... maybe borrowed and unable to be returned, until now. Letters were left, poems, too. Flags and flowers were the most common items placed at the wall.

I walked along the wall, panel after panel of names, a few of which I knew. I don't know why I happened to stop where I did; the panel had no name I knew. I looked down and among the offerings was a clear envelope. Inside were two unused tickets to the 1971 Indianapolis 500, and with it was a toy race car and a brown shaggy teddy bear. Without intention, I began to formulate a story behind the tableau before me. I imagined a father buying those tickets for the race while his son was still in Vietnam. His son was probably "short," not much time left in-country. Perhaps the race was part of a celebration for his homecoming.

Then I imagined the knock at the door. The appearance of an Army officer on your front porch could only mean one thing; your son was coming home in a coffin. I pictured that father once shuttling that little race car across the kitchen floor with his son and tucking him in at night with that teddy bear. And then I thought about my Jenny and my Cathy and how I tucked them in at night, usually after a bedtime story like "The Little Engine that Could" or "The Pokey Little Puppy." I thought about how they would wrap their little arms around my neck and say, "night Daddy, love you," which is just the best feeling in the world. I thought about how I was always so happy to see them after work. I loved hearing them squeal "Daddy's home," just the sweetest sounding two-word combination in the English language.

And I think I knew intuitively then what I know for sure now, that those are the kinds of things that stay with you. And I thought of that father again and knew all of those memories he had of his son could only be bittersweet now. I could only think of how much my girls meant to me, how they made me understand what unconditional love really was, and how they had made me whole. And I knew in my heart that that father, if he was anything like me, would never be whole again.

I began to feel a stinging sensation in my nostrils and some pressure under the bridge of my nose, my eyes began to well up, and my breathing shortened with some halting gasps. For whatever reason, at this time and at this place, after fifteen years of emotional detachment, I was finally able to feel the sadness and the heartache of the war. I was feeling it as a father would, putting my girls in the place of that once little boy with the toy car and the teddy bear.

It took me a while to process what had just happened. The flood of emotion had caught me unaware, the sudden sensibility was something I hadn't thought possible, even though I had longed for it. I guess you could call it an emotional epiphany or maybe a catharsis. All I knew for sure was I felt unburdened. I had finally made the connection— through the power of the wall, the father who left his cherished keepsakes, and my daughters.

EPILOGUE

Dear Jenny and Cathy,

It's been nearly fifty years since my tour of duty in Vietnam. So many things that happened that year are as fresh to me as yesterday, yet, at other times, I have experienced a peculiar sensation where I wonder: "Was that really me?" Those two things seem at odds with each other, but that was Vietnam in a nutshell—a land of contradictions.

Vietnam was beautiful but bloody. It was both boring and exciting. It was an adventure filled with drudgery. I couldn't wait to leave but missed it when I did.

I left Vietnam with my own personal contradiction that the both of you helped me resolve at the Vietnam Veterans Memorial some fifteen years after I left Vietnam. I was fortunate; while my emotional detachment over the war troubled me for those years, it was an internal conflict that was isolated, nobody was aware of it. I had come to accept it and moved on. The flood of emotion that engulfed me at the "Wall" that day proved otherwise. It was truly a relief.

That day was Nov. 11, 1984. Thirty-three years have passed since that day, I'm on the cusp of my seventieth year. Now, an old man stares back at me from the mirror. I'm not too pleased with that picture, but truly, I have no right to complain. Over fifty-eight thousand troops who served in Vietnam never got the chance to grow old. And many, many more of those who did come back arrived home with mental and physical problems that have affected them for life. Issues that have prevented them from forming lasting loving relationships, issues that have destroyed families.

You both are a constant reminder of how blessed I am. It's been wonderful watching you grow up: brownies, girl scouts, dance recitals, softball, school plays and proms. I couldn't be more proud of the beautiful young women you have become. You are both bright, charming, smart and fun to be around. I'd just like to add that being your dad was the best job I ever had.

Finally, thank you for giving me the impetus to write the book. It would never have happened without you.

Love, always, forever,

Daddy,

Nov.11, 2017

Made in the USA
Monee, IL
22 June 2022

98396730R00169